T0247760

Sikh Philosophy

Bloomsbury Introductions to World Philosophies

Series Editor:
Monika Kirloskar-Steinbach

Assistant Series Editor:
Leah Kalmanson

Regional Editors:

Nader El-Bizri, James Madaio, Sarah A. Mattice, Takeshi Morisato,
Pascah Mungwini, Mickaella Perina, Omar Rivera and Georgina Stewart

Bloomsbury Introductions to World Philosophies delivers primers
reflecting exciting new developments in the trajectory of world
philosophies. Instead of privileging a single philosophical approach
as the basis of comparison, the series provides a platform for diverse
philosophical perspectives to accommodate the different dimensions
of cross-cultural philosophizing. While introducing thinkers, texts and
themes emanating from different world philosophies, each book, in an
imaginative and path-breaking way, makes clear how it departs from a
conventional treatment of the subject matter.

Titles in the Series:

A Practical Guide to World Philosophies, by Monika Kirloskar-Steinbach
and Leah Kalmanson
Daya Krishna and Twentieth-Century Indian Philosophy,
by Daniel Raveh
Māori Philosophy, by Georgina Tuari Stewart
Philosophy of Science and The Kyoto School, by Dean Anthony Brink
Tanabe Hajime and the Kyoto School, by Takeshi Morisato
African Philosophy, by Pascah Mungwini
The Zen Buddhist Philosophy of D. T. Suzuki, by Rossa Ó Muireartaigh
Sikh Philosophy, by Arvind-Pal Singh Mandair

Sikh Philosophy

Exploring gurmat *Concepts in a Decolonizing World*

Arvind-Pal Singh Mandair

BLOOMSBURY ACADEMIC
LONDON • NEW YORK • OXFORD • NEW DELHI • SYDNEY

BLOOMSBURY ACADEMIC
Bloomsbury Publishing Plc
50 Bedford Square, London, WC1B 3DP, UK
1385 Broadway, New York, NY 10018, USA
29 Earlsfort Terrace, Dublin 2, Ireland

BLOOMSBURY, BLOOMSBURY ACADEMIC and the Diana logo are trademarks
of Bloomsbury Publishing Plc

First published in Great Britain 2022

Series design by Louise Dugdale
Cover image © mikroman6 / Getty Images

A catalogue record for this book is available from the British Library.

A catalog record for this book is available from the Library of Congress.

ISBN: HB: 978-1-3502-0226-9
PB: 978-1-3502-0225-2
ePDF: 978-1-3502-0227-6
eBook: 978-1-3502-0228-3

Series: Bloomsbury Introductions to World Philosophies

Typeset by Deanta Global Publishing Services, Chennai, India
Printed and bound in Great Britain

To find out more about our authors and books visit www.bloomsbury.com
and sign up for our newsletters.

For Preet

Contents

Illustrations

Figures

Tables

Series editor's preface

The introductions we include in the World Philosophies series take a single thinker, theme or text and provide a close reading of them. What defines the series is that these are likely to be people or traditions that you have not yet encountered in your study of philosophy. By choosing to include them you broaden your understanding of ideas about the self, knowledge and the world around us. Each book presents unexplored pathways into the study of world philosophies. Instead of privileging a single philosophical approach as the basis of comparison, each book accommodates the many different dimensions of cross-cultural philosophizing. While the choice of terms used by the individual volumes may indeed carry a local inflection, they encourage critical thinking about philosophical plurality. Each book strikes a balance between locality and globality.

Arvind-Pal S. Mandair's *Sikh Philosophy: Exploring* gurmat *Concepts in a Decolonizing World* offers readers a rich and multi-layered exposition of concepts, practices and arguments that are central to *gurmat*, the Sikh pathways of thought and practice. Foregrounding their fluid orientation towards self and world, the book carefully works out *gurmat's* intricate intertwining of the human and other-than-human realms. Building upon this orientation, the volume boldly reads Sikh philosophy as an 'assemblage', as a mediation between worlds in which the mediation itself is reconfigured in the process. Similar to a postcolonial diasporic way of being in the world, this fluid *thinking-between* has the potential to enable one to make meaning of changing and new contexts.

Monika Kirloskar-Steinbach

Preface and acknowledgements

Although this book has been long in the making, it was written in a relatively short space of time, much of it composed in 2020 during the first year of the Covid-19 pandemic. My interest in Sikh philosophy goes back more than three decades. In fact the first humanities paper I wrote, after switching career from the natural sciences, was a somewhat confused attempt to understand Sikh sovereignty in terms of its philosophical concepts. The paper was presented at a conference I co-organized at the University of Warwick in 1991, titled 'Sikh Identity in Transition' and privately published in a community magazine (1991). However, during a period of retraining in philosophy, postcolonial theory and Sikh studies in the early 1990s, I soon realized that this early essay had inadvertently inherited a tendency in modern Sikh literature to frame the key concepts of *gurmat* within ethno-nationalist schemas of identity. As I began to dig into the archives, it soon became obvious that the initial formulations of these schemas could be traced back to the intellectual encounters between Sikh elites and Western writers during the colonial period.

The problem with nationalized schemas such as these was that they corresponded neither to the complexities of my subjectivity as a diasporic, postcolonial second-generation Sikh Briton nor indeed to the broad ethos of the teachings of the Sikh Gurus as found primarily in its central scripture, the Guru Granth Sahib. These identitarian schemas had been re-*imagined* by writers in the colonial period partly as a response to the emerging political monotheism of Hindu nationalism in the late nineteenth and early twentieth centuries. Like many others I had uncritically inherited it, which was partly a consequence of the reactionary politics of the 1980s. What I eventually realized was that any Sikh philosophy, to be worthy of this title, (i) needs to remain true to the source of its primary inspiration (*gurbāṇī*), (ii) needs to be deeply attentive to the sociopolitical realm without becoming subservient to the varieties of nationalist tribalisms that afflict the planet today, (iii) needs to be able to speak to the existential and cultural milieu in which it was being received, which is to say that it needs to speak to the lived experiences of people like myself whose lives were situated between encounters between different cultural contexts (Sikh/Punjabi/Indian/British/American/European).

It was precisely the sense of a diasporicity characterized by a process of constantly translating between cultures, which guided the development of my critical thinking through successive MA and PhD dissertations titled

Thinking-Between Cultures: Receiving the Guru Ganth Sahib (1994) and *Thinking-Between Cultures: Metaphysics and Cultural Translation* (1999). These were partly attempts to rethink my own subjectivity, and partly scholarly forays into the intellectual mindset of nineteenth- and twentieth-century Sikh elites as they negotiated imperial encounters between Indian and European cultures. The latter project preoccupied me for longer than I had anticipated. While it enabled me to take a necessary detour into the terrain of colonial history and the study of religion-making and secularism in the Sikh and South Asian context, it also took me away from my primary interest in cross-cultural philosophy.

This particular monograph – *Sikh Philosophy: Exploring* gurmat *Concepts in a Decolonizing World* – builds off these earlier detours and forms part of a trilogy of books that help resituate my research closer to the intersection of the study of world philosophies, decolonization and spiritualities. While this book focuses on surveying, bringing together and explaining connections between key Sikh concepts, a second book *Geophilosophical Encounters* resurrects the earlier 'Thinking-Between' project by placing Sikh thought within the ambit of intercultural philosophizing. A third book *War Machines*, currently underway, investigates the question of sovereignty beyond the constraints imposed by schemas of nationalism, thus taking me back to the 1991 essay that kicked off this entire endeavour. All three of these book projects are experimental in nature. Their collective aim is to demonstrate the possibility of building epistemically empowering frameworks for the study of Sikh concepts (*gurmat*). Empowerment, as I understand it, is an effect of decolonial thinking which extracts Sikh philosophical concepts from their 'original' historico-material contexts, enabling them to adapt to and intervene in new and different cultural, social and political contexts without losing what is essentially creative or spiritually uplifting about them.

*   *   *

The major portion of this book was written during a period of sabbatical leave during winter 2020 generously provided by the University of Michigan's College of Literature Arts and the Science. I want to thank Professor Susan Juster for supporting my application to LSA and for her support from 2018 to 2020 during her time as Chair of Asian Languages and Cultures. Thanks also to Markus Nornes, Reggie Jackson, Nancy Florida and Mrinalini Sinha for their enthusiastic support of my work.

Early versions of Chapters 3 and 4 in this book were originally composed for a lecture series I delivered at the University of London's School of Oriental and African Studies. I want to express my gratitude to SOAS's Department of

Religions, particularly Cosimo Zene and Sian Hawthorne for inviting me to deliver the *Jordan Lectures in Comparative Religion* in 2009.

I want to thank the series editor Monika Kirloskar-Steinbach and the regional editor James Madaio for inviting me to contribute to Bloomsbury Introductions to World Philosophies.

My thanks to George Yancy whose interview with me on 'Sikhism & Death' provided some groundwork for Chapter 5. I also want to acknowledge colleagues, graduate students and friends who have been supportive of my work in recent years: Richard E. King, David Liu, Puninder Singh, Harjeet S. Grewal, Anneeth K. Hundle, Nirinjan Khalsa-Baker, Jasdev Singh Rai, Guriqbal Sahota, Pashaura Singh, Navdeep S. Mandair, Christopher Shackle, Pal Ahluwalia, Gurharpal Singh, Giorgio Shani, Nikky–Guninder Kaur Singh, Raji Singh Soni, Michael Nijhawan, Tavleen Kaur, Jasleen Singh, Pinderjeet Gill, Conner Vanderbeek, Sukhwinder Singh Obhi, Michael Hawley, Nathaniel Eli Gallant, T. Sher Singh, Manoher Singh, Randeep Hothi, Dav Panesar, Virinder Kalra, Tej Purewal, Anne Murphy, Franchesca Cassio, Surinder Singh Matharu, Bhai Baldeep Singh and members of the Naad Pargaas group especially Jagdish Singh, Amaninder Singh, Navjot Kaur and Amandeep Singh Khalsa. Alex Prosi provided much needed help with the diagrams. My local Sikh community in Michigan has always been supportive, and I offer my gratitude to the Sikh Studies Association of Michigan and Mata Tripta Gurdwara in Plymouth (MI) for allowing me to share some of the ideas presented in this book in the form of outreach lectures. As always, Aman-vir and Sukhmani in their very different ways remind me why it was necessary to write this book in the first place. Preet's patience and unflagging support have helped to keep me going even when things seemed to go awry. I dedicate this book to her. For their unstinting *ardās* in support of my academic work, I pay tribute to my mother Parkash Kaur, to my father-in-law Col. Baldev Singh Hundal and to the memory of those who left this world too soon, my father S. Karnail Singh Mandair and mother-in-law Mrs. Gurdev Kaur. Parts of Chapter 7 have appeared in *Sikhism: A Guide for the Perplexed* (2013). My thanks also to Dr. Parvinder Khanuja for permission to use an image from the Khanuja Family Collection (p. 6).

Introduction

This book is a contribution to the study of world philosophies, a branch of philosophy that examines the concepts, practices, arguments and world views of different cultures and traditions, more specifically in this case the set of tradition(s) that are called Sikh. At first glance Sikh philosophy could well pass as a legitimate subfield of comparative philosophy or one of many different world philosophies. From this perspective, Sikh philosophy would be no different from Islamic, Chinese, Hindu, Jewish, Christian or African philosophies insofar as it points to the *philosophical* aspect of an ethnic or religious formation. One could say that 'Sikh philosophy' indicates an originally ethno-religious cultural formation with a capacity for philosophical investigation. Accordingly one finds a number of books and pamphlets dealing with topics like 'Philosophy of Sikhism', 'Teachings of the Sikh Gurus', 'Philosophy of Guru Nanak', Sikh Doctrine and Ideology, almost all of which assume that the term 'Sikh philosophy' refers to an indigenous system of thought, a set of specifically Sikh ideas, doctrines and practices which can be traced back to the original intentions and life practices authorized by its founders, the ten Sikh Gurus and especially the first Sikh Guru, Nanak.

However, some pause for thought is necessary here. First, as I explain in greater detail in Chapter 1, 'Sikh philosophy' is in fact a composite term which first emerges in the context of colonial-period encounters and interactions between categories and concepts of Sikh and Western thought, specifically in relation to the translation of an axial term in the Sikh lexicon: *gurmat* (the logic or teaching of the Guru). From this perspective it may be more helpful to think of Sikh philosophy as an 'assemblage' rather than an autochthonic thought-form. In this sense, secondly, unlike 'Buddhist philosophy', 'Hindu philosophy' or 'Islamic philosophy', 'Sikh philosophy' has not achieved the same level of recognizability within the modern knowledge system. One reason for this might be that Sikhism is obviously much younger than the Buddhist, Islamic and Hindu traditions, whose philosophies (i) derive from long-established indigenous traditions, (ii) are able to draw on the work of iconic exegetes and (iii) have indigenous categories (*darśana* and *śāstra* in the Hindu context or *dhamma/dharma* in Buddhist context) that resonate with the Western category of 'philosophy'.

Yet the Sikh lexicon has similar categories such as *dharam*, which broadly refers to ontology, and the term *gurmat* which refers to the instruction, knowledge or teaching imparted by the Guru and broadly corresponds to what is generally understood by epistemology. In this way the meanings of *gurmat* and *dharam* converge in what might simply be called 'Sikh philosophy'. In this regard there is a relatively voluminous Sikh literature categorizable as broadly philosophical in nature, although thus far it has mainly been restricted to the work of scholars based in the Indian academy. So the question still stands: Why is 'Sikh philosophy' not generally recognized as a knowledge system in its own right, one that is capable of contributing to global thought?

A pertinent answer to this question has to do with the legacies of imperial encounter and the modern knowledge system which reconfigured Sikh categories and concepts through the lenses of religion and theology rather than philosophy. In other words, within the European knowledge system Sikhism was configured primarily as a religious tradition rooted in Punjabi culture with its own beliefs, doctrines and practices, but with no discernible philosophical system by means of which it might be able to participate in the streams of global thought. This in turn affected the ways Sikhs see themselves and how others (especially Western scholars) have seen Sikhs and the conceptual categories of their life-world. To understand how this happened and to establish a useful point of departure for the study of Sikh philosophy, it will be helpful to begin by providing some historical, spiritual and cultural contextualization pertinent to the emergence of Sikh philosophy as an intellectual formation.

Sikhism, *Sikhī* and Guru Nanak

The origins of Sikhism can be traced to the Punjab region of North India (lit. land of the five rivers) five centuries ago. However, the term 'Sikh*ism*' is a Western word coined not by Sikhs but by Europeans, specifically the British, in the nineteenth century. In this sense it is like the words Hinduism, Buddhism, Jainism which also are not indigenous to the Indic lexicons. Sikhs themselves use the term *sikhī* which, like the word Sikh, is derived from the Punjabi verb *sikhnā*: to learn. Unlike Sikhism, the word *sikhī* does not denote an object or thing. Rather, it has a temporal connotation and refers to a path of experiential learning integral to one's life. This of course raises an important question about the very legitimacy of the term 'Sikh-ism' and why it even continues to be used, a point which will be discussed in detail later.

Sikhs are those who choose to undertake a path of self-perfection under the guidance of a spiritual master called Guru (to be distinguished from the lower case 'guru' which is traditionally used in India to refer to any respected teacher). Historically, for Sikhs the Guru (upper case) refers to a succession of ten spiritual masters, each of whom played a role in evolving the path of *sikhī* and a teaching or philosophy known as *gurmat*. But the term 'Guru', as the Sikhs use it, has wider meanings that include the Word of the Gurus as embodied in Sikh scripture (*śabda-guru* as Guru Granth Sahib), the teaching or philosophy of the Gurus (*gurmat*) or the source of inspiration that underpins all of these (the *satguru*). The community as a whole is known as the Panth (also derived from the Sanskrit *pth* meaning path).

The founding figure behind the entire Sikh movement was Guru Nanak whose teachings and life experience became the inspiration and model for the nine Gurus who followed him. The Sikh Gurus passed on their teachings to the community that grew around them, in the form of several thousand exquisitely beautiful poems and hymns enshrined in the two key scriptural texts of the Sikh Panth: the Adi Granth and Dasam Granth, both recognized masterpieces of Indian devotional literature. The Adi Granth is so important in Sikh tradition that it occupies centre stage in the physical layout of all *gurdwaras* (lit. the Guru's Door or Sikh temples) and in ceremonies of worship. It possesses a unique status marked by its honorific title of Guru Granth Sahib. Because of its remarkable influence, and sheer centrality to Sikh practice, devotion, conceptuality, as the single most important textual resource for any Sikh philosophy, and as the repository of sovereign authority, a few words about the development and structural content of the Guru Granth are warranted.[1]

Guru Granth Sahib

Without real parallel in other Indian traditions the importance of the Guru Granth Sahib to the Sikh way of life is most obviously manifested in the central place given to the Sikh scripture in the physical layout of a gurdwara. For this reason, Sikhism is sometimes described as a 'religion of the Book'. But it is in no sense a book containing the sort of laws and rules characteristic of the Semitic scriptures. Rather, the Guru Granth Sahib serves as a hymnal, as the focus of private and communal devotion and as a reference text for philosophical contemplation or spiritual counsel in times of difficulty, and in a way that makes it arguably unique among other scriptures, the Guru Granth Sahib also mediates political-spiritual authority. In this sense it is not mere scripture but the embodiment of the principle of sovereignty itself. If sovereignty can be defined as the 'power to authorize', then this principle was instituted practically and conceptually by Guru Nanak and passed on to his successor Gurus as part of the process of transmitting authority from one Guru to another. Central to this transmission of authority was the tangible presence of a personal living Guru and the intangible presence of the *śabda*

(Word) of *gurbāṇī* (the Guru's utterance) and the consolidation of the latter into a physical text compiled by the fifth Guru, Arjan, and sealed by the tenth Guru, Gobind Singh. During the period of the living Gurus (1469–1708), and in a way that is unique to the Sikh context, sovereignty was diametrically mediated between the person of the Guru and the non-personal form of text as *śabda*. This dialectic of the personal and non-personal came to a close with the tenth Guru. As I explain more carefully in Chapter 2 ('Experience'), the question of tangible and intangible sovereignty becomes a cornerstone of any possible Sikh philosophy. Indeed, Sikh philosophy can be seen as an expression of the sovereign impulse to mediate form and formlessness, visible and invisible, known and unknown, material and immaterial.

If the status of the Guru Granth Sahib as the primary scripture of the Sikhs is a special one, this is due in no small way to (i) the character of its contents which can be regarded as a repository of all major Sikh concepts (hence its centrality to Sikh philosophy), and (ii) its organization, which in its modern form dates from after the introduction of the printing press into nineteenth-century Punjab and has a standard format of 1,430 pages printed in the Gurumukhi script with the text printed in continuous lines, with breaks only for major new sections.[2]

Structurally the Guru Granth Sahib is composed of three main sections of unequal length. The first is a relatively brief opening section consisting of hymns used for liturgical practices. This section contains works that a devout Sikh will recite or sing each day: the *Japji* by Guru Nanak which is prescribed for recitation in the early morning hours and the hymns by the Gurus prescribed for the evening prayers (*Rahiras*) and the night prayer (*Sohilla*). The somewhat longer final section (1353–1430) contains collections of shorter verses by the Gurus and others, along with poems of praise in honour of the Gurus composed by their court poets, the Bhatts.[3]

The main body of the scripture (14–1353) is a vast collection of hymns. As illustrated in Figure 1 its primary arrangement is by means of the *rāga* or musical measure in which they are to be performed. Within the primary category of the thirty-one main *rāgas* which are distinguished as separate headings (equivalent to what might be considered 'chapters' in a typical book), the hymns of the Gurus are next organized by their poetic form, beginning with the shortest, which may occupy only a few lines of text, and gradually progressing to much longer compositions, which may each take up several pages. It is within these categories that authorship is finally distinguished beginning with the hymns of Guru Nanak, followed by those of other Gurus in chronological order. Since all the Gurus used the poetic signature 'Nanak', their compositions are distinguished by the code word 'Mohala', abbreviated as M, so that the hymns of Guru Nanak himself are labelled as M1, those of

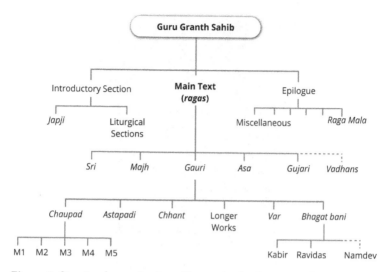

Figure 1 Structural organization of hymns in the Guru Granth Sahib.

the second and third Guru as M2 and M3 respectively and so on. After the hymns of the Gurus, most *rāgas* then conclude with shorter groups of hymns by non-Sikh poets of the pre-Guru period, such as Kabir, Namdev, Ravidas and Farid. These authors are generically known as *bhagats*.[4]

In total, the Guru Granth Sahib contains some 6,000 separate compositions. Of the Sikh Gurus whose works are included in the Sikh scriptures, Guru Nanak has 974 compositions, Guru Angad 62, Guru Amar Das 907, Guru Ramdas 679, Guru Arjan 2,218 and Guru Tegh Bahadur 116. Of the *bhagats*, Kabir has the greatest number, 541, although many of these are very short verses. In the formation of the Adi Granth as a whole, the key figure is the fifth Guru, Arjan, by far the largest contributor.[5] Indeed the organizational structure of the Guru Granth Sahib as a collection stands as testimony to his skill as its chief redactor.

As mentioned earlier the Guru Granth's main body of text (1,340 pages) is arranged not according to concept or narrative but according to musical measures known as *rāgas*. A *rāga* (along with the *tāla* or rhythm) is a traditional melodic type in Hindustani music, consisting of a theme that expresses an aspect of spiritual feeling and sets forth a tonal system on which variations are improvised within a prescribed framework of typical progressions, melodic formulas and rhythmic patterns (*tālas*). The Sikh Gurus were well versed in contemporary styles of Indian music. For example, popular portraits of Guru Nanak depict his constant companion Mardana as a trained musician specializing in the stringed instrument called *rabāb* (Figure 2).

Figure 2 Guru Nanak and Mardana [Khanuja Family Collection].

Guru Nanak and his successors wished their hymns to be sung to *rāgas* that evoked the emotional intensity being experienced and the performance style to be compatible with the meaning of the hymn.

Far from being supplementary to the text, the role of the *rāga* and *tāla* is central to its organization, since according to Indian aesthetic theory, each musical *rāga* in combination with *tāla* evokes a mood or expression that has its own distinctive flavour (*rasa*), which may vary across a spectrum ranging from adoration and rejoicing to desolation and entreaty. To render the *rāga* correctly in performance (*kirtan*) is to correctly express one mood or set of emotions and not another. In order to reproduce a certain mood, traditions of Sikh musicology, variously known as *gurbāṇī kirtan* or *gurmat sangeet*, stress the performance rules and melodic material as the best way of maintaining the individual properties of the *rāga* and of allowing the finer aspect of the hymn to emerge.[6]

Each hymn is therefore set to a predefined *rāga*, and when it is sung, the nature and feelings associated with the *rāga* affect the lyrical interpretation of the text. Sikh music thus has some limitations placed on it so that the aesthetic-spiritual aspect of the performance can be maintained. In performance, therefore, the purpose of setting the Guru's words to a *rāga* and *tāla* is to make an impression on the conscious aspect of the listener's mind in such a way that it can be cajoled into dialogue with its unconscious aspect, the heart or soul. When these two different aspects of the mind speak to each other, it is said to be attuned with its divine ground. The Gurus aimed to convey experience through feelings and moods which make up an aspect of consciousness irreducible to rationalization. And it is always important to remember the significance of this lyrical dimension when approaching the record of the Gurus' teaching contained within the text of their hymns as they appear, silently, on the printed page.[7]

All the compositions of the Gurus are in poetic verse. At the most general level their verse can be defined by common characteristics, shared with most medieval Indian poetry. It is composed of short units, with the end of each line marked by strong rhyme, and with longer lines generally being broken by a marked caesura. Since there is no grammatical run-off from line to line, each self-contained syntactic unit has to be quite short, thus favouring a typically condensed and direct style of expression which relies on such devices as parallelism and varied repetition for its cumulative effects. The verse of the Sikh Gurus is not strictly bound by the exact metrical rules of Hindi poetics, and individual lines or half-lines are often expanded by a word or phrase which is additional to the strict metrical count. This feature is particularly common in the case of the author's signature (*chhāp*), which is a standard mark of closure in all Indian poetic genres. As mentioned earlier, all the Gurus (except Guru Gobind Singh) use the signature 'Nanak', typically as a vocative self-address in the sense of 'O Nanak', or more explicitly spelt out as 'Nanak says'.[8]

Evolution of the Sikh community and polity

No account of Sikhism is ever complete without acknowledging the transition of the Panth from the path of disciplined devotion in the fifteenth and sixteenth centuries to the path of the warrior-saint in the seventeenth century. This transition is normally attributed to two complementary developments. On the one hand, the martyrdoms of the fifth and ninth Gurus, from which point onwards spiritual devotion and militant resistance against all manner of oppression went hand in hand. On the other hand, we see the adaptation, especially by the sixth and tenth Gurus, of Nanak's philosophy of oneness to rapidly changing sociopolitical circumstances at the time prompted by the wars of succession in the Mughal court and the growing intolerance towards minority formations from the Islamic state. The sixth Guru, Hargobind, developed the concept of *miri-piri*, or the oneness of spiritual and political life, and of sovereign violence (inherited from Guru Nanak's philosophy) with the aim of resisting injustice and oppression of the state by violent means where absolutely necessary. The tenth Guru, Gobind Singh, introduced radical new measures (including a new form of initiation, discipline and external form, as well as bequeathing ultimate authority to the scripture) which combined to give the early Sikh community its sense of distinctness from others.[9]

The spirit of political resistance inculcated by the Sikh Gurus inevitably brought the evolving community into conflict with the Mughal Empire. As a result, Khalsa Sikhs were hunted almost to the point of extinction in the early decades of the eighteenth century. Yet they not only survived but, by the early nineteenth century, had risen to establish a sizeable sovereign kingdom that extended from Afghanistan to Delhi. The Sikh kingdom lasted less than half a century until the arrival of the British. Following two bitterly fought wars the Sikh kingdom was annexed by the British who absorbed the Sikhs into the British Empire.

The Sikhs had lost their sovereign kingdom, but far from languishing under colonial rule their encounter with modernity and their interaction with the British proved to be advantageous, enabling a reconstruction of the community's cultural framework through the agency of a lay reformist movement called the Singh Sabha.

Religion-making versus the philosophical: Colonial influences

Most contemporary accounts present Sikhism as a neat package that includes (i) a distinct theology or doctrine whose core consists of an ethico-political monotheism, (ii) a distinct set of beliefs and practices, (iii) a historical founding figure (Nanak), (iv) historical places of worship and pilgrimage (gurdwaras), (v) a community with well-defined boundaries (the Khalsa) and (vi) a distinctly Sikh world view. As noted earlier, this neat repackaging of an internally fluid path (*sikhī*) into a seemingly fixed and immutable entity (Sikhism as a 'religion' among the other religions of the world) that can be reproduced seamlessly in world-religions textbooks, film documentaries and whenever Sikhism is googled on the internet, has certain advantages. For one thing it enables Sikhs and Sikhism to be easily identifiable, although the mechanism of this identification depends on the creation of a superficial relation to Christianity as the essential type for 'religion' in general, and for other 'religions' of the world. Once it is packaged as a 'religion' or an essentially 'religious' community, Sikhs and Sikhism are made familiar to our modern sensibilities. They no longer appear to be perplexing, particularly to outsiders, for the simple reason that everyone is more or less familiar with what religion is.

At a certain level, this kind of representation is by no means unhelpful, especially if all one requires are quick and uncomplicated answers to the questions 'What is Sikhism?' or 'Who is a Sikh?' But when a deeper and more nuanced understanding of Sikh concepts is required – or how such concepts can be applied to rapidly changing circumstances – such representations reveal severe limitations. For example, it characterizes Sikhs and Sikhism as defined objects with a truth-value that corresponds unproblematically to the contemporary lived experience of the community. The apparent truth-value of such definitions renders them difficult to contest and be redefined within the Sikh community, partly because Sikhs themselves have internalized them as truth statements that appear to correspond to their present social form. As seeming truth statements, they elide the fact that 'Sikhism' is not an indigenous term but a colonial construct. The indigenous terms *sikhī, gursikhī, gurmat* or *dharam* are extensively used by Sikhs who speak Punjabi. But in English or other European languages, it is Sikh-*ism* that takes precedence thereby forcing the identification with the category 'religion'.

There is now a great deal of evidence to show that this process of 'religion-making' helped to solidify *sikhī* from a relatively fluid orientation towards self and world, into the rigid objectifying world view that we know as Sikh*ism*. Although the solidification of *sikhī* had already begun during the period of the early Gurus, the colonial period greatly accelerated the concretizing process through the lens of nationalized schemas. The transformation from pre-colonial to nationalized forms was mediated through intercultural mimesis between Sikh and European scholars, a process that disguised itself as natural translation. Native elite scholars internalized the epistemic categories of the ruling global knowledge system, specifically the categories of religion and the secular, and applied them to their own texts, thought systems and communities. By doing so colonial elites subtly recast Sikh tradition as a sui generis religion by channelling it through the modern state's intellectual apparatus. The end result was Sikh*ism* – an entity with a much reduced capacity for making connections to the wider world, to other societies and traditions of thought.

As was the case with other colonial elites, Sikhs began to define themselves as a 'nation' and a 'world religion'[10] separate from but parallel to the rise of the Indian state and global political Hinduism. In an earlier monograph *Religion and the Specter of the West: Sikhism, India, Postcoloniality and the Politics of Translation*,[11] I investigated these processes in some detail. Among its conclusions was that the physical and psychic machinery of colonialism constrained access of Sikh concepts to global arenas of thought. As described later in the chapter, the ability of Sikhs to connect to the world in new and creative ways was disempowered by a colonial machinery, which interpreted and translated Sikh concepts, categories and teachings through the lens of theology. Once theology had become the primary regime of cultural translation, Sikh *thinking* was inevitably tethered to the social and political project of religious identification which was required primarily to facilitate governance of cultural differences or heterogeneity that characterized the indigenous populations. By doing so it effectively locked Sikh activity within the confines of identity politics.

In an intellectually productive period stretching from the late 1880s to the early 1930s in colonial Punjab, Sikh elites and European Orientalists brought some of the central concepts of Sikh thought and practice into encounter with modern Western thought in contexts not too dissimilar to those existing today. As a result of these encounters, Sikh reformists belonging to the Singh Sabha movement pushed key terms such as *gurmat* (teaching/logic/ practice of the Guru) to the forefront of interpretive activity with the aim of delineating clearer boundaries between Sikh and non-Sikh life-worlds. In ways that are only now being recognized, *gurmat* became a conceptual pivot around which reformists framed two overlapping but broadly distinguishable strands of activity, *religious* and *philosophical*.

These two strands can be seen as distinct, though overlapping, expressions of Sikh desire and interpretive capacity, giving rise over a period of fifty years or so, to two different bodies of knowledge. The better-known strand can be traced to the translation of *gurmat* as 'religion' and corresponds closely to the social formation with a well-defined code of social and personal conduct (*Sikh rahitmaryada*) represented in the public sphere as 'Sikhism', the 'Sikh Religion' or 'Sikhism as World Religion'.[12] The lesser-known strand resulting from the translation of *gurmat* as 'the Guru's philosophy or logic' gave rise to a relatively specialized body of knowledge simply known as 'Sikh philosophy' or *Sikh chintan*, which deals with processes of thought vis-à-vis key concepts and how they relate the individual self to the world. Although reformist scholars saw no essential conflict between the religious and philosophical framings of *gurmat*, partly for the sake of convenience and partly because the second strand (*gurmat* as 'Sikh philosophy') is central to this book, I treat them separately.

gurmat as 'Sikh religion' or 'Sikh theology'[13]

In the religious strand *gurmat* became a conceptual vehicle for developing the notion of Sikhism as a world religion. It focused on purifying the domain of ritual practice from what were deemed to be non-Sikh practices and by the mid-twentieth century resulted in the formulation of an official Sikh code of conduct championed by a Sikh political party. Ultimately, the representation of *gurmat* as specifically religious or theological made it easier to capture a broader array of Sikh concepts within the echo chamber of religious identity, an arena of representation engineered and administered by the legal machinery of the modern secular state.

As noted earlier, perhaps the simplest example of the imperial legacy of capture and disempowerment is the term 'Sikhism' – itself a product of colonial encounter – as it is defined by the *Oxford English Dictionary* (OED). While indigenous terms corresponding to the -ism – *sikhī, gurmat, gursikhī, Sikh dharam* – are used by Sikhs on a daily basis, it is the Anglophone category Sikh*ism* which takes precedence, thereby forcing an identification with the category 'religion'. By defining 'Sikhism' as the beliefs and practices of Sikhs, or as an Indian monotheistic religion founded in fifteenth-century India, the OED turns the Sikh aspect into a cliché – a religious type (monotheism), an ethnic type tied to a geographical location (Punjabi/North India) and a historical type (medieval India).

The epistemic narrowing created by the cliché is now increasingly recognized and challenged not only by scholars but, surprisingly, by younger generations of Sikhs working in the public sphere in India and the diaspora. For many, their resistance has taken the form of preference for the term *sikhī* as opposed to Sikhism. As scholars in the field of critical religion studies have noted, the '-ism' in the formation Sikhism represents less a signifier of a certain truth-value than the indication that their users have settled into a comfortable position within the Anglophone consciousness, and through that into the seemingly natural and neutral language of common sense.[14]

What has become increasingly clear to scholars and contemporary generations of Sikh practitioners alike is that what we understand today as 'religion' is not a 'stand-alone category'.[15] As Timothy Fitzgerald reminds us, 'historically and conceptually the idea of religion as a universal essence manifesting in specific religions, that emerged (in English at least) in the late seventeenth century, did not become powerfully institutionalized until the American and French revolutions and their respective problematics of a new world order' (Fitzgerald: 5). In other words, religion as a category is a relatively modern invention that emerged in parallel to the rise of the secular European state and its imperializing project. The purpose of creating the modern category 'religion' was to help authorize and naturalize secular rationality as the dominant form of modern consciousness, and as the essential language of conventional thinking or 'common sense'. It is precisely this common sense which persuades us of the apparent naturalness of oppositions such as religion versus politics, or materiality versus ideality to give two well-known examples. As with the OED entries on 'Sikhism', we tend not to question the framework behind such common-sense definitions because we feel that our everyday language naturally reflects a rationality that any normal person would assent to.[16]

gurmat as 'Sikh philosophy'

The translation of *gurmat* as 'Sikh philosophy' has not been as widely disseminated as 'Sikh Religion' even though there is a considerable body of literature corresponding to the former and the fact that an early form of Sikh philosophy can be traced back to early Sikh tradition in the sixteenth century. However, it is probably correct to say that the modern discourse of 'Sikh philosophy' emerged in the late nineteenth and early twentieth centuries primarily as a way of presenting a distinctly Sikh world view and ethics in response to the more voluminous literature by competing discourses such as Hindu Philosophy, Islamic Philosophy and Christian Philosophy. As a discourse its main purpose was to convey the basic concepts and teachings of the founder of Sikh tradition, Guru Nanak, whose compositions formed the basis of the thought-praxis that Sikhs refer to as *gurmat*.

From this perspective it is possible to discern an *implicit* Sikh philosophy at work going back to the primary source texts of Sikh tradition, the Guru Granth Sahib being the obvious example where the essentials of *gurmat* as a form of thought-practice is expounded by the Sikh Gurus themselves. This in turn gave rise to commentarial traditions beginning with the writings of Bhai Gurdas (a close associate of the fourth, fifth and sixth Gurus and someone who was privy to their thought process), followed by more formalized schools of exegetical commentary regarded today as streams of thought-practice (*prnālī*). These commentarial traditions have an implicit, if not explicit, philosophical orientation and culminate in the Singh Sabha *prnālī* whose writers were strongly influenced by colonial education and European modes of thought.

Despite the fact that Singh Sabha thinkers narrowed the interpretative frameworks for understanding Sikh concepts by tethering them to the modernist religio-secular frame, they nevertheless kept the door open to philosophical thinking vis-à-vis the discursive spheres variously referred to as 'Sikh *chintan*' (thought or philosophy), *gurbānī vichār* (reflection on the Gurus' 'revealed' utterances) or simply *gurmat vichār* (lit. reflection on the Guru's logic). As noted earlier, this discursive sphere corresponds to the second strand of scholarly activity by colonial elites which equated *gurmat* with philosophy. It is this act of *equating* the two discourses – the Indic *gurmat* with the European 'philosophy' – that justifies designating Sikh philosophy as an 'assemblage'. I will say more about this in Chapter 1. For now let us simply note that once it is interpreted as philosophical, *gurmat* includes within its ambit such activities as *chintan* (thought), *viākhiā* (commentary), *vichār* (reflection), *kathā* (oral exegesis) all of which refer to the processes of reflective thought aiming to connect Sikh concepts to the outside world.

Since the early twentieth century these reflective processes have been gradually synthesized into a scholarly and intellectual discourse going by the name 'Sikh philosophy' composed in English and modern Punjabi idioms. Yet despite accumulating a sizeable body of literature over the past century, 'Sikh philosophy' has remained largely ignored by modern scholarship which has, by and large, relegated it to the realm of ideology or doctrine.[17] A detailed analysis of this marginalization is beyond the scope of this chapter and is discussed elsewhere.[18] Due in part to the secularist logic in which modern Sikh studies has been framed, the designation of Sikh philosophy as mere ideology or doctrine is stated in terms that position the primary sources of Sikh literature as essentially devotional or pietistic in nature, and therefore unsuited to the task of philosophical speculation and the broader project of comparative thinking.[19]

However, there is a relatively straightforward rebuttal to this argument, which might go something like this. The source literature may indeed be devotional-poetic-aesthetic in nature. But it has its own form of logic and gives rise to a distinctive mode of thinking which may not be analytic or critical in the way that conventional eurocentric philosophy stipulates. Nevertheless it is thinking, albeit a thinking and logic that operates according to different rules and from a standpoint that is antithetical to conventional modern critique. Moreover, there exists a vast body of secondary literature that has grown up around it, and this secondary literature expounds and explicates the teachings of the Sikh Gurus through modes of reasoning that happen to be current in any social context. Furthermore, there are well-established and vibrant living traditions of oral exegesis (often referred to as *gurmat vichār* or *gurbāṇī viākhiā*) that also expound its core teachings, again, using modes of reasoning corresponding to the social milieus in which they emerged.

While these commentarial traditions (*prnālīs*) are not doing 'philosophy' in the eurocentric sense of the term, it would not be incorrect to suggest that these exegetical traditions are also performing a certain kind of conceptualization, putting into play a thinking based on a devotional logic that helps ordinary Sikhs to reflect on the Gurus' teachings in the context of everyday life. Perhaps the best example is Giani Sant Singh Maskin who was perhaps the leading *kathā vāchic* (oral exegete) of his time. Trained in the Nirmalā tradition, Maskin delivered thousands of lectures elaborating on *gurmat* concepts during his lifetime, many of which were composed into short treatises and published in book form or recorded on cassettes and CDs.[20] By any stretch of the imagination, the nature of Maskin's work was philosophical in the sense that it was not narrow textual exegesis but a thinking about Sikh concepts, teaching his listeners how to connect concepts to the world here and now.[21] It involved forms of public reasoning which suggest that an implicit philosophical endeavour has been underway since the time of the Sikh Gurus, one that became more explicit in the work of modern Sikh scholars due to the encounter with Western modernity.

What is Sikh philosophy *for*?

From the broadened perspective discussed earlier, I would like to offer the following reasons for including Sikh philosophy both as a subfield of world philosophies and as a major growth area within the more specialized but rapidly growing field of Sikh studies.

First: Sikh philosophy can be considered an antidote to the debilitating effects of colonial frameworks inherited by Sikhs and other formerly colonized peoples. Given that one legacy of European colonization was the narrowing and disempowerment of indigenous epistemic frameworks (a process facilitated by the intellectual work of native elites who internalized European systems of knowledge and its attendant matrix of power and governmentality), what the 'assemblage' Sikh philosophy offers is an expansion and empowerment of *gurmat's* epistemic potential. It does this by providing a portal that doesn't simply translate between two different worlds but more importantly reconfigures translation into a process of *thinking-between* the two worlds. Thinking-between is much more than just an act of linguistic translation. It is synonymous with the process of subjectivity itself. In this way, Sikh philosophy not only explores Sikh ways of knowing and existing; perhaps more importantly, it equips Sikh concepts with wings so that they can travel much further than the ethno-cultural milieu which birthed them, find new places to settle and develop new connections to other societies and different thought systems in an increasingly complex world that we all share.[22] In this way the function of the assemblage 'Sikh philosophy' becomes more obvious. While it was born out of debilitating colonial encounters, today it has the potential to develop into a tool for decolonizing the world. Such decolonization involves rectifying the epistemic injustices of the colonial past, not least by embracing hybrid patterns of thought (where 'to think' means to *think-between* different cultures) which in turn arise from intrinsically hybrid subject formations.

Second: stated more succinctly, the purpose of Sikh philosophy is to enable Sikhs and non-Sikhs who use those concepts to intervene in the natural, social and political world in new and productive ways. Or perhaps to apply Sikh concepts with a view to changing oneself, perhaps initiate journeys of self-realization and transform one's consciousness, and in so doing, to change existing and moribund states of affairs. These are precisely the tasks that the modern Western-European knowledge system has appropriated for itself and denied to other cultures. The spell cast by the self-assigned and self-designating dominance of 'white-epistemologies'[23] – which constitutes the core of 'white supremacy' in its religio-secular, racial, casteist and political forms – can be effectively challenged by the emergence of subaltern philosophies or systems of indigenous thinking, knowing and existing in the world.

Third: if the basic components of Sikh philosophy are Sikh concepts, and if these concepts are part of temporal becomings that invite new perspectives on the nature of our lived existence, irrespective of whether this is natural or social, then Sikh philosophy can be more usefully thought of as an 'assemblage', a tool that helps to forge unlikely connections between disparate and diverse concepts and components, with the specific aim of intervening in a particular problematic – namely the actual social field of global modernity and state-ordered society. In this sense Sikh philosophy can be considered an *activist* philosophy.[24] By intervening in and re-imagining the temporal framework of this world, Sikh philosophy has the potential to experiment with new ways of actualizing Sikh concepts debilitated by the epistemic legacy of colonialism. Differently stated, by re-capacitating Sikh concepts and enabling them to move freely from one context to another, we can jolt the underpinning conventions of the dominant system of global thought and bring positive changes to the social milieu in which one lives and operates. Sikh philosophy can achieve this not by sealing itself within a particular ethno-cultural milieu, and thus remain aloof from the dominant social and intellectual field of host cultures, but rather (in a move that might seem counter-intuitive) by *diasporizing* the host culture.

To diasporize the host culture is to simultaneously distort the conceptual matrix of the dominant social field *and* lay claim to it as one's very own. The work of diasporizing a host culture lays the groundwork for dialogue between philosophical traditions and concepts. There is a tendency to assume that 'dialogue' is a process of communication that can be simply plucked off the shelf. True intercultural dialogue happens only when the self corresponding to the host and guest culture *becomes other to itself*. Otherwise, dialogue is simply a schema imposed from above by the dominant culture. As I have argued elsewhere, Sikh philosophy has an action-orientation enabling individuals to intervene in and change existing states of affairs by experimenting with Sikh concepts in the field of life and applying them to everything from the political (international/national), society, through journeys of self-realization or as a mode of social resistance. It is an invitation to explore and experiment with *gurmat* concepts with the aim of connecting with and making positive changes to the world rather than being hermetically sealed from it.

Fourth: Sikh philosophy can be re-imagined as a mode of 'lived abstraction', a wide-ranging practice grounded in everyday life *and at the same time* a practice of forming and reforming Sikh concepts in relation to whatever one's life encounters. Stated differently, the practice of everyday life – which incorporates the ongoing attendant negotiation of identity and difference, the processes of selfing and de-selfing that are continually going on – is inseparable from the making and re-making of Sikh concepts. Sikhs perform both in some manner or another, often without realizing that they are doing it.[25]

Fifth: the decolonization of the knowledge system. Conventionally this has been the task of critical and cultural theory. However, a major criticism of critical theory, even its most progressive versions, is that it assumes an understanding of critique that is limited only to European concepts and models of thought.[26] By operationalizing Sikh concepts and rethinking the model of critical and cross-cultural thinking, it may be possible to develop a 'post-Western' system of knowledge which is able to internally pluralize the epistemic machinery of the humanities, social and natural sciences. This in turn would allow the knowledge system to recognize and deploy the concepts of different cultures to solve social, political and spiritual problems. Concepts of Sikh philosophy could then be made available and deployed within disciplines such as sociology, anthropology, psychology, art, religious studies, music, politics and philosophy, as well as fields such as Asian studies, postcolonial studies and diaspora studies.

Overview of chapters

The primary aim of this book is to introduce and examine some of the central concepts of Sikh philosophy, to ask what these concepts tell us about the nature of reality, the nature of mind/self/ego, and whether it is possible to discern broad contours of a Sikh logic, epistemology and ontology. Additionally, the book looks at how these concepts address broader themes such as the body, health and well-being, creation cosmology, death, immortality and rebirth, the nature of action and intention, ethics and, a theme that undergirds every chapter, spirituality.

Chapter 1 charts the development of Sikh philosophy from its pre-philosophical roots to an intellectual field in its own right during the colonial period. By focusing on the axial concept *gurmat* (logic or teaching of the Guru) this chapter traces a genealogy of the major interpretive traditions (*prnālīan*) of Sikh thought from the sixteenth century to the modern period, highlighting the key conceptual moves by which *gurmat* undergoes a secular translation into the new assemblage 'Sikh philosophy'. The bulk of this chapter will look at the encounter of Sikhism with modernity through the work of leading Sikh thinkers of the twentieth century and the way in which the term *gurmat* becomes representative of Sikh thought and practice.

Chapter 2 shifts the book's focus back to the present by asking: Where does a contemporary Sikh philosophy begin? From where does it attain its authority as a discourse? Sikh thinkers have been fairly adamant that the authoritative source of *gurmat* must be the defining spiritual experience of Guru Nanak. Although the question of authority is reasonably well established in the writings of the Sikh Gurus, the nature of this experience has been interpreted in a variety of different ways ranging from the politico-ethical monotheism favoured by modernist Sikhs to a more open way of thinking about experience which favours the discourse of consciousness and spirituality, often (and I would argue wrongly) categorized as monism.

My discussion navigates between the two options showing how the choice between monotheism and monism is a misleading one, resulting in an either/or oppositional thinking which in both cases devalues the role of the world. The logic underpinning such categories as monism, monotheism and pantheism is derived from a Christian world view and inherited from the Euro-Christian colonial knowledge system. Instead, I point to a different way of thinking about experience, one that reappraises the central tendencies within *sikhī* or *gurmat*. More specifically, my discussion asks whether this experience is directed towards a world or reality *beyond* this one, in which case its primary tendency might be described as religious/ascetic and remains rooted in a particular historical ethno-religious milieu? Or is the experience directed primarily towards *this* life and *this* world, in which case it would manifest as a desire to intervene in psychic, social and political formations for the betterment of the world beyond the milieu in which one is initially situated? Inevitably the discussion also touches on the question of revelation – a term that is used somewhat loosely as a synonym for transcendental experience. I ask whether, and to what extent, the term 'revelation' is applicable to *gurbāṇī*. If so – and most Sikhs seem to agree about the suitability of the concept of revelation – does this necessarily mean that *gurmat* is essentially theological (monotheistic) in its impulse? Or, can the Sikh notion of revelation be understood according to a radically different model, one that follows Guru Nanak's advice, that to properly understand the nature of spiritual experience, one needs to pay closer attention to the internal revolution within one's psyche? In other words, Guru Nanak's own testimony moves the discussion of experience and authority towards ego-death, which in turn requires a radically different notion of epistemology or way of knowing.

Accordingly, Chapter 3 explores what would normally go by the name 'epistemology'. However, rather than following eurocentric understandings of knowing, this chapter deepens the discussions of experience and ego-death to redefine the meaning of epistemic logic in Sikh philosophy. Any discussion of logic has to examine an axial concept of mainstream Sikh thought and practice: the concept of *śabda-guru* (Word-as-Guru). Chapter 3 raises important questions, for example, when Guru Nanak claims that it is the 'Word that speaks' rather than the human mind (which must be silent to hear the Word speak), what does this mean? How can mere words or language possibly be regarded as the ultimate authority in Sikhism? What is the relationship between the principle of *śabda-guru* and the nature of thought? What kind of thought is opened up by the realization of this principle? If the realization of *śabda-guru* is intimately connected to egoloss, what is the relationship between thought and egoloss? Is thought separate from affect? Furthermore, what implications does the concept of *śabda-guru* have for the idea of a personal God? Can the principle of *śabda-guru* provide an alternative notion of the secular?

Chapter 4 builds on the foregoing investigation of logic to examine what a Sikh ontology might look like. A useful insight into the nature of Sikh ontology can be found in one of Guru Nanak's major compositions, the so-called *Rāga Marū* hymn, a profound meditation on the nature of reality that begins by contemplating the age-old theme of creation *ex nihilo*. What becomes evident in this hymn, however, is that Nanak may simply have been using creation cosmology as a heuristic that helps relocate the creative impulse to the interiorizing functions of the human mind/self, as can be seen in an individual's quest for self-perfection through the process of egoloss. Working between the cosmic and the psychic dimensions, Nanak shifts the question of ontology into the language and realm of consciousness. By reconceiving reality in terms of an expanded notion of consciousness, the way is open to more fruitful discussions of human freedom, the nature of

'God' and towards the question of health, well-being and liberation explored in Chapter 6.

Chapter 5 explores the interlinked notions of death, life and rebirth in Sikh philosophy by way of the following questions: What is death for the Sikh Gurus and how do they approach it in their writings? Why do we fear death? How can we face death? Is death final? Or is there life after death? Do we have immortal souls? Can a philosophical understanding of death help us to live our lives in certain ways rather than others? How does Nanak's view of death relate to his understanding of life itself? Is there any point to thinking about the question of life after death? How does the notion of transmigration (the idea that we are reborn into different life forms after we die until we gain liberation) be compared to other theories of life after death? Discussions of life, death and rebirth in Sikh philosophy are usually connected to the notion of *karma*. I examine the Sikh theory of *karma* through the writing of Bhai Jodh Singh, an influential Sikh thinker of the twentieth century. Does the Sikh understanding of *karma* point to an inexorable law as it does in Hindu and Buddhist philosophy, or does it point elsewhere in Sikh thought? In this chapter I lean towards the latter perspective as Nanak's writings are rich in allusions to the idea of action and activism as a process of writing or imprinting the individual self (and the fabric of life itself) – a process that is in turn connected to the work of memory.

An immediate implication of our earlier examinations of the concept *śabda-guru* (Word-as-Guru) is that it opens up a model of the human psyche based on the intrinsic relatedness of ego and non-ego. This means that a discussion of affect (connected to non-ego) is absolutely central for understanding soteriology which, in the Sikh context, is refracted through the discourse of perfection. Basically, what this leads to is the application of Sikh theory to its practice, which becomes the topic of Chapter 6, 'Self-Realization: Liberation and Health'. The relationship between practice and theory in Sikh philosophy forces us to take the body seriously, not only as something represented or brought to mind but as a physical site where the application of techniques and concepts of self-perfection can be worked out. The main part of this chapter will be devoted to understanding mental and physical health through an examination of the emergence and manifestation of '*kléshas*' – literally emotions that (i) result in mental conflict as opposed to oneness, (ii) distort perception and (iii) result in a dualistic world view. The main innovation of this chapter will be to bring a discussion of *kléshas* (referred to by Guru Nanak as the 'five thieves' or 'five enemies') into philosophical discourse and show how they fit with a broader theory of liberation.

The book concludes with a brief discussion on the potentially important role of Sikh philosophy in the twenty-first century. I argue that the importance of philosophical investigation and the kinds of questions it raises is tied, one way or another, to questions of sovereignty. This is a pertinent discussion today because, as a stateless minority, Sikhs are faced with difficult choices as the nature of polity in the Punjabi 'homeland' is rapidly being transformed by a Hindu nationalist regime determined to unify all Indians through Hindutva ideology. Because some on the fringes of the Sikh community have been engaged in political conflict with the secular Indian state for several decades, the question of sovereignty is even more urgent.[27]

Discussion questions

(1) What are the implications of saying that 'Sikh philosophy' is a composite term, or an assemblage, rather than an autocthonic thought-form?

(2) Assess the impact of colonialism on Sikh thought and praxis.

(3) Under the influence of colonialism the primary sources of Sikh philosophical project were designated 'religious' or devotional, and therefore unsuited for the task of philosophical speculation. How might this argument be rebutted?

(4) In what ways can Sikh philosophy contribute to the task of decolonization?

(5) How can the field of Sikh philosophy be of practical use? For whom?

Emergence of Sikh philosophy

This chapter provides an overview of the development of Sikh philosophy from its pre-philosophical roots to the formation of 'Sikh philosophy' as a field in its own right during and after the colonial period. To say that Sikh philosophy emerged from pre-philosophical roots is also to suggest that Sikh philosophy can be considered an 'assemblage'. I borrow the term 'assemblage' from the conceptual toolbox of Deleuze and Guattari for whom it signifies processes that associate 'multiple and heterogenous elements' in ways that give rise to new experiences, new meanings and new possibilities.[1] This broad sense of the term 'assemblage' can be usefully adapted to describe what happened to Sikh concepts as they encountered Western thought. Thus, in the colonial context assemblage can refer to a coupling of an ensemble of collected material parts resulting from colonial encounters between a Sikh category (*gurmat*) and a European category ('Philosophy'). Yet the nature of this coupling is such that it produces a mutually synergizing consistency despite the differences.

The focus of this particular chapter, however, is the axial concept *gurmat* (logic or teaching of the Guru) which is a cornerstone of the various interpretive traditions (*prnālīan*) of Sikh thought from the sixteenth century to the modern period. Our survey will highlight the key conceptual moves by which *gurmat* undergoes a translation into the new assemblage 'Sikh philosophy'. The latter part of this chapter will look at the encounter of Sikhism with modernity through the work of leading Sikh thinkers of the twentieth century who collectively promoted the term *gurmat* as representative of Sikh thought and practice. Although the impetus behind the development of Sikh philosophy was to explain Sikh concepts at a time when India's various communities were becoming nationalized, encounters with British imperialism were impacting the Sikh world, coercing its elite scholars to internalize structures and presuppositions of Western thought through colonial education and governance.

One such presupposition in Western philosophy was an ideology of translation which helped reformist elites reshape the nature of Sikh thought in the image of political theology. As a result, political monotheism in parallel with an imagined ethno-national identity became a conjoint baseline for early expressions of modern Sikh philosophy and continues to cast a shadow over Sikh thinking even today.

gurmat – a conceptual pillar of Sikh philosophy

According to a leading scholar of Sikh scriptural tradition, the term *gurmat* 'designates the Gurus' view or doctrine that is at the same time a living practice among Sikhs'.[2] Its meaning incorporates, but is by no means limited to, the Guru's instruction, the wisdom of the Guru, the Gurus' system or logic; the Gurus' philosophy of life as a whole; the teachings of the Guru. Terms that are 'related to *gurmat* include *gurdarsan* and *gurshabad* (which indicate) the Guru's world view or philosophical system'.[3]

The word *darsan* (vision, viewpoint) is of course reminiscent of the six schools of Indian philosophy also known as the six *darsanas* because they provided different visions, perspectives or viewpoints on the nature of reality which eventually became a central pillar of orthodox Brahmanic doctrine. As is well known the historical Buddha challenged the notion of a foundational standpoint by replacing the term *darsana* with *yānā* (way or vehicle). The Sikh Gurus did something similar but without letting go of the word *darsan*, instead of associating it with the term *gurū* or *gur*. Hence *gurdarsan* or *gurū kā darsan* qualifies the meaning of *darsan*. Thus, in contradistinction from the six Hindu philosophical systems (Samkhya-Yoga, Nyaya-Vaiseska, Mimāmsā-Vedanta) prevalent in medieval North India at the time of the Sikh Gurus (and which they refer to as '*khaṭ darsan*' lit. sour or incomplete viewpoint), the third Sikh spiritual master Guru Amardas explains the distinctive nature of Guru Nanak's philosophical system (*gurdarsan*):

> Though the six Hindu philosophical systems are all-pervasive,
>   The Guru's philosophical vision (*gur kā darsan*) is beyond these
>   systems.
> Liberation and attainment of perfection come directly through the
>   Guru (*gurmat*)
>   When Oneness takes abode in the heart/mind/soul.
> In the Guru's system
>   Whoever cultivates love and devotion is liberated.
>
> (GGS 360–1)

Two ideas seem to be central to Guru Nanak's system: the immediacy or directness of liberation and the need for inner transformation. In order to attain perfection-liberation, a certain turning or conversion needs to take place in the heart-mind-soul complex. But any such turning requires the intervention of an authentic spiritual preceptor or *satgurū*. In mainstream Sikh tradition, however, the *satgurū* does not correspond to the category of 'person' signifying an individual subject as the natural container of thought, or the idea that thought belongs to a single consciousness which exerts sovereign ownership over it.[4] The *satgurū* is better described as a trans-personal principle responsible for mediating inner transformation of the psyche. We shall look more closely at the term *satgurū* in Chapter 2, which explores its relevance to spiritual experience, authority and sovereignty. In fact, after the line of living Gurus was brought to an end in 1708 by the tenth Nanak (Guru Gobind Singh), the *satgurū* came to be recognized less as a person than as a mystical impersonal principle embodied in the word (*śabda/bāṇī*) or instruction (*updēsh*) of the Guru – a principle that could effect immediate or direct enlightenment, perfection and emancipation for anyone willing to kill ego. In a unique and seemingly counter-intuitive system of logic (*mat*) where *satgurū* is *śabda*, and *śabda* is the sword needed to slay ego and attain perfection, the central term is Guru or Gur which relates not only to the historical person Guru Nanak (and his nine successors and body of writings) but even more importantly to a trans-personal figure known as *gurmukh*.

A unique development in the *bāṇī* of Guru Nanak, the figure of the *gurmukh* signifies a sense of personhood yet-to-come; it points to the state of perfection implied in Nanak's teaching, towards which this particular person here and now (*manmukh*) can and should be moving. The *gurmukh* is therefore always nameless, a *conceptual impersonae*,[5] meaning that anyone can potentially access and attain enlightenment providing one follows a specified instructional practice and logic (*gurmat*). If it can be potentially accessed by anyone without discrimination, it follows that *gurmat* as a practical logic is not necessarily bound to the Punjabi ethno-cultural milieu from which it arises. In other words, *gurmat* has a pluriversalizing dimension as attested to by the leading reformist scholar Bhai Kahn Singh Nabha. In his monumental work *Gurśabda Ratnākar Mahānkōsh*, Kahn Singh provides the following meanings for the two linguistic components of *gurmat(i)*, namely, the terms *gur(ū)* and *mat(i)*, both of which appear to converge around the operation of the mind:

mat(i)[6]

- *āhamkār* = forms of individuation ('I' making)
- *antahkaran* = faculty for processing raw sensuous data of perception by interiorizing it

- *mat(i)* has four essential faculties – *mn, buddhī, chit* and *āhamkār* – but is identifiable with the fourth part *āhamkār*
- *mn*: faculty for concept creation (*sankālap*) and making determinate choices (*vikālap*)
- *buddhī*: faculty of reflection or thinking
- *chit*: faculty of memory (synthesizing of past/present/future)
- *āhamkār*: individuation of the type where the self learns to distinguish between itself and other things or entities
- *mati* is identifiable with the fourth faculty (*āhamkār*) insofar as *āhamkār* involves the process of synthesizing the other three into a single faculty of individuation or self-making

gur(u)[7]

- the principle that is causative of effort/elevation/self-death
- from the root *gṛh* to swallow or take in
  - hence one who ingests a learner/devotee's state of unenlightenment/ darkness, thereby enabling the devotee to directly realize the essential wisdom
- a spiritual preceptor with gravitas capable of divulging instruction
- preceptor of *mat(i)* capable of reaching the deepest part of the learner's mind (thought/desires/speech formation)
- divine instructor of the gods (Bṛhaspatī/Devgurū)
- *antahkaran* or *mn*
  - the kind of individuation proper to a Guru

Following Kahn Singh's commentary, if we combine the two terms *gur(ū)* and *mat(i)*, the synthesis results in *gurmat(i)* – a form of thinking or practice imparted either through the agency of a spiritually endowed preceptor or through the trans-personal agency of *śabda* (word). In a manner of speaking, *gurmat* can be considered a higher plane of thinking-practice. It is this sense of *gurmat* that becomes increasingly pronounced in the writings and practices of everyday life taught by Guru Nanak and his successor Gurus.

As the Sikh community evolved between the sixteenth and eighteenth centuries, the term *gurmat* remained a key pillar of Sikh praxis. Over time it was subjected to reinterpretation in the form of textual exegesis, hagiographical literatures and commentarial traditions but was rendered equally amenable to being translated into other languages and frames of modern understanding such as religio-secular liberalism. It is through the lens of the latter that *gurmat* became amenable to the work of philosophical investigation and reflection, ultimately giving rise to the modern formation 'Sikh philosophy'. The scholar Taran Singh refers to these evolving modes of *gurmat*'s reinterpretation as *prnālīan* – literally systems, techniques or schools of interpretation.[8]

Prnālīan are relatively distinct but continuous techniques of exegetical, interpretive, translational practice – continuous in the sense that interpretive activity has been going on since the time of Guru Nanak – each distinguished by one or more dominant thinkers or techniques of learning reacting to changing historical contexts and challenges.[9] A closer look at these *prnālīan* can show us how each successive *prnālī* – which I prefer to render as schools of thought-practice rather than as strictly hermeneutical schools – shaped the reception of *gurmat* as it exists today and eventually laid the ground for the emergence of the modern formation 'Sikh philosophy'.

Major systems (*prnālīan*) contributing to Sikh thought-practice (*gurmat*)

Taran Singh's important work *Gurbānī Dīan Viākhiā Prnālīan* is the first systematic attempt to survey the major systems of Sikh scriptural interpretation. Despite its signal contribution, however, one of the limitations of Taran Singh's approach is his narrowing of the scope of *prnālīan* to *viākhiā*, which basically refers to exegesis and extended commentary. In this sense *viākhiā* is limited to scriptural hermeneutics. However, *viākhiā* is but one of four strands of a broader activity of interpretive thinking called *vichār*, or when applied more specifically to the poetry of the Sikh Gurus, *gurbānī vichār* or *śabda vichār* (lit. contemplative reflection on the Guru's Word). The other three components of *gurbānī vichār* are *śabda-artha, tīkā and parmārath.* As Pashaura Singh notes,

> There are four standard techniques of Indian scriptural interpretation that are employed in Sikh exegetical methods. The first is *śabda arth* (meanings of the words) which provides synonyms as well as the meanings of difficult words in a particular hymn. The second is *tīkā* (commentary) which provides the meaning of a particular hymn with comments in simple language. The third is *viākhiā* (exegesis) which provides a detailed exegesis and extended commentary on a particular hymn from a particular angle. The last is *parmārath* (sublime meaning) which provides the scriptural meaning of a particular hymn. Thus, interpretation begins at a discursive level, at which one deals with the literal sense of *gurbānī*, but goes deeper as one contemplates the divine mysteries by gradually penetrating into subtler levels of meaning.[10]

My point is that the category *prnālī* offers a wider catchment that incorporates contemplative thought-practice and does not need to be limited to *viākhiā*, which remains fixed within exegetical commentary. The designation of *prnālī* as hermeneutics is also limiting for several reasons. First, it reduces both *prnālī* (technique or system of learning) and *gurśabda/gurbānī* to a purely textual clericalism, whereas *gurbānī* is intrinsically associated with non-textual techniques and functions, notably music and the function of the body–mind complex as a receptacle of the effects of *gurbānī*. Second, the activity of *vichār* (thought-interpretation) within different *prnālīan* incorporates a variety and complexity of modes of thought, all of which interact to produce meaning in different ways. These include complexities of reasoning, beginning with purely calculative reasoning such as *tarka* (measured or calculated judgement used in debate and argument), *vādī* and *sōch* (everyday thinking), *khōj* (deeper searching), *vichār* (contemplative reflection); *aql-siānap* (reasoning directed towards practical or pragmatic ends); *manan/mannai* (thinking that results in changed habits and frames of mind). And these modes of reasoning in turn give way to progressively deeper forms of knowing and understanding such as *sunniae* (the deeper art of listening-understanding), *giān* (wisdom acquired through mastery of the above), *sojhī* (ethical discernment), *dhyān* (focused meditative state of mind) and *bibēk* (awakening).[11]

Broadly speaking then, if we incorporate all of the above into the scope of what a *prnālī* is, it is closer to the kind of thought-practice taught by the Sikh Gurus (*gurmat*) rather than a narrow clerical method of textual analysis or philology. Having made this clarification, we can return to providing a brief overview of the main *prnālīan* of Sikh thought-practice.

Bhai prnālī

This school of interpretation can be traced to Bhāī Gurdās (1540–1630) who was a contemporary of the early Sikh Gurus and a scribe and amanuensis chosen by the fifth Guru Arjan during the final stages of composing the Adi Granth. He received the honorific 'Bhāī' (lit. brother or elder) for his contributions to the early Sikh community. Bhāī Gurdās composed 675 poems in Braj dialect. Much of his poetry is a direct exegesis of the Gurus' teaching which he uses to expound their philosophico-theological message in relatively simple and accessible style. Central to his interpretation is the concept of Guru as *śabda* (*śabda-gurū*), which identifies the physical living Guru with his Word in a spiritual sense. Bhai Gurdās is therefore rightly credited with establishing the doctrinal basis of Sikh tradition as centred around the concept of *gurmat* on the basis that his exegesis elaborates themes that continue to be central to Sikh thought and practice: the unity of Guruship, Sikh way of life (*gursikhī*), right community (*sādh sangat*) the ideal Sikh (*gurmukh*).[12]

Udāsī and Nirmalā *prnālīan*

Though nominally distinct, these two schools of interpretation have one thing in common, namely the influence of orthodox Hindu or Brahmanical philosophies as a framework for interpreting the poetry of the Sikh Gurus. The Udāsī school is associated with the Udāsī sect, the ascetic disciples of Bābā Sri Chand who was the eldest son of Guru Nānak. Sri Chand rejected the worldly path of the householder-warrior espoused by the house of Nānak, opting instead to become a wandering ascetic or *sādhū*. Udāsīs are itinerant *sādhūs* who expounded aspects of Gurū Nānak's message during the course of their travels throughout the Indian subcontinent. Although their discourses were limited to oral exegesis, an early literary record of the Udāsī school of thought is to be found in Sādhū Anandghān's exegetical commentary (*tīkā*) on Guru Nānak's *Japji*, *Ārati*, *Siddh Gōsht* and Guru Amardas's *Anand*.[13] These *tīkās* were most likely composed between 1795 and 1802 at Kāshī, the centre of Hindu orthodoxy also known as Vārānāsī where Anandghān received his philosophical training.

According to Rattan Singh Jaggi, Anandghān's interpretive technique (*prnālī*) resembles the style of a formal symposium: 'Wherever an important point is to be explained, he follows the question-answer format.'[14] Thoroughly conversant with the tools of philosophical commentary Anandghān writes with conviction, argumentative verve and arrogance most likely derived from a preconceived superiority of the Vedantic framework of Brahmanical philosophy within which he was trained. Likewise, Taran Singh notes that for Anandghān, Guru Nānak's entire *bāṇī* was nothing more than a reflection of the Hindu philosophical systems and particularly the *saguna bhaktī* school.[15] This is best seen in his interpretation of the line from the fifth stanza of Japji where Nānak writes: 'Shivā, Brahmā, Vishnū, Pārbhati are but manifestations of one eternal guru (*satgurū*).'[16] In this way Anandghān reverses Guru Nānak's own perspective, making the latter a disciple of the Hindu deities. Motivated by an underpinning process of state formation in the late eighteenth century when Sikhs were becoming the dominant political force in North India, Anandghān's vision appears to have been driven by a desire to strengthen alliances between Sikh and Hindu communities by reducing Sikhism to a sect of *sanātan dharma*, the form of orthodox Hinduism that gravitates around belief in 'eternal law' specified by Veda. This reductive technique would become a feature of commentaries in the late nineteenth century when the process of state formation took a decisively different turn under British colonialism.

Unlike the Udāsī *prnālī*, the Nirmalā *prnālī* has produced a significant literature since the late eighteenth and nineteenth centuries and has come to be regarded as an important scholastic school specializing in philosophical interpretations of central Sikh literatures. The expositions of Nirmalā scholars have generally tended to lean towards the Advaita Vedanta school of Hindu philosophy. This has led some observers such as Sher Singh to note that 'the resemblance between the two systems [*gurmat* and Advaita Vedanta] is so great that most of the Nirmalā writers have been holding, at least on the theoretical side, the two systems to be absolutely identical.'[17] Sher Singh may be overstating the point here as closer inspection reveals that most Nirmalā scholars, despite working within the dominant framework of Vedantic philosophy, nevertheless managed to maintain a degree of difference between the two traditions.

The origins of the Nirmalā school are somewhat obscure and seem to go back to a prevailing myth that the tenth Guru, Gobind Singh, sent five Sikhs from Paonṭa Sāhib to Kāshī in order to acquire training in Hindu classics and philosophy. Lack of evidence for this story notwithstanding, it is clear that during the late eighteenth and early nineteenth centuries, many centres of higher learning (or *akhāṛā*) run by Nirmalā scholars were established in cities and villages across Northern India. These Nirmalā scholars were well grounded in Indian philosophy and many specialized in deploying Advaita Vedanta as a theoretical frame for religio-philosophical discourses (*gōsṭi*) and oral exegeses (*viākhiā*) on Sikh scripture. By doing so they helped to bring Sikh concepts in line with early Indian philosophy.

One of the earliest scholars of the Nirmalā school was Pandit Gulāb Singh (b. 1732). Born into a low caste *jaṭ* peasant family Gulāb Singh attained a high level of proficiency in Sanskrit but was summarily ejected from the seminary at Vārānāsī when his teacher discovered he was not a Brahmin. All of Gulāb Singh's works are composed in Braj but written in Gurmukhi script. Chief among his works is *Mōkh Panth* (1778) or 'Path of Liberation' which is a comparative exercise of sorts that attempts to expound doctrines of *gurmat* and *gurbāṇī* in dialogue with prevailing schools of Hindu philosophy including Yoga, Nyaya, Mimāmsā and Vedanta. Another of Gulāb Singh's important works is the *Bhāvarasamrit* (1778 – 'The Essence of Immortal Nectar') which is a treatise on rationalism and detachment. The text opens with invocations of the Sikh Gurus before expounding on themes such as *ardās* (prayer), *nām*, divine love, *karmā*, detachment, heroism (*virya*) and *dharma*. Although Gulāb Singh's prose is steeped in Vedantic terminology, his touchstone remains the teachings of the Sikh Gurus concerning which he explicitly states, 'I am a follower of Guru Gobind Singh.'[18]

A renowned Nirmalā scholar during the height of Sikh political power in the early nineteenth century was Kavī Santōkh Singh. Better known for his historical accounts of the Sikh Gurus in works such as *Guru Nānak Parkāsh* (1823) and *Gurpartāp Sūraj*, he also wrote an influential *tīkā* on the Japji popularly known as *Garabganjanī Tīkā* – 'A Commentary to Humble the Pride (of Udāsī Anandghān)'. In this commentary Kavī Santōkh Singh strongly criticized Anandghān's interpretation in an effort to return the focus back to Guru Nānak's own system.

By the late nineteenth century Nirmalā scholars were regularly producing works of an explicitly philosophical nature but with a more doctrinal bent. A good example is Pandit Tārā Singh Narotam's treatise *Sri Gurmat Nirnai Sāgar* (1877 – 'A Treatise on the Nature of Gurmat'). Written at a time of heightened political tensions between Hindus, Muslims and Sikhs under British rule, the title *Gurmat Nirnai Sāgar* gives an indication of the increasing centrality of the term *gurmat* in philosophical and religious disputes between various Sikh schools of interpretation and even more so in helping to demarcate and solidify sociopolitical boundaries between Sikhs and Hindus. Narotam's treatise was a major attempt to expand the fundamental concepts of the Sikh Gurus, albeit from the traditional Indian non-dualistic standpoint. For example, Pandit Narotam interprets a line from Guru Nanak's composition *Bāburvānī* in which Nanak narrates to Lālo how the 'Word' comes to be revealed to him:

jaisī mai āvē khasam kī bāṇī taisaṛā karī giān ve Lālo
As my Beloved's Word comes to me, so I narrate it to you, O Lālo.

(SGGS, *Bāburvāṇī*)

Pandit Tārā Singh Narotam's strategy in his exposition is to show the impersonal manner in which the Word comes to Nānak. By selecting verses from the Guru Granth Sahib as his principal source, he correctly highlights the nature of the impersonal in the emergence of Guru Nānak's speech (i.e. personal sovereignty has to be annihilated), but he justifies his interpretation by way of reference to some of the great philosophers of Hinduism such as Śankara and Ramanuja, even as he fully engages the writings of mainstream Sikh thinkers such as Bhāī Nand Lāl, Bhāī Gurdās and Bhai Mani Singh.

Giānī *prnālī*

During the early decades of the twentieth century, the rise of nationalist sentiment and antagonism between North India's Hindu and Muslim communities had an analogous polarizing impact on the internal politics of the

Sikh community. As we shall see later in this chapter, it was the modernizing reformist Sikh organizations backed by the British imperial administration with a proclivity towards nationalization of the Sikh community who, being in a position to redefine what is Sikhism, or who is a Sikh, gained political ascendancy and in the process marginalized groups perceived to be un-Sikh. Despite their influence in the early to mid-nineteenth century, the Udāsī and Nirmalā schools fall into this latter category. This trend was noted in the 1930s by the Sikh philosopher Sher Singh who wrote that 'the philosophical activities of the Nirmalā school seem to have come to a close in the twentieth century. This appears to have been the effect of the modern revival of Sikhism under the influence of British rule in the Punjab.'[19] What Sher Singh is alluding to here was the rise of the Singh Sabha movement and its direct political descendant the Shiromani Akali Dal – the revivalist party of Sikh nationalism.

It needs to be stated, however, that the transition from pre-modern to modern schools of interpretation mediated by the Singh Sabha *prnālī* was nowhere near as stark as the reformist literature suggests. Complicating the premodern/modern divide, or to put it more accurately, embodying the premodern/modern gap, was the Giānī *prnālī* or Giānī *samapradaya* as it is often called, whose scholarship imbibes premodern and modern influences, but at the same time embodied the split in the Singh Sabha movement between the conservative Amritsar faction and the progressive Lahore faction (see later in this chapter).

The term *giānī* is a Punjabi derivation of the Sanskrit *jñāna* or *jñāna mārg* or path of high learning or deep wisdom. In Sikh tradition the Giānī *prnālī* is said to have originated with Bhāī Mani Singh (d. 1737) and Bābā Deep Singh, both trusted devotees of the tenth Guru Gobind Singh during his stay at Damdamā Sahib. Mani Singh was authorized by Guru Gobind Singh to take charge of the central Sikh shrine, the Harimandar Sahib.[20] At Amritsar Bhāī Mani Singh founded a *taksāl* or centre of higher learning, and also developed the art of *kathā* – the delivery of oral discourses expounding the teaching of the Sikh Gurus based on close exegesis of a given *śabda* or verse from the Guru Granth Sahib. *Kathā* is now regarded as integral to the practice of *gurmat* and is specifically tied to the Giānī school. Bābā Deep Singh, however, stayed at Damdamā Sahib and founded a similar *taksāl*. These two centres of learning, the Damdamā and Amritsar *taksāls*, gave rise to influential lineages of scriptural scholarship and oral discourse which in turn evolved into 'the established form for clerical interpretation of the sacred text'.[21]

But the Giānī school has also been instrumental in disseminating the philosophical aspects of the Gurus' teachings either in the form of *kathā* or in the form of dialogues. A very particular form of their expertise consisted in combining philosophical explanations of the Guru Granth Sahib with tales from the life stories (*sākhīan*) of the Sikh Gurus. Examples of scholarship that weave expertise in metaphysical philosophy with the art of storytelling can be found in works such as *Sikhan dī Bhāgat Mālā* and *Giān Ratnāvalī* (Bhāī Mani Singh), *Prayai Guru Granth Sahib* (Bhāī Chandā Singh), *Sri Guru Granth Kōsh* (Bhai Hazarā Singh), *Gurbāṇī Vyākaran* (Bhai Bhāgvan Singh), *Tawārikh Guru Khālsā* and *Giān Prabōdh* (Giānī Giān Singh).[22]

By the close of the nineteenth century a notable shift is discernible in the scholarly output of the Giānī *prnālī* with the production of complete or partially complete commentaries on Sikh scripture. One reason for this was the situation created on the one hand by Christian missionaries, and on the other hand the disparaging remarks made about the Sikh religion by the Orientalist scholar Ernest Trumpp in his partial translation of the Adi Granth in 1877 (see Singh Sabha Prnali).[23] The first such commentary was the *Farīdkōt Tīkā* written by multiple authors belonging to different Sikh schools of interpretation, but under the overall charge of Giānī Badan Singh, a Nirmalā Sikh from Sekhavan. Although the *Farīdkōt Tīkā* project was undertaken as a response to Trumpp's English translation and introduction to the teachings of the Sikh Gurus, it did not make anywhere near the impact for which it was intended. There are several reasons for this.[24]

First, the lateness of its publication in 1905 ensured that the *Farīdkōt Tīkā* was superseded and made irrelevant by the modernist literature of the Lahore Singh Sabha, also known as the Tat Khālsā faction. Second, its idiom emulated Braj literature rendering it inaccessible to a wider Sikh readership. More importantly, however, it continued the trend within Nirmalā schools of self-consciously and unproblematically framing its hermeneutic squarely within the Vedic paradigm. A good example of this can be found in its preface (*bhūmikā*), where Giānī Badan Singh argues that the correct interpretation of the teachings of the Sikh Gurus (*gurmat*) is unattainable by those persons whose faculty of inner consciousness is not pure or correctly attuned (*shuddh*):

> *asmdadi jīvan dē antahkaran shudh nā hōṇ karkē gur asyā nū anubhav karnā hōr bhī kaṭhan hai*[25]

For Badan Singh the interpreter's focus should be on understanding meaning through intuition (*anubhav*). If intuition is not fostered, then the meanings of *gurbāṇī/gurmat* will go astray:

> *je gurbāṇī dā artha keval viddyā dī chattrī nāl kītā jave aur anubhav dī sahaytā nā kītī jāve tad arth de an ras ho jande han*[26]

Furthermore, the method of intuitive interpretation, Badan Singh argues, can only be developed in the company of 'enlightened souls' (*mahātmā dī nikdārī*) referring to a practice that has specifically been fostered and transmitted from mind to mind (*sine-be-sine*) within the *sanātan* tradition of oral exegesis:

> *jo sanātan sampraday arthan dī sine-be-sine chalī auondī sī*[27]

Giānī Badan Singh's reference to Sanātan traditions of oral exegesis, and his further claim that this Sanātan exegesis is by default the pure or authentic tradition (*shuddh sampardayā*) that has retained its form intact despite the changes of time, suggests that he located the intellectual work of the *Farīdkōt Tīkā* within the Hindu orthodox tradition of *sanātan dharma* whose Vedic-Brahmanical heritage of exegesis was governed by the theological paradigm of 'eternal Sanskrit'.[28] This is immediately evident when we read the first lines of his exegesis on the *mul mantar*, and particularly the syllable *ik oankār*, with which Guru Nānak begins his major composition the Japji and opens the Guru Granth Sahib itself. Badan Singh's opening line is: '*Ved rūp updesh meh ...*' – that is, 'according to the teaching of the Veda', following which he delineates the non-duality of the syllable *ik oankār* by way of reference to the tripartite system of the Hindu syllable *ōm/aum*.

At the heart of this interpretive strategy is the question of authority, or sovereignty, if one pushes the context of authority a little wider to include the context of modernity within which Giānī Badan Singh was writing. According to Sanātanists like Badan Singh, the notion of *gurmat* espoused by Guru Nanak derived its foundational authority and meaning from the Vedic tradition. As such only those 'enlightened souls' who received their training within a strictly oral tradition of Sanātan lineage could gain the capacity for intuiting the purity of authentic meanings of the text.

Of course, the deployment of terms such as 'intuition' and 'purity' of meaning can be read as rhetorical claims to authority based on the 'theology of eternal Sanskrit'[29]. According to the metaphysics of sacred sound which undergirds the theology of 'eternal Sanskrit', only a particular kind of consciousness could be properly attuned, or not attuned, on account of its purity (*antahkaran shuddh nā hōṇ karkē*). And clearly, any rhetoric which measures consciousness in terms of its purity or correctness of atonement is simply a philosophical justification of caste lineage (kinship lines or biological race) to which the interpreter belongs. Sanātanist claims to authority thus amounted to little more than invocations of an ancient Brahmanic caste ideology.

As the literature on colonial-period Punjab shows, such questions over authority were vigorously contested within Sikh interpretive circles.[30] By the end of the nineteenth century these contestations reached new levels of theological, philosophical and sociopolitical complexity, driven in part by the rise of a radically new interpretive paradigm based on the encounter between modern Western thought and existing schools of Sikh thought-practice. It is this peculiarly modern encounter which led to the emergence of the assemblage 'Sikh philosophy'. To understand how this happened, we need to look at the Singh Sabha *prnālī*, the school of interpretation which has not only dominated Sikh thought since the colonial period but, through its inadvertent alliance with religio-secular regimes of translation, served as an apparatus for capturing the sovereignty of Sikh concepts within a nationalist paradigm.

Singh Sabha *prnālī*

Colonialism and the deterritorialization of *gurmat*

Before it became a school of Sikh thought in its own right, the Singh Sabha started out as a social and religious reform movement. Its aim was to revive traditional Sikh values while remaining open to engagement with modernity's different forms, specifically British colonial governance and Western modes of critical reasoning and philosophical speculation. The nature of the Singh Sabha's engagement with Western thought is difficult to gauge without understanding the political context of Punjab in the nineteenth century. Of central importance is the struggle between the dominant sociopolitical forces in the region. These include, first, the two forms of Christian presence in Punjab: Evangelical missionaries and secular British governance; and second, the increasing nationalization of Hindu traditions by revivalist organizations such as the Sanātanist Hindu Dharma Sabhas and the Arya Samaj; third the Muslim reformist movement, Ahmadhya Anjuman; and fourth the Singh Sabhas.[31]

From the Sikh perspective the story effectively begins in 1849 with the fall of the Sikh kingdom, at which point Punjab went from a half-century of sovereign Sikh rule over a majority Hindu and Muslim population to subjugation under British rule. Between 1849 and the 1860s the machinery of British imperial government operated a dual policy towards indigenous cultures, allowing Christian missionaries a free hand to convert natives, while officially it operated a policy of secular rule based on 'non-interference' in indigenous cultures. Although the British portrayed their governance as resolutely secular and balanced in its approach towards different 'religions' of Punjab, Indians saw them as fundamentally Christian. The reason for this perception lies in the major reversal in the colonial administration's implementation of secular governance culminating in Thomas Macaulay's infamous *Minute on Indian Education*.

Passed by the British parliament in 1835, Macaulay's *Minute* effectively delegitimized indigenous forms of knowledge and education which early British Indologists, with their philosophically Deist orientation, had portrayed in relatively positive light on par with Western philosophy and Christian revelation. This policy had prevented early Christian missions from spreading and upsetting the delicate balance of trust between indigenous communities in North India and the British administration. A more insidious aspect of Macaulay's *Minute*, however, was that it enabled the transmission of Christian ideas and morals into native communities by actively promoting the teaching of ostensibly secular English literature in government-sponsored schools – also known as Anglo-Vernacular schools – where English literature and the native vernaculars were taught side by side. Anglo-Vernacular schools served a dual purpose. On the one hand, the teaching of English literature enabled a secularized translation of Christian values of the colonizer into the supposedly neutral medium of literature, language and history. On the other hand, the same process of secular translation helped to create a new class of Indians with a modernized mindset more likely to break with indigenous systems of education, thereby facilitating the creation of a modern colonial subject.[32]

Although the Administration's secular education policy made considerable inroads into Sikh, Muslim and Hindu communities in Punjab, native elites were not entirely fooled by the show of British 'impartiality'. Indeed, each of these communities reacted to the colonial education system by establishing voluntary organizations that took part in the newly emerging public sphere. This development was exemplified by the emergence of Hindu, Sikh and Muslim reformist organizations which included (i) Arya Samaj representing Hindus, (ii) Ahmadiyas representing Muslim interests, (iii) the Singh Sabha which advocated for Sikh interests. Cities across northeastern India such as Calcutta in the 1820s, followed by Benares in the 1840s, had already witnessed such developments with the formation of voluntary reformist societies such as the modernist Brahmo Samaj and the more conservative Hindu Dharam Sabhas. But in the northwestern region of Punjab the spark for this process was provided by the presence of the Hindu preacher Dayanand Saraswati who published a polemicizing work *Satyarath Prakāsh*.

Dayanand directly countered the Christian influence of missionary and secular English education by reinterpreting Hindu doctrines, refracting them through a Christian lens in such a way that Hindus could claim they possessed a monotheistic concept of God, a divinely revealed text (the Veda), and that they were racially Arya(n). Moreover, Dayanand claimed a more ancient lineage for Hindu doctrine by arguing that Sanskrit was an older and purer predecessor of European languages.

Initially, Dayanand was welcomed by some Sikhs who found his anti-Christian stance appealing. But their admiration was short-lived when Dayanand was found to be claiming that the teaching of Guru Nanak (*gurmat*) was derived from the Veda. Such a claim resonated with the rhetoric of Sanātanist Hindus who made a similar claim for the authority of Veda in relation to Nanak's teachings. Sikh elites soon realized that Dayanand and his Arya Samaj posed a greater threat to them than Christianity, as it was part of a massive nationalizing construction of Hindu consciousness throughout India. Feeling threatened by Christian and Hindu proselytizing, Sikh leaders began to convene a series of meetings in Amritsar which culminated in the formation of a body called the Sri Guru Singh Sabha. Better known as the Singh Sabha for short, this body evolved into a movement whose success was premised on an engagement with the British imperial state and modernity per se.[33]

The original Singh Sabha based in Amritsar was established by conservative Sikhs belonging to the upper castes, some of whom were descendants of the early Sikh Gurus. The conservatism of this group stemmed from their tendency to regard the teachings of Guru Nānak (*gurmat*) and the Sikh *panth* itself as one among many streams of doctrinal thought constituting *sanātana dharma*, the so-called perennial tradition which identifies its source of authority as the Veda. Doctrinally, these self-styled 'Sanātan Sikhs' considered Guru Nānak to be an incarnation of the Hindu deity Vishnu and thus aligned with Brahmanical social structure and caste ideology. This conservative ideology invited strong opposition from more socially progressive Sikh elites educated in Anglo-Vernacular schools and fully attuned to the modernizing process. Styling themselves as 'Tat Khalsa' these new elites believed that ultimate authority in Sikhism resided in the principle of *śabda-gurū* (lit. the Word is Guru) as manifested in the dual institutions of Guru Granth (text) and Guru Panth (Khālsā). By 1879 the differences between these two views had become irreconcilable with the result that the more progressive Tat Khālsā group established separate headquarters in Lahore and began the task of modernizing both the life-world and world view of Sikhs.[34]

Over the next half-century, the Lahore Singh Sabha's combination of grassroots activism and sustained intellectual labour coordinated by a group of scholarly elites helped redefine popular ritual and practice to distinguish Sikh from 'Hindu' practices, and in the process evolved a more concretized form of Sikh identity. Key to this effort was the creation of a new interpretive paradigm centred around the production of detailed philosophico-religious commentaries on central texts such as the Guru Granth Sahib. Though rarely acknowledged, motivating the creation of this new school of thought was sensitivity to a new era in which representation of Sikh teachings through English language and an engagement of Sikh concepts with Western concepts was beginning to assume critical importance. As noted earlier, in earlier periods Sikh thought had remained intimately connected to its native Punjabi cultural, ethnic and linguistic milieu. There had been no incentive to disturb this close association. But by the late 1870s, for the first time, Sikh elites were coming face to face with the dangers and the potentials of translation, where the stakes were nothing less than a displacement and deterritorialization of indigenous Sikh categories in relation to Western/Anglophone categories.

One event in particular marked this new era of conceptual encounter with the West. This was the commissioning of an 'official' partial translation of the Adi Granth by the British Administration in Punjab and its eventual publication in 1877 by the German Indologist, Ernest Trumpp. This translation by Trumpp, and even more so the introductory section entitled 'Sketch of the Religion of the Sikhs', can be considered an event of cultural translation in two different but related senses. First, it provided a philosophical and theological framework for understanding Sikh concepts in English – a framework to which all future translations were beholden. Second, in a way that might seem counter-intuitive, the rationalizing process within this European philosophical framework was internalized by Sikh elites through their native language via a process of intercultural mimesis, and from there it was seamlessly incorporated not only into exegetical commentaries but, as we shall see in the remaining sections of this chapter, into early expressions of Sikh philosophy.[35]

The central thesis of Trumpp's *Sketch* consisted of an attempt to demonstrate the lack of conceptual rigour of Guru Nanak's notion of oneness of the Supreme Being. Influenced by the Brahmanical leanings of his Nirmalā collaborators, Trumpp argued that the notion of unity of the Supreme Being in the Adi Granth could not be reasonably differentiated from orthodox Hindu philosophy. Accordingly, Trumpp translated the first line of the Adi Granth by missing out the numeral 'One' altogether, substituting the term *ōm* for Guru Nanak's *ik oankār*. Since Hindu philosophy had long expounded the meaning of *ōm* in terms of a pantheistic unity of the deities Brahma, Vishnu and Shiva, which suggested that Hindu thought was unable to transcend multiplicity and achieve a sufficiently exalted (which is to say, monotheistic) notion of unity, it followed that Nanak's conception of oneness similarly lacked the requisite degree of transcendence and systematic unity.[36]

Trumpp's argument achieved several things at once. First, it suggested that prevailing British depictions of Sikhism as a 'moralizing deism' were mistaken since Nanak's teaching was 'Hindoo' in its orientation. Second, Nanak's teaching could be considered neither a proper religion nor a philosophy, as it did not have a 'sufficiently exalted idea of God'.[37] It could not prove the existence of God, and if it failed to do this, there could be no basis for any ethics, and thus no possibility for self-governance for Sikhs. As with the 'Hindoos' from whom they had arisen, the evidence of their own scripture justified colonization of Sikhs by a European power. Third, and perhaps most importantly, it shifted the conceptual terrain for future Anglophone encounters between Sikh and Western concepts towards a form of dialectical negativity engineered by Hegel, specifically the latter's master-slave dialectic.

In political terms Trumpp's thesis had the potential not only to undermine the British Administration's established view of Sikhs as a distinct nation among other nations in India, with its own system of ethics and self-governance, but to legitimize the Arya Samaj's claims that the teachings of Guru Nānak were just one of many strands of Hindu philosophy. As such it presented the Singh Sabha's leading scholars with an urgent and clearly defined task: of proving that Guru Nanak's doctrines were philosophically and theologically distinct from Hindu thought. This task was incorporated into a long-term project of formulating new commentaries in modern Punjabi prose on the teachings of the Sikh Gurus. As we have seen, one of the first to be commissioned was the Farīdkōt Tīkā, compiled by the self-styled Sanātan Sikh, Giānī Badan Singh. By the time it was published in 1905, the Farīdkōt Tīkā had been superseded by more accessible works composed by Singh Sabha intellectuals such as Kahn Singh Nabhā, Bhāī Vīr Singh and Teja Singh. In the 1890s Kahn Singh Nabha published two important works, *Gurmat Prabhakar* (Divine *Gurmat*) and *Gurmat Suddhakar* (Essence of *Gurmat*) both of which listed key concepts of the Sikh Gurus arranged in alphabetical order and supported by a litany of scriptural quotations. In 1931 Nabha produced his monumental *Gurshabad Ratnākar Mahānkōsh* (Great Dictionary of the Guru's Lexicon) which continues to be an indispensable work for research into Sikh philosophy and theology.

The late 1920s and 1930s were fruitful decades for Sikh philosophical exegesis with the production of works such as Bhai Vir Singh's seven-volume *Santhya Sri Guru Granth Sahib*, and his *Guru Nanak Chamaṭkār* (Radiance of Guru Nanak); Teja Singh's four-volume *Shabadarth Sri Guru Granth Sahib*, Sahib Singh's ten-volume *Sri Guru Granth Sahib Darpan* and Jodh Singh's *Gurmati Nirnai* (Treatise on the Guru's Philosophy). Almost all of these works are concerned primarily with establishing doctrinal integrity of Sikh concepts rather than producing a work of systematic philosophy. In this sense they mark a successful culmination of fifty years of interpretative activity in modern standard Punjabi that effectively defined the nature of the early Singh Sabha *prnālī*.

The one possible exception is Jodh Singh's *Gurmati Nirnai*, which because of its succinctness (one volume as opposed to the multivolume nature of other Singh Sabha works), its conceptual and schematic organization (other Singh Sabha works were straightforward textual exegeses) and its accessible style (it reads like a transcript of public lectures), can be regarded as the prototype for properly philosophical works on Sikh philosophy that would appear later in the twentieth century. For this reason *Gurmati Nirnai* needs to be discussed further before turning our attention to the second phase of intellectual activity by Sikh thinkers who inherited the ethos and legacy of the early Singh Sabha *prnālī*. This second phase (post-1940s or post-partition) was dominated by Sikh scholars who utilized English language more frequently, and in doing so began to popularize the term 'Sikh philosophy' in a more systematic manner.

One of the striking things about *Gurmati Nirnai* is its broad schematic arrangement, which appears simply to have transplanted the Kantian ontotheological schema of God-World-Man for organizing the main chapters in the following way: (i) God (*akāl purakh*), (ii) World (*sristī rachnā*), (iii) Man (*manukh*), (iv) the Guru (*Guru*) . . . (ix) Word (*śabda*), and so on.[38] The first chapter is essentially an extended argument for the need to comprehend the existence of God in terms of a static immutable One. The crux of his argument is to demonstrate, very much in the style of his mentor Bhai Vir Singh, the transcendental nature of the One, which allows him not only to reproduce an intellectual separation between God/World/Man in the early chapters but, by the time he comes to discuss the nature of community in chapter 14, to use ontological separation as a basis for establishing an epistemological distinction between Sikh and non-Sikh world views.[39] In short, Jodh Singh harnesses both Christian and secular schemas for translating the key concepts of the Sikh Gurus in a short and accessible form. *Gurmati Nirnai*'s achievement was to package the essence of Sikh thought (*gurmat*) into something resembling a creedal statement. The whole purpose of a creedal statement is that it provided succinct access in modern Punjabi to a schema that could be easily reproduced by Sikh publicists, literary figures and preachers who could rapidly deploy the newly formulated credo to combat other creeds – Hindu, Muslim, Christian and secular.[40]

In many ways, *Gurmat Nirnai* was the bridge to the next generation of Sikh thinkers, particularly those writing in English, and more specifically those scholars who used its readily accessible schema to materialize a 'Sikh philosophy' based on a modernized interpretation of *gurmat*. It was, in other words, the bridge that created the appearance of a faithful and unhindered passage of meaning (akin to what Talal Asad calls a 'secular translation'[41]) from *gurmat* to 'Sikh philosophy', giving the impression that the two are exactly the same. By ensuring conformity of philosophical-theological concepts of *gurmat* to Sikh notions of self or Sikh identity, it was in many ways also a work of political theology.

Entering the comparative arena: Sher Singh's 'philosophy of Sikhism'

There is something of a consensus that the first work of systematic Sikh philosophy is Sher Singh's *Philosophy of Sikhism* (1944).[42] Sher Singh's book is also the first to bring Sikh ideas into a comparative framework.[43] Writing in the mid- to late 1930s the author is acutely aware of breaking new ground as can be noted in his somewhat nervous attempts to justify the use of 'philosophy' in the title of his book: 'What justifies the title of my work is the angle, the viewpoint, from which I have approached Sikhism'.[44] This new perspective, he argues, is one based on 'rational conviction' and 'impassionate criticism' which alone can succeed 'in exercising a rational check on biased opinions issuing from. . . . [t]he fact of my being a Sikh by birth'.[45]

Clearly, Sher Singh is rehearsing the kind of secular translation, which since Descartes's *Meditations* has defined philosophy as a discipline vis-à-vis the claim that its mode of knowledge is not tainted by prejudice, belief or opinion. I point this out because this is probably the only occasion that the genre of Sikh philosophy has aspired to this neutral standpoint. After 1947 practically all works in this genre tended to assume that Sikh philosophy could not be separated from its Punjabi-Sikh milieu and cultural roots.

Equally noteworthy in this preface is Sher Singh's apology for 'indulging in comparisons between concepts held by the Guru and those held by some Western thinkers'.[46] 'I realize', he goes on, 'that this was not very necessary and could be safely avoided. I have done so in the hope that *such a comparison may render an Eastern concept more intelligible* to the Western or non-Sikh reader' (emphasis mine).[47] Again, this kind of confession will never be heard in future attempts to establish Sikh philosophy. So what is its significance?

I would like to suggest that this is much more than secular apologetic. Rather, it is a clear indication that Sher Singh was very conscious about the mode of thought he was operating in. He seems to have come to the realization that the *operations of thought* in which he was trying to interpret the concepts of Guru Nanak were neither transparent nor seamless. The process of thinking, or the plane of encounter on which 'Eastern' and Western concepts are allowed to approach each other, appeared to him to be riddled with interdiction, which in turn engendered a problematic situation. Namely that the 'Eastern concept' is *unable to stand of its own accord* (it was not as 'intelligible' as it could be) within the medium of thought he was working in. To make Guru Nanak's concept 'more intelligible to the Western reader' required the aid of – that is to say, comparison with – the Western concept which *helped to hold it in place*.

Without saying it in so many words Sher Singh brings attention not only to the fact that he is working *in translation*, and therefore thinking about Nanak's concept in English, but that the form of this translation is representation – in the sense of constantly presenting the Sikh concept to the mind. But perhaps more importantly, that by itself the Sikh concept is not able to *stand sufficiently still*, suggesting it is not adequate to the function of representation. Something in addition to representation is needed to make it 'more intelligible'. And that something more is the work performed by comparison, where a foreign concept or thinker enters the plane of encounter and vouchsafes or speaks on behalf of the 'Eastern concept' (e.g. 'Yes! It is a proper concept; it means this; it is like our Western concept . . .'). In this way, the work performed by comparison provides the 'Eastern' concept with an identity recognizable as similar or different to the host concept. Once the Sikh is given an identity, it can become exchangeable, substitutable, translatable within the global arena of thought.

I labour this point for three reasons. First, it is acknowledged by Sher Singh as an impediment to the potential freedom of a Sikh concept (its capacity to be itself by differing from itself) residing in an Anglophone medium. And this insight only comes to him because, at the time he composed *Philosophy of Sikhism*, he was living as a diasporic Sikh in London, trying to engage in philosophical reflection as a Sikh and within the Anglophone medium. Or, to put it in the language of 'diaspora', he was trying to *find a home* for the Sikh concept *away from home*. Second, because it points to comparison not as a mere supplement to normal thought but as intrinsic to the proper operations of Anglophone thought, especially when trying to think (about a Punjabi concept) in translation. As I have argued elsewhere, comparison is in fact a mode of translation, or at least a mode of encounter that prefigures the work of actual translation.[48] Third, and this seems to be telling, comparison will never be overtly acknowledged *as an impediment* again after Sher Singh, even though comparison becomes a routine practice in post-partition works of Sikh philosophy. The difference here is that after 1947 all work in Sikh philosophy is carried out by Sikh scholars in their native Punjabi milieu where they are never removed from their ethnic, cultural or linguistic sensibilities, even when they write in English. Comparison only becomes a *problem* for those who experience diasporicity simultaneously as an existential predicament and promise.

Despite being a pioneering work, Sher Singh's *Philosophy of Sikhism* did not gain much traction. It remained relatively obscure partly due to the timing of its publication in 1944 – barely three years before the devastating partition of India, with the Sikh heartland being split into two regions, the Western half going to Muslim-dominated Pakistan, the other half going to Hindu-dominated India. In the migration from West to East, Sikhs not only lost some of their main pilgrimage sites, including the birthplace of Guru Nānak; they also lost their intellectual centre, Lahore. During these years, Sikh intellectual elites were more invested in putting together the case for Sikh political autonomy than the more 'leisurely' pursuit of Sikh philosophy.

By the late 1960s, though, Sikhs had resurrected their fortunes and achieved some measure of economic and political success resulting in the creation of two new universities Guru Nanak Dev University (GNDU) and Punjabi University Patiala where the formal academic study of Sikhism was re-established. Coinciding with the 500th birth anniversary of Guru Nānak (1969) and tercentenary birth anniversary of Guru Gobind Singh (1967), the early leadership of these universities was entrusted to scholars reared in the intellectual frameworks created by the Singh Sabha *prnālī*, notably Dr Bhai Jodh Singh who became the first vice chancellor of GNDU. While much of the scholarship from these institutions tended to reproduce the two main identity markers of the Singh Sabha *prnālī* – 'Sikhism as a World Religion' and 'Sikhs as a Nation' – there were sporadic attempts to rearticulate the discourse of Sikh philosophy. This can be seen in works such as Ishar Singh's *Philosophy of Guru Nanak* (1978), Daljeet Singh's *The Sikh Ideology* (1979) and Sohan Singh's *The Seeker's Path* (1957).

It is only in the 1980s and 1990s that a new wave of publications with an overtly philosophical orientation begins to emerge. English-language works exemplifying this new approach include Avtar Singh's *Ethics of the Sikhs* (1983), Gurnam Kaur's *Reason and Revelation* (1990), Nirbhai Singh's *Philosophy of Sikhism* (1990), Himmat Singh's *Philosophical Conception of Śabda* (1985), Jasbir Singh Ahluwalia's *Sovereignty of the Sikh Doctrine* (1983/2005) and Nikky Guninder Kaur Singh's *Physics and Metaphysics of the Guru Granth Sahib* (1987). Notable Punjabi-language works focusing on Sikh thought include Harinder Singh Mahboob's *Sahaje Rachio Khālsā* (1988) and Jasbir Singh Ahluwalia's *Sikh Falsafe dī Bhūmikā* (Preface to a Sikh Philosophy) and his *Sikh Chintan: Darśanak ate Sansthāmik Vikās* (Sikh Thought: Philosophical Vision and Systematic Development).[49] Also important here are the works of the Sikh postmodernist thinker and literary critic Gurbhagat Singh, notably his *Vishwa Chintan ate Punjabi Sahit* (World Thought and Punjabi Literature), *Sikhism and Postmodern Thought* and *Western Poetics and Eastern Thought*, the title of which playfully reverses the Indian philosopher Sarvapalli Radhakrishan's classic text: *Eastern Religions and Western Thought*.

What sets these works apart from others is the more or less systematic engagement with key Western philosophers and philosophical themes. Much as Sher Singh seems to have anticipated in the early 1930s, the engagement with the discipline of philosophy is in some senses indicative of the fact that the material and ideal element in which Sikh thinking is conducted can no longer pretend to be isolated from the West. Though none of these philosophers overtly admit to it, there is an unconscious acceptance that the meaning of a Sikh concept is not made in a self-enclosed Sikh-Punjabi world. Even if such a self-enclosed world existed, colonialism effectively displaced its ability to provide ultimate value and meaning. Even though these writers all lived in Punjab and assumed Sikh-Punjabi-Indian identity, any attempt to express Sikh concepts and establish their meanings was now necessarily rerouted and referenced through the modern Western paradigm of reality and knowing. This trend is amply illustrated in the works of Nirbhai Singh, Himmat Singh and Gurnam Kaur, which in different ways attempt to discern 'the philosophical Sikh world view' through a systematic survey of its key concepts drawn from the Sikh texts and specifically in relation to Kantian metaphysics.

For example, by his own admission Nirbhai Singh's *Philosophy of Sikhism* attempts to establish an ostensibly authentic standpoint on Sikh philosophy by examining 'the nature of Reality as conceived in Sikhism'.[50] And mind you, not just any reality, but the 'Ultimate Reality' which the author sees as a 'central problem for most philosophies of religions'.[51] Nirbhai Singh seems oblivious to the fact that the word or concept of 'Reality' or 'Ultimate Reality' does not find very good matches in the Sikh lexicon. The nearest terms are *yatharathvād* (depth), *vāstikvād* (thingness), *tatvikta* (essence) or the more mundane term *aslīat* (truth).[52] These are composite terms that are almost never used by the Sikh Gurus. On the other hand, the nature of reality or ultimate reality have been and continue to be a central concern of post-Kantian philosophy and especially the philosophy of religion. Accordingly, core chapters in Nirbhai Singh's book reflect key Kantian and Hegelian themes: 'Reality in Sikhism' (Chapter 3), 'Reality and its Attributes' (Chapter 4), 'Appearances and Reality' (Chapter 5) and 'Reality and Experience' (Chapter 6). Similarly, Gurnam Kaur's *Reason and Revelation* tries to construct a Sikh epistemology but again through a framework that is essentially Kantian.

If there is a problem with these works, it is *not* that they should have avoided engaging with Western frameworks. On the contrary, as we learn from Sher Singh's experience, such engagement was, and remains, necessary and part and parcel of what it means to think in a global context. Rather, it is that they attempt to develop sui generis accounts of Sikh concepts by unconsciously translating them into frameworks of secularity. There were two major consequences of these secular translations. First, they reconstructed categories of the Sikh life-world, such as *sikhī* and *gurmat*, as religious categories, while simultaneously implanting it within a secular humanistic understanding of reality whose sense nevertheless remains broadly Christian/Kantian. This process of replicating concepts as religious identities before embedding them in a comparative schematism representing present 'Reality' can be regarded as a 'capture' of Sikh concepts. Second, they continued to treat Sikh philosophy as an autochthonic thought-form, which it clearly is not. As noted earlier, the term which better describes the nature of Sikh philosophy is 'assemblage'. Contrary to what some may think, to describe Sikh philosophy as an assemblage in no way weakens its relationship to *gurmat*. In fact treating Sikh philosophy as an assemblage strengthens the outward reach of *gurmat*, its ability to translate into and connect to other cultures, and particularly to the current arena of global thought. There is strong evidence that even iconic figures of Sikh exegesis such as Bhai Vir Singh made vigorous efforts to connect *gurmat* concepts to the thought of philosophers such as Henri Bergson. We see this in exegetical texts such as *Guru Nanak Chamatkar* (the 'Radiance of Guru Nanak') where Bhai Vir Singh tried to create transversal connections between Guru Nanak concepts and those and Bergson in his own native language of Punjabi – a perfect example of how using Sikh philosophy as an assemblage widened the reach of *gurmat* concepts.

Discussion questions

(1) Why is *gurmat* such an axial concept for Sikh philosophy? Are there concepts that might play a similar role in, say, Buddhist, Hindu or Islamic philosophies?

(2) Although this chapter, especially the section on 'Singh Sabha Prnālī', deals with the encounter between Sikh concepts and Western philosophy during the era of European colonialism, can we use this case study to reflect upon similar encounters between Western and non-Western traditions of thought? Provide examples.

(3) What is the significance of translation as it pertains to encounters between different philosophical traditions? How did the translation of Sikh concepts into the religio-secular framework displace native concepts and understandings of reality with Euro-Christian modes of epistemology and ontology? How was this accomplished?

(4) What lessons do we learn about comparative philosophy from Sher Singh's *Philosophy of Sikhism* (1944)?

(5) What are the advantages of thinking about Sikh philosophy as an assemblage? Explain using concrete examples showing how Sikh concepts can be connected to the wider world.

Experience

Where do we begin a contemporary Sikh philosophy? Establishing a standpoint and context for any philosophy is neither easy nor a trivial matter, for it is also connected to the question of authority – in this case the authority of Sikh philosophy as a discourse. Fortunately, though, the question of authority is fairly well settled in Sikh studies. Most scholars in this field agree that the voluminous compositions of the Sikh Gurus, and particularly Guru Nanak, as we find them in Sikh scripture such as Guru Granth Sahib, were not only authored and edited by the Sikh Gurus themselves, but that these compositions stem from direct and profound experiences of the im/material reality generally referred to as *nām*. Eschewing any straightforward representation, *nām* can be comprehended philosophically only from a trans-personal or trans-individual perspective; as such *nām* refers to the primary consciousness that pervades all existence and non-existence, while from a personal perspective *nām* constitutes the beloved object of spiritual search, which has infinite names (god/God, the divine, Madho, Hari, etc) yet remains One in nature.

But while there is a consensus that any discourse going by the name 'Sikh philosophy' has to take its bearings from this direct experience, there is less agreement about its nature. Is it an experience that happened once-and-for-all in a particular historical moment, or can it be repeated again, differently, here and now, and in the future? Establishing the nature of this experience is important as it has implications for understanding the central tendencies within *sikhī* or *gurmat*. More specifically, is this experience directed towards a world or reality *beyond* this one, in which case its primary tendency might be described as religious/ascetic? Or is the experience directed primarily towards *this* life and *this* world, in which case it would manifest as a desire to intervene in psychic, social and political formations for the betterment of the world beyond the milieu in which one is initially situated? If the latter is the case, a further question that needs addressing is whether the experience is inextricably tied to a particular historical ethno-cultural milieu, or whether the experience can be transplanted in different cultural and conceptual terrains, and in effect undergo repetition differently.

Again, it is not difficult to establish the basic tendencies of the experience. One can go straight to the source – that is, to the revealed utterances of Guru Nanak (*gurbāṇī*) which contains its own testimony to the authority. Although I'll explore *gurbāṇī* as a primary source for Sikh thought, I also want to consider the meaning of 'revelation' itself – a term that is used somewhat loosely as a synonym for transcendental experience. How does the term 'revelation' apply to *gurbāṇī*? Given that most Sikhs seem to agree about the suitability of the concept of revelation, does this necessarily mean that Sikh philosophy is monotheistic in its impulse, and therefore comparable to other monotheisms? Or, can the Sikh notion of revelation be understood in a radically different way?

While these are important questions, I want to begin our philosophical inquiry by appealing to a more narratological genre known as *janamsākhī*. Commonly associated with devotional piety than philosophical thought because of its hagiographical style, the *janamsākhī* are basically life narratives of the Gurus and particularly Guru Nanak, the founder of Sikh tradition. For devotees, the attraction of the *janamsākhī* is not that it facilitates rational interpretation of meaning, but that the listener is emotionally swept up by the ethical force of the story in a way that helps the devotee to reconfigure one's self or mind in a transformative event. What specifically interests me about *janamsākhī*, and one in particular, the so-called *Puratan janamsākhī*, is that aside from providing biographical details about Guru Nanak's life, the life narratives provide interesting, if somewhat unlikely, clues about the motivational impulses underpinning Guru Nanak's engagement with the world around him, his spiritual formation, the teachings arising from his authentic writings, and, by no means least, provide clues about the nature of revelation in the context of *gurbāṇī*.[1]

Life of Guru Nanak

The *Puratan janamsākhī* (*PJS*) divides Nanak's life into five relatively distinct phases: early childhood (age zero to nine years), adolescent development (age nine to eighteen), early manhood (age nineteen to thirty-three), period of travels (age thirty-three to fifty), settled mature phase (age fifty to seventy). Although many of the anecdotes in the life narratives speak about Nanak's predilection towards spiritual greatness, with accounts often embellished by supernatural details, one of the most interesting though overlooked aspects concern Nanak's encounters with the outside world and the effect these interactions had on his psychic and spiritual development.

The *PJS* tells us that Nanak received his early education from both Hindu and Muslim tutors. Nanak's father provided him with a decent education in the hope that it might lead to suitable employment perhaps as an accountant or a mercantile trader. He was initiated into the Veda and the six systems of orthodox Hindu philosophy, after which he was sent to learn Arabic and Persian in order to learn about Islamic philosophy, scripture and law. It seems, however, that Nanak found a classical education deeply dissatisfying and preferred to spend more time discoursing with wandering ascetics, *sadhus* or visiting Nath Yogis and Sufi masters. Through these more informal channels the young Nanak imbibed much of the oral poetry and spiritual wisdom of spiritual adepts such as the *bhagats* and soon began to formulate his own experiences into lyrical-poetic verse. By age thirteen he was already so deeply immersed in his own spiritual journey that he strongly resisted the conventional path desired by his parents, flatly refusing to undergo initiation and wear the sacred thread of twice-born orthodox Hindus. Nanak's refusal to be initiated in Hindu tradition caused a stir in his village and was seen as an act of revolt against a foundational pillar of Vedic orthodoxy and the first sign of his eventual split with the Hindu tradition of his ancestors.[2]

The *janamsākhī* tells us that shortly after this event Nanak immersed himself more deeply in a spiritual quest and became intransigent towards worldly affairs. His parents sent him to herd cattle, to till the land and lent him a considerable sum of money to start a business, and even married him off so that he might be able to settle. But all to no avail. As Nanak reached adolescence, signs of a psychic malaise characterized by periods of depressive melancholia punctuated by bouts of ecstatic joy and deep sadness began to manifest themselves in Nanak's personality. He began to withdraw from society and worldly activity. Alarmed at the apparent deterioration of his mental health, his parents counselled him to cease weaving unpractical discourses. The talk of the village was that Kalu's son had become a 'crazed fool' who was slowly losing his senses.[3] During these years Nanak would often lie down, refuse to eat, become inactive or simply remain sitting transfixed for days. Moreover, Nanak regularly fell into trance-like states giving the impression of being possessed. At this stage the family feared for Nanak's state of mind and called a *vaid*, or village shaman, for help, asking him to prescribe a remedy for his psychological ailment. The *vaid* duly arrived and began to take Nanak's pulse. But Nanak resisted, withdrawing his arm and asking the *vaid* what he was doing. 'I'm here to diagnose the sickness that has disturbed your health', the *vaid* replied. Nanak laughed and responded with the following words which later came to be recorded in Sikh scripture under the musical register of *Rāg Malar*:

They call a *vaid* to diagnose my pain:

   He takes my arm to feel its pulse.

But the ignorant fool knows not that the pain exists in my mind.

   O *vaid* go home and take not my curse with you.

   How can this medicine remedy the ailment of my lovesick soul?

The *vaid* wants to cure me with his pills,

   Yet my body weeps, my soul cries out in pain.

Go home *vaid*, take your medication with you!

   The One who gave the pain will remove it. (p. 20)

Shortly after this episode Nanak left his ancestral village to find work at Sultanpur, where his brother-in-law procured a post for him as a village accountant. As Nanak began to earn his keep, he sent for his wife, Sulakhni, to join him. He was nineteen at the time. Over the next few years his life settled into a more regulated pattern. As Nanak became adept in controlling the trances, earlier cycles of melancholia and enstasis were productively channelled into spiritual activity. During the day Nanak would diligently look after the village accounts. Most of the night, however, was reserved for spiritual cultivation through practices such as *kirtan* (meditational music), often followed by *katha* (a form of mindful exegesis), to a community of devotees. At dawn Nanak would bathe in a nearby river, then sleep for a while before going back to work. During his stay at Sultanpur, Nanak was reunited with his childhood friend Mardana, a gifted Muslim *rabaab* player who provided musical accompaniment to Nanak's songs.

Twelve years passed in this way. Nanak and his wife settled into the comfortable life of the trading classes and had two sons. However, the regularity of this life was interrupted at around the age of thirty-three when Nanak failed to return from his morning ablutions near the river Bein. For three days no trace of Nanak could be found. The villagers believed that he had drowned. Then, on the fourth day Nanak reappeared as dramatically as he had disappeared, but his demeanour had changed. He had once again become silent and reclusive. When questioned about the state of his health, he responded with a perplexing statement: 'There is no Hindu; there is no Muslim', leading people to suspect he was possessed or had gone mad.

Often referred to as the Sultanpur event, this episode is generally recognized as a culminating point in Nanak's journey towards spiritual perfection. While the *janamsākhīs* embellish the experience with hagiographic details centred around a personal communion with the divine, it is possible to read the Sultanpur event as marking Nanak's achievement of perfection, his becoming a spiritual master in his own right, one who would from thereon undertake a mission to bring others to a new path based on a mindful practice known as *nām simaran*, sharing one's wealth with the needy (*dān*), regularly immersing the mind in the divine name (*isnān*) and living a life of service to others (*sevā*).

Soon after the Sultanpur episode, the fully enlightened master, now called Guru Nanak, began to attract his first followers or Sikhs (lit. learners travelling on a path to perfection). Over the next seventeen years he travelled extensively throughout the Indian subcontinent and as far west as Baghdad, undertaking teaching tours or *udāsīs* where he encountered and interacted with a wide range of religious, philosophical and political systems and personalities. The teaching tours continued until Guru Nanak had reached the age of fifty, by which time he had garnered considerable fame as a spiritual master. Casting off the *udāsī*'s garb Nanak settled down and established a community. He also began the process of compiling his poetic compositions into a transmissible form and formalizing a set of teachings which came to be known as *gurmat* (lit. the Guru's logic, instruction or teaching), essentially a combination of spiritual theory and practice centred around the life of a householder. By the time of his death in 1539, Guru Nanak had left behind a young but vibrant community with its own distinctive practices, a rite of initiation and a successor fully authorized to continue development of the fledgling community.

However, the key legacy that Guru Nanak left to his successor Angad and to the early Sikh community was a collection of his own compositions containing the first statement of *gurmat* in the form of an authentic teaching and practice of living. At the heart of Guru Nanak's compositions is a set of concepts closely centred around terms such as *satguru* and *śabda-guru* (Word-as-Guru). Both *satguru* and *śabda-guru* are closely intertwined and carry connotations of sovereign authority. For example, *satguru* essentially means the true or authentic Guru and refers to a spiritual preceptor who has genuinely undergone the highest form of spiritual experience, which authorizes him or her to transmit the teaching and the experience to others. The question here is how the preceptor actually transmits authentic experience, or whether anything is transmitted per se. This is where the concept of *śabda* takes on central significance in Sikh thought and practice as it performs an interiorization of experience by enabling each individual to undergo experience for herself. In other words, it enables direct spiritual liberation and insight thereby doing away with the need for a flesh-and-blood person to mediate the process.

In this sense, the *śabda-guru* concept-cluster is an extraordinarily important one in the Sikh philosophical and spiritual lexicon, but its significance is difficult to comprehend without taking the historical context into account, which includes the following aspects. First, its emergence in

relation to actual events of early Sikh history especially the transmission of
authority in the form of Guruship from Nanak to his successors. Second,
the evolving form taken by *śabda*, ranging from its incarnation within the
body and consciousness of the Guru as a living person to its co-incarnation
within a canonized text (Adi Granth) at which point the *śabda* is co-present
in the extant living Guru authorized by the name 'Nanak'. Third, following
the death of the tenth living Guru (Gobind Singh), the sealing of authority
within the canonized text which henceforth becomes Guru Granth Sahib –
the text that is the repository of *śabda*.

Fourth, the embeddedness of the principle of *śabda-guru* in the lived
context of contemporary Sikhism, and its potential for catalysing philosophical
reflections and 'lines of flight' that can be extracted and transplanted into
the context of global thought.[4] All of this suggests that while *śabda* emerges
within actual historical contexts, nonetheless, its operation is not necessarily
bound to or imprisoned within any material historical context. From this
perspective, *śabda*'s paradoxical nature, its ability to work within a specific
historico-cultural context and at the same time to be free of any particular
context, its ability to traverse and hold different senses of time and ontology,
its ability to operate in material and immaterial contexts together place it
at the centre of any investigation into Sikh philosophy. To see how this can
make sense we need to explain some other key concepts of Sikh thought and
practice. In order to do this I'd like to make an additional remark about the
janamsākhī genre in relation to the idiom of Sikh philosophy.

If I make a distinction between the teaching of Guru Nanak and what
later becomes known as 'Sikh philosophy', it is primarily to distinguish,
on the one hand, between what Guru Nanak might actually have taught
during his lifetime to his immediate circle of followers, to the dignitaries
representing the prevailing spiritual and philosophical systems of his time, to
his immediate successors. And on the other hand, the modernist discourse of
Sikh philosophy which takes its central inspiration from the earlier teachings.
Clues about the nature of the early teachings can be seen in the *janamsākhī*
and other literatures of the sixteenth and seventeenth centuries.

Before turning to look at Nanak's teaching, let me return to the point made
earlier about the relevance of devotional literature such as the *janamsākhī*
to the discourse that came to be known as Sikh philosophy. What makes
the life narratives of Guru Nanak *philosophically relevant* is that, in different
ways, they both situate the central concepts of *gurmat* within the context of
an engagement with the world. Although the *janamsākhī* is embellished with
supernatural events of all kinds, which are clearly there to enhance Nanak's
social and spiritual status among his followers, nevertheless, what makes the
janamsākhī so effective in communicating central concepts and teachings is

that they are set in ordinary temporal and human contexts: Nanak's family, the village, other diverse places, his interactions with various people. Each episode presents an encounter or engagement between Nanak and the world, in such a way that both Nanak and the world enter into a negotiation and association in which change is brought about to prevailing states of affairs. Thus, in his early life, the young Nanak encounters a world of oppressive conventional orthodoxy, religion, superstition, politics, all of which interdict his conative self-expression. Nanak's response to this encounter is to initiate an internal self-struggle followed by a path towards self-perfection, which resulted in creative points of intersection. Later in life he encounters forms of cultural diversity, spiritual and political figures and rulers.

The point here is that Nanak's experience begins in *this world*, in *this life*. It evolved in *this world*, in *this life* and was applied *to this world*, to *this life* in order to change it. Thus the relevance of Nanak's life story for philosophy is that it forces us to reassess the kind of exceptionalism normally attributed to his personhood.[5] Perhaps what is truly exceptional about Nanak is how he deconstructs the tendency towards personhood by signalling towards the axial principle of his teaching – that his own Guru was not another human being but the direct experience of *śabda*. As we explore later, the implications of this are politically and spiritually profound, for Nanak is basically saying: experience *śabda* yourself, experience it directly, and by experiencing it yourself *become sovereign*! The possibility of this sovereign experience is available to everyone irrespective of caste, class, race, colour or religious creed. Moreover, the nature of this experience is not only internal (resulting in what can variously be described as self-transformation, inner conversion or a change of heart) but equally one that affects every encounter we have with the external world, other selves and societies. To put it slightly differently, each encounter provides a shock to conventional, orthodox, commonsensical thought, pushing it towards new searches. We see this in the way that Nanak takes over existing concepts and recreates them through the crucible of his own encounters with life, world and self.

Guru Nanak's teaching at a glance

Guru Nanak's teaching shares an important thematic inheritance with a loose lineage of spiritual masters such as the Sufi master Sheik Farid, or the *bhagats* Ravidas, Namdev and Kabir. Like Nanak these masters combined the search for spiritual perfection with devotional discipline and their teachings contained insights in common with Islamic, Hindu and Buddhist mysticism. These were individuals who experienced the highest states of spiritual enlightenment through psychic transformation, but then went out into the world to help others achieve that same experience.

Certain social characteristics were also shared by these masters. With the exception of Nanak they came from the lowest rungs of Hindu and Muslim society; they were uneducated and denied access to Vedic philosophy and Sanskrit, so their poetry was expressed in the local dialects. Like Nanak they all worked for a living; they were all householders who cultivated family and social ties. Moreover, they shared a disdain for asceticism, for organized religions and rigid belief systems, and not least for dogmatic forms of authority. Their writings strongly emphasize the unique opportunity presented by human life, urging their followers to develop the capacities of body and mind, but at the same time to maintain intense awareness of life's shortness and the ever-presence of death.

Where Guru Nanak and the nine Sikh Gurus who succeeded him differ from the *bhagat* inheritance is in the degree of systemization and institutionalization of the above-mentioned tendencies and ideas. This is especially the case with the teachings of Guru Nanak which not only place greater emphasis on certain themes and concepts that remained either undeveloped or loosely articulated in the *bhagats* but translate these concepts into the context of this life and this world. Let me therefore introduce a few of Nanak's key concepts in the form of a brief overview, which will be developed in the chapters that follow.

The 'Beloved' as figure of non-oppositional oneness

At the heart of Guru Nanak's teaching is an absolute sense of oneness. Absolute here means that it is a oneness that brooks no opposition between the One (*ēk*) and the Many (*anēk*) – it is both simultaneously. This non-oppositional logic of the One-Many (*ēk-anēk*) pervades all existence and non-existence, all matter and consciousness, in such a way that matter and consciousness are part of a continuum of oneness. In the writings of the Sikh Gurus, this absolute oneness cannot be known or experienced from a distance – that is, from a position occupied by a mind that observes it externally. It can be known and experienced only as an *immediacy*, that is to say, without mediation. Such immediacy can be attained by those who struggle with the tendency of the human mind to insert distance and therefore separation from the experience of oneness.

In other words, this direct experience can be attained and for those who do so, it manifests as a state of sovereign consciousness marked by immediate self-proximity. Oneness *is* immediate self-proximity, and it is a state that can be achieved by all and is open to all. To exist in this state is to exist in a state of unconditional love for everything that exists, all living things, beginning with an absolutely intimate relation of proximity or loving oneself. It is described as a state of absolute bliss or absolute joy.

At this point a certain difficulty arises with such descriptions of oneness. Although these attributes of oneness can certainly be gleaned from Guru Nanak's writings, descriptions of this kind are somewhat abstract and impersonal. It might suit those with a philosophical sensibility but not the mystical sensibilities of someone like Nanak who experienced it first-hand, and therefore often used a much more personal tone, a tone imbued with the intensity, depth and intimacy of feeling when speaking about oneness. However, the feelings associated with the personal tone are not only sensations of joy and ecstasy but are also tinged with feelings of pain and sadness, all of which converge into a pining for something lost – sentiments we would normally associate not only with human nature but with the nature of life in general.

It is worth asking, therefore, whether Nanak's notion of oneness is impersonal or personal? Or perhaps both? If both, would this not be a logical contradiction? The *janamsākhī* episode referencing Nanak's adolescent experience holds further clues that can help us answer these questions.

When the *vaid* (village doctor) arrived to attempt a cure for Nanak's suffering, Nanak refused treatment. But at the same time, in a series of verses, he provides helpful clues as to the nature of his suffering. According to Nanak's own testimony what the doctor failed to realize is that the kind of pain he was suffering from was not a normal bodily pain that neither drugs nor herbal concoctions might have alleviated. Rather, Nanak provides a peculiar image for the pain, describing it as *karak*, a piercing pain that went right through the body, tearing into his heart-soul-mind (*kalēja*). *Kalēja* is the Punjabi term for colic or black bile produced by the liver and widely known to be the seat of the kind of melancholia normally associated with the painful experience of mourning or pining that a lover feels when separated from the immediate proximity of her Beloved's embrace. Indeed, in the next lines of the verse, Nanak identifies the cause of his suffering: 'My body and soul weeps for my Beloved . . . , If you're to know the nature of my suffering. . . . Only the Beloved who gave me this pain can remove it.' When the *vaid* pressed Nanak to describe the symptoms of his illness, Nanak replied that 'I feel first the *intolerable pain of separation* (from the One) followed by a *pining* to join my Beloved'.[6] (emphasis mine).

What seems to be clear from Nanak's own testimony is that this peculiar state of mind-body, which is neither purely a separation nor purely a fusion of the lover and the Beloved but, rather, both separation and fusion at the same time, is not the same as mystical union or any experience of rapture. Rather, it seems to be initiated by a *wound in the very fabric of love*. In the Punjabi tradition of spiritual mysticism, this wound has its own name: *birahā* – which is perhaps best described as a feeling of ecstatic joy accompanied by piercing feelings that are intensely bitter/intensely sweet, intensely painful/ intensely pleasurable. What's interesting about *birahā* as a concept is that it challenges simple theological prescription. One of Nanak's predecessors, the great Sufi master Baba Farid, describes the singularity of this state:

birahā birahā tu sultān

Oh *birahā*! You alone are sovereign!

What Farid suggests here in characterizing *birahā* as sovereign (*sultān*) is that the wound of love is both the most intense and the most authoritative of experiences because it needs neither man nor god to validate it. In other words *birahā* signifies a state akin to the primordial state of being; it is the original state, signifying God's simultaneous presence-absence, the simultaneous transcendence-immanence at the same time. *Birahā* is therefore imbued with the creative principle from which all things come into being. It is the state in which the mortal (lover) becomes co-present and co-implicated in the divine treasure that it seeks (the Beloved).

To value *birahā* as supreme or sovereign (*sultān*) in this way is to value the bond or relation signified by the intertwined figures of lover and Beloved. Given that this bond is the relation to one's life that is slipping away, what the spiritual masters suggest is that the figure of the Beloved (and therefore *birahā*) intensifies the value of this life. As explained in Chapters 2 and 3 the creation of the bond itself is dependent on *nām*, but for now it will be helpful to note that the effect of force within the figure of the Beloved seeks to capture simultaneously the pain and joy intrinsic to the finitude of mortal life – a life that is always already life-death in the sense of a being who suffers loss, can die at any moment, but precisely because s/he can lose this life, has a realization of the preciousness and value of this life and the world in which this life is situated. This valuation of life matters for it determines the nature of Guru Nanak's encounter and engagement with the world. In turn, this encounter and engagement determine Nanak's philosophy as a whole encompassing epistemology, ontology, sociology and his ethics.

This co-implication and co-participation of the lover and the Beloved, with its attendant movements of separation and fusion, is a ubiquitous theme not only in Sikh scripture but also in Indian devotional literature, irrespective of its religious or sectarian origins. However, influential strands of scholarship in the history of religions have continued to translate and interpret states such as *birahā* through the logic of ontotheology, which is essentially a form of Christian philosophy according to which all reality (ontology) and ways of knowing (epistemology) are based on the existence of an eminent divine, a monotheistic God often represented as the highest Being.[7] As I have noted elsewhere,[8] ontotheology pervaded the conceptual frameworks of orientalist scholars, and through their translation of indigenous texts, it was able to impose secularizing interdictions on the perception of Indic concepts and phenomena. For this reason alone ontotheology, and the seemingly universally translatable figure of 'God' it transmits, warrants further contextualization and explanation.

Representing 'God': Aporias of time

There is a substantial body of scholarly research which has shown that since the late nineteenth century, Western historians, theologians and Indologists have been unable to present ideas, concepts and practices of Indic philosophy and culture other than through the lens of Christian theology central to which is the existence of God.[9] The foundational (and seemingly indisputable) logic of God's existence provided the framework for analysing the nature of Indic devotion which, because it was deemed to be inherently religious (evidence of the only true religion), could be divided into two types: *saguna bhakti* and *nirguna bhakti*.

The former (*saguna bhakti*) refers to a personal God who exists, has attributes, qualities or form and can be represented through imagery, iconography and idols.[10] In contradistinction *nirguna bhakti* is devotion to a God who cannot be represented in any form, shape or attribute and is therefore non-existent. Indologists have mistakenly attributed this notion of God to the philosophy of Guru Nanak.[11] Since the focus of devotion is a formless divine, the experience of this non-existent God is ineffable and gives rise to a strictly interior mode of piety, one that is amenable to secularity and privatization and therefore less likely to produce conflicting truth claims that might lead to communal violence.

There are two major problems with this model. First, the strict opposition between *saguna* and *nirguna bhakti* was itself an orientalist construction with roots in nineteenth-century colonial Indology which has continued in the work of prominent modern historians of religion. It has little relevance either to actual Sikh piety or to Sikh philosophical interpretations. Indeed, neither Guru Nanak nor the *bhagats* before him use the term *saguna* or *nirguna bhakti* to name their definitive experience. Second, European scholars framed Indic forms of experience (which far from being conceptually opposed to each other, actually flourish through a non-oppositional synthesis) within Enlightenment Christian frameworks.[12] Devotion was understood in the Christian sense in terms of the ontotheological axiom: God exists and cannot *not* exist. As recent continental philosophers of religion have argued, logical formulations about God's non-existence are ultimately based on the law of non-contradiction, also known as the philosophical law of identity, whose canonical formulation is found in Aristotle's *Metaphysics*: 'the same attribute cannot at the same time belong and not belong to the same subject'.[13] This principle became axiomatic to the normative discourse of religion so that it could be translated and applied to all cultures.

But what's rarely remembered is that the attribution of theo-logic to Indic concepts and phenomena represents just one aspect of a Janus-faced reality whose other dominant side is the operation of secularity. It is now generally accepted that theological prescription is actually tied to secularizing moves which establish a normative distinction in one's consciousness between the real world and the illusory world.[14] The real world is the one that is out there, empirically and objectively available to our consciousness, whereas, the illusory world is the one that is only subjectively and therefore privately available to us. And it is within this private world that divine entities such as 'God' and psycho-somatic states such as *birahā* are segregated. As thinking, rational 'subjects' we are expected to sort through our sensations and ideas in order to separate out those among them that represent genuine external objects (designated real) from those that are merely internal subjective mental states.[15]

Introduced by late nineteenth-century orientalist scholars, these secularizing moves were internalized by Sikh scholarly elites in the twentieth century. The result was the prevalent representation of Guru Nanak's teachings as *essentially theological*, and therefore *essentially religious*, which dominated post-Singh Sabha scholarship until fairly recently. As I have noted elsewhere,[16] the most refined expression of this theological paradigm can be found in W. H. McLeod's influential works, especially his chapter on 'The Teachings of Guru Nanak'.[17] In this chapter McLeod follows the Singh Sabha thinker Bhai Jodh Singh in framing Guru Nanak's teaching around a definition of God as an eternally existing, eminent Being, which both scholars regard as equivalent to Nanak's concept of *akāl purakh*.[18]

This translation of *akāl purakh* as an immutable monotheistic Being hinges around two key interlinked assumptions. First that *akāl* signifies a negation of historical time (*kāl*). Second, because God's most important attribute is transcendence of ordinary, human, historical time, this leads to the translation of *akāl* as eternal or immutable – both key characteristics of God's existence.

While not entirely wrong, this theologized translation suppresses a more complex and deeper meaning of *akāl* which, rather than negating historical time, points to an ontologically richer dimension of time that subsists simultaneously with *kāl* but cannot be accessed in the same way. This is because *akāl* as a concept does not refer to anything *beyond* the time of this world. It does not answer to a *theo*-logic and cannot therefore be classified as 'religious experience'. Rather, *akāl* refers to the time of life as it is being experienced, a richer and creative mode of time that resists the conventional duality of eternity versus temporality, allowing both to coexist in this life. This more complex notion of time (*akāl*) demands an ontology more closely attuned to immaterial transformations within subjectivity. In other words *akāl* is more suggestive of the absolute entanglement and non-oppositionality between immanence and transcendence. McLeod's separation of *kāl* and *akāl* – corresponding to the separation of human-time and divine-time, the time of this world and the time of God – is a fundamentally secularizing move which segregates (or privatizes) Nanak's concept to the realm of interiority,[19] in the process ensuring that religion does not enter the public sphere.

A further consequence of this secularizing logic is to classify states like *birahā* as devotional/religious/non-worldly. From here on, all talk of the lover-Beloved, of *birahā*, refer not to the external public world of time, space and material cause but to an illusory world that can only exist as an interior impulse that must be confined to the depths of human interiority. Its claim to sovereign experience (*birhā tu sultān!*) is undercut by regimes of translation that interpret the relationship between the experience of oneness and/or the Beloved through a lens that is at once secularizing and orientalizing, insofar as it classifies *birhā* as 'essentially religious'.

In stark contrast to this secularizing orientalist schema, Guru Nanak's own writings render the opposition between *nirgun* and *sargun* meaningless as the following verse clearly indicates:

sargun nirgun nirankār, sun samadhi aap
aapan kiā Nanakā, aape hī phir jaap.

In trance-like void Oneness subsists, imageless, with and without form.
From the same impulse, O Nanak, creation happens, and is eternally
    repeated.

Through a characteristically simple form of non-oppositional logic Nanak articulates a different way of thinking about the sovereign experience of absolute oneness and/or the Beloved. He says that if we are to discuss this experience in propositional terms, we need to adopt a logic that corresponds to an experience of oneness that is absolute. Absolute here does not mean one and only one but a one that is at the same time many or a many that is simultaneously one. It is an experience and a logic that keeps opposites together in a mutually enhancing oneness. The practical implication of this non-oppositional logic is that we can certainly think of this oneness in personal terms, as a feeling of an infinitely close presence, and we can give the feeling of such a presence a variety of names: Hari, Ram, Gobind, Gopal, Mukand, Narayan, Allah, Ghani, Haq, etc.

But at the same time, this oneness can also be referred to as *anām* (Nameless), thereby suggesting that it is an experience of a divine *person* with whom one can have an intimate relationship, as lovers do with their Beloved. But whether we think about it as personal or impersonal, or neither, we do so *in this life* that we are in the process of living. And the conventional or normative experience of living is one that is subject to a form of time (*kāl*) that is by default inherently constricted. Synthesized according to the demands and limitations of our ordinary field of consciousness, or mind, it is a form of time that constricts time to the passage of instants which come and go, arising and disappearing as they're presented to the mind. As long as this mode of time dominates life and living, the Beloved is always experienced as constantly slipping away, becoming absent in the very moment that we try to establish its presence. Unable to grasp the unicity of the Beloved as it comes to presence and becomes absent in that very moment, our mind processes this event as an either/or dualism: either the Beloved is present or it is absent; but not both, and not at once. On the other hand, the concept and lived reality *akāl* deals a death blow, not to time as such but to the impoverished, dualized, oppositional form of time to which we unsuspectingly subject life.

akāl – the time of my beloved

While Western philosophy and theology have struggled with this duality – *either God exists or God does not exist, but surely not both!* – Indic wisdom traditions have dealt with this conundrum by directing it back at the mind, and Guru Nanak's approach is not essentially different in this regard. As I explain in greater detail later in this book, the problem resides in the *contracted* nature of human consciousness, that is to say, the mind's tendency to squeeze the experience of infinity into a limited time frame (*kāl*). For Guru Nanak, the true form (*murat*) of the Beloved cannot be experienced in the constricted mode of *kāl*-time, which filters out all experience of reality that the mind deems incompatible with its personal gratification. To attain experiential vision (*darśan*) of one's Beloved requires immersion and participation in a different mode of time that Nanak names *akāl*.

In some ways the term *akāl* is so central to Sikh tradition that it could justifiably be regarded not only as the essential attribute and/or predicate but as the Name of the divine par excellence. A case in point are the terms *akāl purakh*, *akāl murat*, or the common Sikh greeting: *sat sri akāl* (the nature of reality is *akāl*) which are used as evidence that Sikh thought cannot be divorced from the notion of a personal God or from the idea that Sikhism is monotheistic. However, things are not quite as simple as they might seem.

While it is certainly a prevalent term in the writings of the Sikh Gurus, *akāl* is often interpreted as a negation of ordinary historical time (*kāl*), a move which has led most modern translators and exegetes to interpret *akāl* as 'immortal' or 'eternal' signifying a key characteristic of God's personhood (namely 'his' immortality). Again, while not incorrect, this theologized translation suppresses a richer and deeper meaning of *akāl* which, rather than transcending historical time, or simplistically expanding it into an infinite succession of homogenous moments, points to an ontologically richer dimension of time that subsists simultaneously with *kāl* but cannot be accessed in the same way. This is because *akāl* as a concept does not purport to transcend the time of this world. Rather, *akāl* refers to a deepening of the time of this world, in the sense of creatively multiplying time from within. From this perspective, to affirm *akāl* is to make time heterogeneous, in the sense that each passing present doesn't simply disappear but splits into unlimited pasts and unlimited futures. This is not contracted time-consciousness (*kāl*) but infinitely expanded time-consciousness (*akāl*) beyond the three modes of ordinary successive time (*satto gun*, *tamo gun* and *rajo gun*) that pertains to an infinite freedom normally associated with the divine.

Furthermore, and this is perhaps the crucial point, far from being the negation or transcendence of time, *akāl* refers to the time of life *as it is becoming*, as it is being experienced, as it is being lived, but perhaps most importantly, to a form of life that connects each thing to everything else. In other words, *akāl* is the time that names relation or relationality, the pure interconnectedness of all things, existent and non-existent, which demands an ontology more closely attuned to immaterial transformations within subjectivity. Thus *akāl* does not signify a transcendence of human life but instead gestures towards a participatory mode of living, in which one is continually attached to one's Beloved, namely, to the creative impulse (*akāl purakh*) that sustains and underpins all life. At the risk of sounding provocative, it can be suggested that *akāl* as a concept makes completely redundant the religio-secular logic of modernity and the oppositional mode of thought and time.

manmukh (contracted consciousness)

It is perhaps a little clearer why Nanak favours the figure of the Beloved to express an experience of oneness that is absent-present, personal-impersonal, One-Many, finite-infinite, at the same time. It is because the figure of the Beloved expresses a logic which gathers contradictions into a singular experience that is at work in *every moment* of our lives. Indeed, the point about experience is not that it is some otherworldly mystical attainment, but that it is all about deepening the experience of living this life that has been made available to us. Where Guru Nanak's teachings seem to score over other Indian devotional, mystical or philosophical movements is in articulating a logic that is deceptively simple yet immensely practical because it is grounded not in any otherworldly theo-logic but in the logic of life.

The only problem is that this logic is inaccessible to those of us who live, work, sleep, dream in the shallowness of an everyday existence and ordinary states of consciousness that are geared around self-interest and self-attachment. Guru Nanak calls this degenerate, egocentric state of mind in which humanity is congenitally trapped: *manmukh*. To experience the logic of life as a oneness, with the intensity of the figure of the Beloved, is to cultivate the experience of self-loss or egoloss, which to the *manmukh* state of mind is antithetical. Hence, the *manmukh* trapped in its egotistical bubble works against the logic of life. Instead of struggling against this everyday state of consciousness in which it is effectively imprisoned, the *manmukh* routinely objectifies the experience of oneness into a social construct 'God', which, in turn, can be manipulated by wider social forces.

We can show how this works by recalling the example given by Guru Nanak. Both Hindus and Muslims, he argues, say that God is one, but the problem is that they objectify this oneness, albeit in opposing ways. While Hindus objectify God as infinitely near to us and try to express his proximity through idols and images, Muslims regard this one as transcendent, infinitely beyond us. In their efforts to outdo each other, both groups miss the *experience* of oneness, instead wrapping the Beloved in a social projection of God, on the basis of which they pit themselves against each other. As the focus on God or oneness disappears, it is replaced by a focus on social or individual identification: 'I am Hindu' or 'I am Muslim'. It is in response to this individualizing and boundary-making 'I am' that, according to the *janamsākhīs*, Guru Nanak stated: 'There is no Hindu. There is no Muslim' implying that the followers of each creed had forgotten what it meant to be Hindu or Muslim and replaced it with the anxiety of a deluded ego. In view of this problem, Nanak and his close contemporary Kabir suggest a more

practical formula to the figure of an eminent, monotheistic deity, as indicated
in the following couplets:

NANAK

When I act in ego, you're not present
  When you're present, ego is absent.
O'Nanak repeat these words: I am that One, that One is me,
  Within this One the three worlds are merged.

(GGS: p. 1092)

KABIR

When I am, my Beloved is not.
  Now my Beloved is here, and 'I am' no more.
By saying 'You, You', I have become you.
  The 'I am' is no longer present in me.

(GGS: p. 1375)

The formula suggested by these couplets is both simple and practical: human
ego (I am) and 'God' (or the Beloved) cannot be in the same place at the same
time. When one is present, the other is absent. When I am, God does not
exist. When God exists, I am no more. To approach God, to become divine,
one must lose oneself, hence egoloss. The question then becomes: How does
one act, think and live in the world if one relinquishes ego? Given that we
must remain in the world and engaged with it, should we not simply let go
of ego or the 'I am', which is the very basis of our being in the world in the
first place?

The clue that Nanak offers for solving this puzzle is to think of the ego
as a paradoxical enigma whose contradictory sides must be held together.
As we shall see in the next two chapters, Guru Nanak's approach is to shift
attention back to the nature of the ego: it is what *prevents* the experience of
oneness, and yet it is also the *very means* by which we can experience the
world. Holding this thought together is no easy task. Indeed, it is literally a
struggle – the very same struggle by which the lover strives to prevent the
Beloved slipping away, out of mind, at each moment. In other words, how to
bring about this experience of fusion-separation in which one exists as fused-
joined with the Beloved, even as the Beloved is continually slipping away?

According to Nanak's own testimony, in order to make such an experience
possible a profound transformation of the normal human psyche is required.
This is precisely the struggle described in the *janamsākhīs*, a struggle that
Nanak underwent during the period of adolescence culminating in the
Sultanpur experience. It was a journey towards self-perfection lasting twelve
years or so, during which time Nanak submitted himself to and developed his

own techniques of spiritual discipline (*sadhana*). Of course, these techniques were not entirely unique to Guru Nanak. As his own writings make abundantly clear, Nanak inherited certain broad concepts and techniques which had been cultivated by a long line of spiritual masters before him. Several such practical concepts stand out in particular – *satguru*, *satnām*, *satsang* and *vismād*.

While these first three terms, *satguru*, *satsang* and *satnām*, refer to an actual discipline or practice through which one can attain transformation of the psyche, they are also conceptually vibrant and can be regarded as pillars of a system of practical or experiential logic developed by Guru Nanak, which came to be called *gurmat* (lit. the logic, teaching, instruction or philosophy of the Guru).

Philosophically *satguru* beckons towards epistemology, *satnām* signals towards ontology, while *satsang* provides access to a potential sociology. Although later chapters in this book closely examine the philosophical, psychological and spiritual operations signified by these terms, it will be helpful to introduce them here.

satguru: *śabda* and revelation

The term *sat* means truth or existence and *guru* refers both to a living spiritual master and an axial principle which helps a devotee achieve enlightenment. In combination *satguru* refers to a true or authentic source of enlightenment. In Indian wisdom traditions a teaching, instruction, technique, path leading to perfection is usually provided by a living person acting as a *guru*.

By contrast, Nanak's deployment of the term *satguru* indicates that the kind of spiritual transformation he teaches about should not be reliant on a living human preceptor or personal guru. It does not have to be mediated via another person. Rather, it is better to try and attain it directly from the divine source through one's own effort, for the simple reason that this spiritual transformation is singular in nature. It is not only unique to each person but it consists in *immediacy*. That is to say, it takes place immediately, without distance, within the interiority of one's consciousness, in the sense that it transports alterity into the heart of one's subjectivity, one's sense of who 'I am'.

As Nanak himself tells us in his compositions, his singular experience and therefore his own authority as a Guru came from a non-human source which resides in each of us as a potentiality. For this reason, although *satguru* is rather conveniently equated with 'God', more precisely it refers to an absolutely interior wellspring, a living force inherent in life or existence, that remains hidden from us. But this wellspring can only be accessed if we are able to properly attune our consciousness. As we shall see in Chapter 3, Nanak is very specific about what *satguru* is. It is *śabda* (lit. the Word or language) which is also referred to as *anhad-śabda* (lit. the Unpulsed Word), a pure form of egoless speech/thought that resonates with the underlying sonic-mnemic theme of creation (*nām*) and, in resonating, unlocks and reveals the creative potentials inherent within human consciousness.

From this perspective it would not be incorrect to suggest that *śabda* is the non-human agent of revelation. I use the word 'revelation' with some caution here, for I want to underscore that it does not necessarily correspond to the Abrahamic notion of revelation as the literal speaking of God's Word to man either directly or through the agency of supernatural beings such as angels. Revelation in Guru Nanak's philosophy is intrinsically tied to the role of *śabda* as the non-anthropomorphic agent of spiritual self-realization.

In this sense *satguru* can be more productively regarded as the force immanent within us that creates a conversion from ordinary ego-centred consciousness to egoless consciousness. The clearest expression of this transformation can be found in the nature of the language we utter, such that ordinary self-centric language gives way to the poetic language of self-loss. The agent of this transformation is *śabda* or *anhad-śabda* – the unpulsed or Unspoken Word – which is produced not by our everyday consciousness but by the non-conscious part of the psyche. Chapters 3 and 4 examine the connection between *satguru* and *śabda* (Word) more carefully as this principle is axiomatic for Sikh philosophy. For now it should suffice to say that the concept of *satguru* functions to displace the need for human mediation in achieving perfection. As a principle it indicates both the immediacy of the spiritual experience and that it is open to anyone. Because a human agent is unnecessary, the sovereign experience through which this language is released (or revealed) itself becomes the touchstone of all authority in a way that has implications for social and political praxis.

However, this paradoxical ability of *śabda-guru* to operate simultaneously in the realm of external time (history) and in the interiorized time-consciousness of immediate experience seems to have baffled modernist scholarship in Sikh studies. Most scholars have simply evaded it by working uncritically with Western epistemological frameworks that designate historical time as the legitimate framework for explaining the transmission of authority from one Guru to another, or to the text, in rational terms. Concepts such as *satguru* and *śabda-guru*, which are resistant to being rationalized and explained within the parameters of historical materialism, are reduced to theological metaphor. We see this especially in the kind of secularized narratives that attempt to explain a phenomenon which is crucially significant to mainstream Sikh tradition. The phenomenon is crucial because not only did it involve a series of actual events (the transmission of authority from one Guru to another) that occurred in historical time; these events were simultaneously experiential transformations that occurred not in external datable time but *within* and *as* interiorized time-consciousness. So the conundrum is how to narrate an event that is datable (external) but at the same time ineffable (interior). How to retain the paradox at the heart of the transmission of authority from one Guru to the next? The secularized narratives followed by historians of religion exhibit contours similar to the following:

> During his lifetime Guru Nānak wrote down his compositions (*śabda-guru*) compiling them into a *pothi* or manuscript which he passed onto his successor Angad, who in turn added his own compositions and passed them on to his successor and so on for at least 6 of the 10 living Sikh Gurus. The fifth Guru, Arjan compiled all the extant compositions of his predecessors, his own voluminous poetry, and the chosen works of the *bhāgats* (saints and mystics who taught a very similar message to Guru Nānak) into a major text called the Adi Granth (the original book) which was formally installed in the central Sikh shrine. Until the time of the last Sikh Guru, Gobind Singh, the Adi Granth was revered, not only as the definitive collection of the teachings of the house of Nānak, but with the same veneration accorded to the living Guru. Shortly before his death in 1708 it was Guru Gobind Singh who took the decisive steps of (i) closing the line of living Gurus, (ii) formally passing spiritual authority to the Adi Granth, which thenceforth became known as the Guru Granth Sahib. Since then Sikhs have treated the Guru Granth Sahib as a living Guru insofar as it takes center place in Sikh gurdwaras and is central to all Sikh ceremonies, rites of passage and collective worship.

Because it is grounded in materialist (*kāl*-centric) epistemology, what seems to be erased from such narratives is anything to do with experience as such, which now becomes automatically routed through the realm of transcendental metaphysics and/or theology, from which the historical materialist keeps a safe distance.

In contradistinction, the kind of narratives used in early Sikh textual and oral traditions deploy pluralist epistemologies that enable the reader or listener to keep historical and 'theological' (I prefer philosophical) elements in a mutually enhancing relationship. They do this by being able to access the radically different, but equally real, mode of time-consciousness (*akāl*) which *reveals* – in the sense that the revelatory process unravels the layers of our consciousness – the experience central to the transmission of authority. This experience is not to be found in the materiality of merely written or printed texts or historical data but within the im/material force of affects that are released in the process of undergoing the self-transformatory experience of egoloss, which is to say, an internal transformation of the psyche. Thus, a narrative that is both philosophically literate and resonates with the epistemologies prevalent in early Sikh texts, practice and tradition[20] should be able to explain and narrate the meaning of *satguru* and/or *śabda-guru* as historically situated and experiential at the same time. Such a narrative might go something like this:[21]

Guru Nanak's spiritual experience, his claim to authority as *Guru*, derives from his undergoing an experience with *śabda* which provides an episte-mological sword that kills ego, releasing his psyche into a state of bliss and equipoise (*anand, sahaj*). . . . Nanak had experienced the sublime truth of existence at the most profound level, which he was convinced could change the nature of the self and society. Yet the complexities of the social, political and cultural milieu in which he lived prevented him from com-pleting his task before the end of his life. Clearly, it was necessary to find some person who could continue Nānak's work in accordance with the founder's own intentions.

But what was to be the touchstone for choosing a new successor? If the touchstone was proximity to the master himself, then an obvious choice might have been Guru Nanak's own family, perhaps one of his own two sons. However both sons 'proved intractable and disobedient', and failed a number of tests that were designed by the Guru to probe his disciples' inner qualities.[22]

The person eventually chosen to succeed him was Bhai Lehna whose service, devotion and humility were recognized by Guru Nanak and his inner circle who regarded Lehna as an exemplary and inspirational figure. The various tests to which Lehna was put displayed his proximity to the cardinal virtues that Nanak desired in his successor: humility, complete devotion, respect for the householder's life, but perhaps most importantly a mode of consciousness that drew from the same wellspring of spiritual experience as Nānak. Central to achieving this mode of consciousness was the concept of *śabda-guru*: the idea that the ultimate Guru (or *satguru*) is the *śabda* (Word), rather than a living human guru. And this non-human principle can only be realized by 'dying to the Word', by sacrificing ego on the sword of the Word. In order to succeed Nanak as the new Guru, Lehna would have had to demonstrate this principle to his mentor. It is this qualitative proximity that the *janamsākhīs* speak of as the passing of light from one body to another. Accordingly, to indicate the succession of Guruship, in the last months of his life Guru Nanak renamed Lehna as Angad (lit. part of my own body). Prostrating himself before his successor, Nanak proclaimed to the Kartarpur community that Angad would be their new Guru, the new 'Nanak'.[23]

This act of prostration of the master before his disciple was a profoundly important event in the formation of the early Sikh community and carried strong philosophical and social meaning that sent out several important signals. First, that Nanak intended for his work to be continued. Second, that it was possible for any of his Sikhs to achieve the perfected state of *gurmukh* within one's lifetime, and that the positions of Guru and Sikh were interchangeable – they were not divinely ordained. In other words, there was, potentially at least, no difference, spiritually, poetically, philosophically, between the founder and his successor(s), between master and disciple.

But, in order for the transmission of authority between master and disciple to take effect, it was necessary for the disciple's act of surrender / devotion/self-sacrifice to be equalled or surpassed by the master who, by surrendering to his disciple, committed an act of ultimate sacrifice in the form of *self-violation*, a violence to the perceived image of him as divine. In order to put the succession into motion, Nanak had to *publicly enact self-loss*, a death of the self premised conceptually on the principle of *śabda-guru*. It is this free and willing exchange of egoloss (one by the Sikh, the other by the Guru) that not only set in motion the historical transmission of Guruship but provided philosophical focus and continuity of practice for the early Sikh community as it would evolve over the next two centuries. Indeed, this paradoxical doctrine of egoloss as dying to the Word encapsulated the sovereign principle of Guru Nanak's teaching (*gurmat*). If the sovereignty of this teaching is defined by a violence directed towards the desire to concentrate sovereignty in one's own self, then sovereign violence resides at the core of Guru Nanak's teaching.

The performative transmission of sovereign consciousness was similarly repeated in the case of the third, fourth and fifth Gurus, Amardas, Ramdas and Arjan. According to early Sikh sources such as Bhai Gurdas, the transmission of sovereign consciousness from the incumbent to the incoming Guru came to be known as *jotī jōt samāṇā* – the passing-on of light from one to the next by fusing or merging one consciousness with the other. But the process as such was probably less a handing-on of a torch from one to another, than a devotionally induced process of self-transformation centred around dying to the Word/Self and ending in self-illumination. In other words, each incoming Guru had to demonstrate self-perfection to the incumbent Guru by willingly dying to *śabda-guru* – the absolute acknowledgement that one's authority and self-perfection came from *śabda-guru* and not from a living person. In this way, what is renounced is any notion of personal sovereignty. The category of person is now secondary to the principle of *śabda-guru*.

We see this performative depersonalization of the category of 'Guru' especially during the tenure of Guru Arjan, the fifth Guru. One of Guru Arjan's major achievements was to compile the writings of his predecessors and a variety of spiritual masters whose basic philosophy was in accordance with that of Guru Nanak. The result was the Adi Granth, a major scriptural text running into 1,431 pages, centred around the authority of Guru Nanak's compositions, and to which Arjan himself contributed the majority of hymns. Completed in August 1604, the Adi Granth was ceremonially installed in the inner sanctum of the Harimandar, the holiest shrine of the Sikh faith. During the installation ceremony Guru Arjan prostrated himself in front of the Adi Granth in a performative gesture demonstrating to his followers that sovereign authority was now vested in the Granth.

This spectacle of investing sovereign authority in the Granth was a landmark event in Sikh memory, equally momentous to that of Guru Nanak's transmission of spiritual authority. Whereas with Arjan's predecessors, the body and voice of a living flesh-and-blood (*dehdhārī*) Guru had been the sole locus of authority and focus of devotion, Sikhs now came to see the Adi Granth as signifying an equal and legitimate sovereignty. Apart from putting an authoritative seal on the physical text itself, more importantly, it signalled a change in the external manifestation of authority and that Sikhs were to regard the central principle *within* the text – *śabda-as-guru* – to be above the living *dehdhārī* Guru. Moreover, it signalled with absolute clarity that spiritual authority lay not 'literally' in the physical volume itself but in the potential of the *śabda* to interact with and transform the living consciousness of its devotees.[24] This ability to change an individual's consciousness is also the ability to change the individual's sense of reality, clearly indicating that *śabda* has an intimate connection to making, breaking and transforming reality. Indeed, as we'll see in more detail in Chapter 3, the concept of the *śabda* as Guru (Word as Guru) was invoked by Guru Nānak himself when he was challenged by rivals to reveal the source of his authority: *The Word is my Guru; Consciousness attuned to its message, is the disciple* (Siddh Gosht).

The later Sikh Gurus (Hargobind, HarRai, Har Krishan and Tegh Bahadur) all continued the spectacle of dual authority venerating the Adi Granth as repository of sovereign *śabda-guru* principle, even as they themselves physically occupied the seat of Guruship (*gurgaddhī*). This continued until the tenure of the tenth and last human Guru of the Sikhs, Gobind Singh. According to historical sources, shortly prior to his death Guru Gobind Singh declared that the sovereign role of the Guru would pass to the Adi Granth, which was henceforth sealed and known as Guru Granth Sahib, and to the corporate community which was to be led by the Khalsa. Hence the doctrine of dual authority: Guru Granth (Guru as text) and Guru Panth (the order of the Khalsa as the body designated to uphold Nanak's core principle of *śabda-guru*, from which the Khalsa could not deviate, at the cost of life itself).

satnām

If, as we have established earlier, concepts such as *satguru* and *śabda-guru* operate in both historical and experiential contexts, it follows that anyone today should be able to access the wellspring from which they emerge. So the question arises: If *satguru* as *śabda-guru* implies a direct unmediated experience, how does one go about actually achieving it? What is the most suitable method for attaining it? For Nanak the preferred method for achieving enlightened states cannot be limited to conceptuality. Rather, it has to be cultivated through contemplative practices which aim to recentre our lives in relation to *nām* – a term that is conventionally translated as the 'divine Name' or the 'Name of God'. Accordingly, *satnām* is rendered as the 'True Name', 'Truth by Name' or 'One whose Name is Truth'. As noted already, theologizing translations such as these are more of a hindrance than a help, in as much as they conceal the richness, depth and mystery of *nām* itself. The next two chapters will provide a more detailed treatment, but for now it may be helpful to risk a few interconnected clues registering what *nām* might be.

Insofar as *nām* is what *names-without-naming the Beloved*, it is the singular Word for the creative essence inherent within all existence and non-existence. The creative essence is that which ensures the continuity or permanence of a thing even as that thing changes in time; *nām* refers to the sonic-mnemic principle that orders, interconnects and provides direction for all existence. It is not uncommon for practitioners and scholars to reduce *nām* to a mere mechanical repetition of the divine names or some mantric formula. The Sikh Gurus were adamant, however, that *nām* needs to be understood in relation to mental concentration and the devoted practice of orienting one's consciousness around *nām*. In this sense *nām* signifies an inner communion of the heart, that is, the soul-mind-body complex which involves the engagement of one's entire personality in relation to the world outside us. As a practice it begins with a mnemo-technique, a method of vocal and mental repetition which, after diligent practice, leads to an alignment of personal and cosmic consciousness. The basic techniques are *nām japna*, the chanting or vocalized repetition, which leads to *nām simran* or mindful meditation or contemplation. The technique favoured by Guru Nanak was devotional singing to the accompaniment of musical measures (*rāgas*) of North Indian music (*gurbāṇī kirtan*), in order to produce effulgent states of consciousness. *Kirtan* was favoured by Guru Nanak for two reasons. First, it already incorporates the essential meditative elements of *nām japna* and *nām simran* as mindful remembrance is enhanced by the nature of music accompanying the poetic verses to be sung. Second, *kirtan* is meant to be performed in association with others, that is, within a gathering of individuals devoted to the same spiritual journey. Such a gathering is known as *sangat* or *satsang*.

satsang/sangat

In the Sikh context, the term *satsang* or simply *sangat* (lit. being-with-others, or gathering together) refers to the community of like-minded individuals drawn together by their devotion to a true spiritual master or *satguru* and by a common method of adoration based on mindful remembrance of *nām*. A *satsang* refers to a gathering or association of those who travel together on the path towards deliberative experience. As such the path is the journey between life and death, a path that is essentially temporal and temporalizing. A deeper philosophical foray into *sangat/satsang* may reveal a pluriversal aspect of these terms, namely, the idea of a community of those who have nothing in common, or to a notion of relation grounded in difference rather than identity.

Taken together, and in conjunction with a variety of other key terms, concepts such as *satguru, satnām* and *satsang* comprise the nuclear elements of a life-world, whose common focus is a desire on the part of individual travellers to attain an experience of the Beloved. This is not to be confused, conflated or reduced to the memory of an actual experience – for example, Guru Nanak's Sultanpur experience – which would result in creating an idolization of that event.[25]

Rather, it is a way for each person to actively strive to learn to experience life and world anew, and therefore to experience creatively and in such a way that newness is created in the world. The language of the Beloved is an allusion to a form of lived experience in which one strives to rest with the object of one's love. This *resting-in* is another word for contemplation. To contemplate is not simply to reflect or think upon something deeply, but even more so it is a participatory event, a being-at-home-in, or being-at-home-with, the object of one's contemplation.[26] It is a practice of living, a way of life (*panth*) in which *the knower is always already with the known*, in a state of adoration or wonder that the Sikh Gurus refer to as *vismād*.

Vismād: Passion evoked by wonder

In some ways *nām* is the essence of *gurbāṇī* and therefore of Sikh philosophy. It is that paradoxical essence of reality (*sat*) towards which Sikh philosophy as a whole is orientated. For, on the one hand, the Sikh Gurus describe *nām* as ineffable and indefineable. On the other hand, they don't hesitate to provide detailed descriptive clues about *nām*. However, these descriptive clues are not objectifications of *nām*, for example, as the Name of an eminent Being (Madho, Hari, Ram, etc.) which can be repeated as a magical-mechanical formula to attain personal benefits. To the extent that it can be objectified as the name of an entity, this entity is the Beloved. Hence, *nām* can maximally be objectified only as the Name-of-my-Beloved.[27] Rather, what the Sikh Gurus provide are descriptions of subjective mental states, specifically feelings. Thus, I can only know my Beloved through specific feelings. The nature of these feeling-states is beyond adequate definition, but its *expression* can nevertheless be described in words. Expression is therefore important as it refers to the manifestation of *nām* in and as a subjective mental state. Guru Nanak calls this expression *vismād*.

Though difficult to pin down with a description, *vismād* refers to the element of wonder, the element of uncontrollable surprise registered by an individual when her consciousness is in communion or pure relationality with the All. There is no psychical or physical distance between the One and the All, between the lover and the Beloved. This lack of distance or expansion into pure connectivity is experienced as pure enjoyment, and it is this 'enjoyment-element' which the Gurus particularly emphasize in their descriptions. The person in a state of *vismād* experiences indescribable intensity, which can be described as *suād* (lit. taste). Stated differently, in the state of *vismād* one tastes the infinite enjoyment of fusion. In this state one gets a taste of the divine, and this taste comports the taster to forget herself and feel the All by distancing oneself from one's ego. This state of *vismād* or wonder results in a definite, concrete perception of reality through one's sensory organs, but it is synthesized in such a way that the data supplied to the senses is not presented as a duality. The intellect (*buddhī*) retains a oneness-in-Manyness, identity-in-difference, basically a state of fusion that is entranced with colour, smell, taste or sound of the object experienced, whether this is a flower, another person or nature in general. To quote Sher Singh, in the state of *vismād* the 'inner organ – the *anubhav* – call it intuition, feeling, insight, enters into the very nature of the thing and feels quite at home because there is no difference, there is no differentiation' (Sher Singh: p. 238). *Vismād* as a state of wonder and enjoyment signifies a perfection of one's relation to nature, a state in which the individual consciousness is greatly sensitized to the environment, in turn attuning one's thoughts, desires and actions towards an attitude of selfless service and sharing of the environment with other people, creatures, indeed the whole universe.

Discussion questions

(1) What relevance does the 'life of Guru Nanak' have for Sikh philosophy?

(2) What are some key concepts that contribute to a Sikh theory of experience? How does the Sikh concept of experience mitigate some of the problems of Western religio-secular frameworks in which we continue to do our work?

(3) Ought we to differentiate between 'Sikh philosophy' and 'Sikh theology'? How do the Sikh Gurus deal with the problems created by classical monotheism?

(4) What do *kāl* and *akāl* mean? Explain the relationship between these two terms. How is the question of time relevant to the notion of the Beloved?

(5) Explain the importance of the term *satguru* and its link to the concept *śabda-guru*. How does Sikh tradition explain the workings of these concepts in Sikh?

(6) What do you understand by the concept of *vismād*?

(7) Are there limitations on applying categories such as monotheism, monism, or pantheism, to *gurmat*? Why?

Epistemology

(*giān*)

In modern academic philosophy there is a prevailing tendency to assume that every culture, every society possessing its own thought system must, at the very least, have an implicit theory of knowledge, perhaps even something akin to an indigenous or folk epistemology according to which an individual or a society is able to order knowledge and understanding of the world. In the modern period, formalized systems of knowledge have become foundational for defining the philosophical system of a culture. Is there, then, something akin to a Sikh epistemology or theory of knowledge, a specific way in which Sikhs think and act according to performative categories designated by the founders of this tradition?

The body of literature categorized as 'Philosophy of Sikhism' and composed in the twentieth century seems to unambiguously suggest that there may indeed be a uniquely Sikh form of epistemology, and its writers accordingly outlined its various components and categories. From this perspective the work performed by Sikh philosophy does not function so very differently from the variations of Indian philosophy composed in the early twentieth century by iconic figures such as S. Radhakrishnan and S. N. Dasgupta who went to great lengths to configure Indian theories of knowledge.

Once again, however, one needs to pause here and ask whether, and to what extent, scholars writing in the heyday of European colonialism were inadvertently influenced by its knowledge system. My own approach to the question of Sikh epistemology, or whether it is possible to think in a specifically Sikh way, will proceed by first registering an ambiguity. While Sikh thinkers in the twentieth century did a fine job of identifying and assembling the nuts and bolts of a Sikh theory of knowledge, their work inadvertently reproduced key aspects of the colonial European-Christian world view. The core of this dominant world view consisted of a political theology, which neatly combined the ideologies of liberal secular humanism and Christian theology by fusing their two key components into a belief system.[1] These two components were: (i) the assumption that thought belongs to a single consciousness, a person who owns her or his own thought; (ii) the anthropocentric belief that, having been placed by God at the centre of creation, man becomes the 'relational center'[2] of all things in the world by exerting an 'epistemic sovereignty'[3] that once belonged to God.[4]

Such a starting point is anathema to any possible Sikh epistemology. Although it is possible to identify similar components and functions to the European or Indian, the starting point for any Sikh epistemology is quite different from the Western one in its understanding and evaluation of what knowledge is. As will become clear in the pages that follow, whereas modern Western philosophy begins with ontology – which sets out what exists, the being of things, leading to a hierarchical ontotheological classification according to which all beings are measured in relation to an eminent Being (God), so that epistemology is always a knowledge of the sanctioned order of things – in contradistinction, *gurmat* co-relates ontology and epistemology. Sikh epistemology can only begin if we break out of a human-centred way of knowing disguised as Sikh theology which inveigled its way into Sikh thought through the work of orientalists and modern colonial elites.[5] In other words, only by breaking out of anthropocentric epistemology can we get to any worthwhile ontology. Having registered this important fact, let us work our way through the received wisdoms in order to move towards a Sikh epistemology.

*   *   *

In the Sikh philosophical system known as *gurmat*, the function of epistemology is generally thought to come under the purview of the term *giān*, which is a Punjabi cognate of the much older Sanskrit word *jñāna*. Traceable to the ancient Upanisadic texts, *jñāna* specifies the path of wisdom or enlightenment acquired through processes of learning that teach us how to see the nature of reality correctly. The orthodox schools of Indian philosophy, which emerged from the Upanishads, placed major emphasis on the need to believe in the nature of Vedic knowledge as revealed (*śruti*). According to its circular system of reasoning, *śruti* provides validity and ultimate authority to this way of seeing and knowing reality. Orthodox schools of Hindu philosophy later enumerated what they understood to be the valid sources of knowledge or *pramanas*. The main *pramanas* are perception (*pratakshya*), inference (*anuman*), analogical comparison (*upmana*), derivative postulation (*artha patti*), implicative reasoning (*sambhava*), cognitive proof (*anupalabadhi*) and Word (*śabda*) or the verbal testimony of a reliable witness.[6] In the Indian systems *pratakshya* or direct perception is intimately associated with *śabda*, the instructive verbal testimony of a self-realized person (*rishi* or *guru*). These two sources of knowing, *pratakshya* and *śabda*, work in parallel and contribute to the prevalent Indian proclivity to believe the verbal testimony of a personal *guru* or *rishi* who is believed to have gained exceptional insight into the nature of reality. Indeed, as a source of valid knowledge, the word or testimony of a personal *guru* or *rishi* is considered superior to the perceptive capacities of ordinary thinkers, no matter how great the capacity for deductive reasoning.

Despite superficial similarities, the Sikh philosophical system of *giān* differs from the classical Indian systems in two key respects. First, the *gurmat* system does not distinguish between different kinds of *pramanas*. Instead, *giān* refers to interpenetrating forms of knowledge gathered together into a unity of consciousness (knowing) – which happens to be the important aspect of *giān*. Second, *giān* as a system of knowledge bypasses the mediating influence of personal *gurus* or *rishis*. This Sikh system of *giān* is centrally focused on *śabda* (Word), but with the difference that *śabda* is not the verbal testimony of a person but, rather, indicates a system for perfecting our means of knowing directly through a combination of revelation (as described earlier) and intuition (*anubhav*) in a way that is distinct from other *pramanas* (perception/reasoning). In fact *śabda* in the *gurmat* system works in a manner sufficiently different from the classical Indian system that it restructures knowledge (*giān*) in such a way that any system of *giān* is derived from *śabda*, rather than the other way around. In the *gurmat* system, *śabda* does not belong to a person or personal consciousness. Rather, it is what emerges or unfolds when attachment to personal consciousness is relinquished. As indicated earlier, the concept and operation of *śabda* in *gurmat* co-relates ontology and epistemology which, as we see later, prevents the kinds of problems that arise with theo-centrism (Christian), cosmo-centrism (Vedic) and anthropo-centrism (secular humanist).

But what kind of knowledge is this? What kind of knowledge is it that cannot be contained in a personal consciousness, yet provides direct access to reality? To understand the unique significance of *śabda*, it is helpful to return to Guru Nanak's own writings. Of course, any astute reader will no doubt balk at this suggestion, for have I not just stated that *śabda* in the Sikh system doesn't require the verbal testimony of a person (even Nanak)? Objections notwithstanding, there is clear evidence in Nanak's writings of a unique system of logic (what might be called the *Guru-logic*) that is irreducible to belief in a person or her testimony, but instead, it gives rise to a distinctively Sikh understanding of how we know and think, or what thinking is.

Word-as-Guru (*śabda-guru*)

In a famous composition called *Siddh Gosht*, Guru Nanak presents a debate between himself and a group of spiritual adepts known as Siddhas.[7] Trained in yogic techniques the Siddhas were part of the order of Nath Yogis who derived their authority from the great master Gorakh Nath and were a force of major significance in the northwestern regions of India between the twelfth and fifteenth centuries. The *Siddh Gosht* uses the form of dialogical debate to present Nanak's own understanding of key concepts like the nature of void or detachment (*sunya/sunnan*), the nature of the Self (*haumai*) and Word (*śabda*), with the aim of presenting Nanak's teaching as superior in its insight into reality. In stanzas 43 and 44 the debate reaches a kind of climax as the Siddhas directly confront Nanak about the source of his knowledge and therefore about the source of his authority as a spiritual master.

Siddhas (43)
What is the origin (of your power)?
    What system of knowledge commands respect today?
Who is your guru? Whose disciple are you?
    Which knowledge leads to detachment?
Let Nanak speak and explain to us
    Which Word (or teaching) can liberate us?

Nanak replies (44):
Breath is the origin (of my practice and power).
    The Gurus logic is the knowledge in this age.
The Word is Guru: Consciousness attuned to it, is the disciple.
    Through the Un-pulsed/Un-spoken Word, detachment can be
    attained.
Only through the Word (*śabda*) can the state of Oneness be described,
    Embodying Oneness/detachment, the *gurmukh* quenches the fire
    of ego.

What stands out straight away in these two verses (the main themes of which are repeatedly stressed throughout the dialogue) is the importance given to Word (*śabda*), to its role in attuning consciousness and as the means for attaining liberation without the need for a mediator, either in the form of a person or a belief system. The central idea here is immediacy, or directness of liberation and insight. Moreover, such immediacy or directness is implied in the reference at the end of verse 44 that it is more helpful to understand oneness as a detached state of mind or self-relinquishing, rather than what we normally do, which is to objectify oneness as an external entity, a thing out there among other things in the world. The central focus of Nanak's reply is pure interiority (which is not to be confused with the liberal secular ideal of privatized interiority), one that is more akin to immanence as a way of living that connects the mind (microcosm) to everything else in the universe (macrocosm). Oneness is therefore something that can (and should) be lived rather than represented, and it is the Word that enables this interconnection.

This, of course, raises a number of questions. What *kind* of Word is it that leads to a state of pure interiority or oneness? How does this Word differ from what is conventionally understood as word(s) or language? Nanak gestures towards something called the Unspoken Word (*anhad śabda*) – but this is no less enigmatic and seems a contradiction in terms, a paradox at best, or at worst, illogical/irrational. Is Nanak gesturing at a *logic specific to the Word* – a logic that does not aid representation but rather makes things happen, enables a certain kind of action, which is also conducive to liberation/interiority? If so, how does this logic relate specifically to *giān*?

Elsewhere in his writings Guru Nanak provides more direct clues as to the working of the logic of Word (*śabda*) and how it both underpins and connects epistemology and ontology for Sikh philosophy. One of the more obvious places where such an explanation can be found happens to be the first few stanzas of the *Japji* – widely regarded as Guru Nanak's most authoritative composition. As I go on to show in this chapter, later verses in the Japji also provide structural elements for a theory of *giān* as knowledge and consciousness.

Japji (The recitation)

Composed by Guru Nanak during his mature years, the *Japji* is rightly considered the most authoritative hymn in Sikh scripture. Its authority is reflected in the fact that pious Sikhs regard its daily recitation as a cornerstone of Sikh contemplative practice of which the Gurus speak continually in their teachings. As such it is used not only for the purpose of recitation (*jap*: to recite), or as a practical aid for altering and expanding one's state of consciousness, but also as a terse expression of *gurmat*, the Guru's logic, in so far as it brings together almost all of the key themes articulated in Sikh scripture around its central core devoted to adoration of an unknowable One. Tied up with this adoration are subtle hints about the nature of reality culminating in a distinctive description of realms of consciousness (*khands*) that link the rhythms of individual consciousness to infinite consciousness.

The importance of the *Japji* as a resource for Sikh philosophy is underlined by the prevalence of substantive exegeses by Sikh commentators in the early twentieth century focusing on *Japji*'s opening creedal statement or *mul mantar*, and particularly the enigmatic syllable *ik oankār* with which the *mul mantar* itself opens. This is perhaps not surprising given that the *mul mantar*, as a foundational statement, is repeatedly invoked in shortened form on every page of Sikh scripture. The writers of the modern commentaries, and many Sikh thinkers who followed their lead, interpreted *ik oankār* as an ontotheological statement about the existence and identity of God.[8] Their extended commentaries on the nature of oneness effectively became proof for the existence of a personal God, which, in turn, not only helped to differentiate Sikhism from other world religions by pushing Sikh thought into the realm of political theology, but also designated *ik oankār* as a statement of fundamental ontology where ੧ (1 or One) signifies the nature of God's being as eternal and *oankār* (ਓ) designates a creationist sense of world-making. The key point about the modernist ontology with its translations of ੧ਓ as 'One God exists' or 'One Being' is that it set up an order of things under the control and supervision of a supra-natural Being whose immutable identity became the touchstone for cosmic, societal, psychoanalytic and political ordering. Once this secular Christian ontology was established as a belief system, the rest of *Japji* (indeed Sikh philosophy in general) was interpreted accordingly.

Yet despite the fact that this interpretation was a foreign implant and has held sway for almost a century and a half, the text of the *Japji* itself pulsates with resistance to the colonial matrix of modernist ontology. To actualize this resistance into a positive mode of thought, one needs to bracket the belief system and to think of *ik oankār* [੧ਓ] experientially. That is to say, ੧ਓ is more helpfully understood as a statement about *this life* and about the nature of the self and world, than it is about a supernatural eminent entity. Because the human mind not only craves permanence but has a proclivity for investing permanence in a personal form, there is always the danger that this theistic entity can become an idol for the mind.

A better approach to interpreting the symbol ੧ਓ is to see it as the most pertinent descriptor or attribute not only of an eminent being or beings, of and about whom one can be conscious in an objective manner, but as absolute subjectivity, or consciousness per se, which can be understood 'only without distance, without external observation, in an immediacy'.[9] From this perspective it is possible to see the numeral ੧ not as a characteristic *of* a thing or object attributed *by* a self-conscious mind but, instead, as oneness-without-separation or distance, which is to say, an im/material non-duality as the primary attribute of consciousness itself. This in turn implies that if consciousness is oneness, and oneness is consciousness, then consciousness is im/material or simultaneously psychic and cosmic at the same time, a point that will be explored further in Chapter 4. Thus, from the perspective that ੧ਓ is an expression of absolute consciousness, we can proffer a more apt interpretation of ੧ਓ, one that is more in tune with the rest of Japji. Such an interpretation might go something like this:

> Oneness, Infinite eternal becoming actualizable in Word-Thought-
> Action (*ik oankar*)
> Unfolding as the infinitely creative impulse within all existence
> (*satnām*)
> Embodied in creative agency (*karta purakh*), . . .
> Without fear (*nirbhau*),
> Without enmity/oppositionality (*nirvair*),
> Whose form is beyond human time (*akāl murat*),
> Without Cause (*ajūnī*)
> Self enlightening/Self enjoying (*saibhang*),
> Given through the Guru's grace (*gurprasad*).

> Recite (*japu*):
> Primordial Truth-Reality (*adi sach*),
> Truth-Reality in ages of time (*jugadi sach*),
> True or real now (*hai bhi sach*)
> Will remain true or real in the future (*hosi bhi sach*).

However, an important question arises here. If, as Nanak states, the reality of oneness is its unchanging nature, how can this oneness be *experienced in time*, that is, in the world of temporality in which we live our lives? Doesn't the element of time, which underpins and defines all existence (*samsāra*) as coming and going, make an experience of oneness impossible? Moreover, if reality is oneness, what is it that prevents each and every person from realizing this all the time? What kind of repetition is Nanak asking us to imbibe as the experience of oneness?

Although it is not immediately obvious from a cursory reading, these questions are answered in stanzas 1 to 4 of *Japji* through a series of questions and answers that appear to provide an informal logic. For the sake of pedagogical clarity these moves can be reduced to the following four steps.[10]

Step 1: How to become self-realized?
(*kiv sachiārā hoiae?*)

What prevents us from experiencing oneness as a totality of consciousness is the extremely limited individualized nature of normal everyday consciousness. The nature of our individualized consciousness is such that it keeps us fundamentally separated from absolute oneness or from experiencing consciousness in its true reality. Our individualized sense of self creates a barrier by generating its own sense of unity which deludes us into believing it is the centre of all reality. This individualized consciousness creates a barrier, a wall of delusion around us preventing us from actualizing oneness in our lived existence. It is this barrier that helps propagate a delusional form of individuation driven by an oppositional sense of unity. The delusion resides in the tendency of the individual self to believe it is sovereign, self-authorized, the cause of its own existence and reality, and as such must stand over and against anything that is different from it. On the basis of this deluded sense of individuation, individuals try to retain their sense of oneness through conceptual thought and ritual purity (*sochai sōch*), or by practising silent austerities (*chupai chup*), or by trying to materially satisfy our innermost cravings (*bhukhian bhukh*). Yet all of these methods of repetition fail. How then, asks Nanak, can these illusory barriers be broken (*kiv kurai tutai paal*)? How is it possible to actually *experience* the reality of oneness and, in so doing, become truly self-realized (*kiv sachiārā hoiae*)?

Step 2: Accept the sovereignty of *hukam* and
move in accordance to its command
(*hukam rajai chalana*)

Nanak answers the question in stanza 2, which introduces the concept of *hukam*. The wall of delusion is broken, and oneness realized by comporting one's self in accordance with an imperative that is always already inscribed within every person's consciousness. This imperative is pre-written within the nature of all that exists (*hukam rajai chalana, Nanak likhiā nāl*).

Nanak's name for this imperative is *hukam* – a term derived from Arabic/Persian languages which ordinarily means imperative, order or command, but also has connotations of call, command and will. In ordinary parlance *hukam* carries the sense of two other terms: *hāk* – the call or voice that calls and *hākam*, the one invested with the power of authoritative command, the one who calls. In the language of ontotheology, the word *hukam* carries the sense of divine will of an eminent deity through which existence arises and disappears.

For Nanak, however, it refers less to the will of a deity endowed with personal consciousness than to a universal sense of being, an imperative to recognize that everything coming into existence is subject to one and the same imperative, even though the source of this imperative cannot be defined (*hukmī hovan akār, hukam na kahiya jae*). From this same imperative all life evolves (*hukami hovan jian, hukam milai vadiyai*). From the same imperative humans develop individuation, awareness and discrimination (i.e. a sense of differentiation) resulting in sufferings for some, joy and rewards for others (*hukmī utam nich, hukam likh dukh sukh paaiah. . . . ikna hukmī bakshish iku hukmī sada bhavaiae*). By the same imperative some are favoured, while others continue the same habitual cycles.

In short, the imperative (*hukam*) can be considered an immanent plane of consciousness on which all beings coexist, encounter and are interconnected, and in relation to which there is no outside (*hukmai andar sabh koi, bahar hukam na koi*). One possible consequence of this important stanza is that the concept of *hukam* makes the usual distinction between transcendence and immanence completely redundant. Far from being a transcendental law that operates from afar, *hukam*, as Nanak describes it, is a law of absolute relationality. Everything, psychic and cosmic, existent and non-existent, is intricately related to everything else, and nothing is beyond this pure connectivity. Chapter 4 takes a closer look at the immanence-transcendence equation.

For now, it should suffice to note about *hukam* that it indicates an immanental plane of consciousness on which, and in which, all things, material and immaterial, coexist. Hence *hukam*, for Nanak, provides a means for speaking about the workings of consciousness and the consequences of this non-oppositional, immanental-transcendental law. All life is subject to change and becoming with whatever consequences this brings. *Hukam* applies to all things, at all times, even before time begins. All life is time, and all time is life. As a universal law it takes effect as soon as something comes into existence. As the fundamental law of all existence and non-existence, it also speaks the truth of existence. As such *hukam* can be regarded akin to an 'order-word' that names the univocity of Being – that Being's central attribute of oneness resonates everywhere, and at all times, in the same way.

Dialectic of *hukam* and *haumai*

Step 3: How to understand the workings of *hukam*? (*Nanak hukmai je bujhai?*)

Towards the end of stanza 2 Guru Nanak asks the all-important question which connects to the previous one: if *hukam* is necessary to breaking the walls of self-delusion that limit our individual consciousness, in order to become self-realized (*sachiārā*), how are we to comprehend how *hukam* operates in practice? How can we recognize it? If the imperative is inscribed within (*likhia nal*) all sentient and non-sentient forms of existence, and if living and non-living things are constituted within the plane of consciousness, if *hukam* is not merely immanent but immanence as such, how can this 'within' be located? And if it could be located, how does one go about actualizing it? Nanak's answer is enigmatic yet deceptively simple. He states:

> *Nanak hukmai je bujhai*
> *Tan haumai kahai na koi*

> O Nanak, if one desires to recognize this imperative
> Then avoid saying: 'I am myself'

It is important to note here that Nanak insists on two things simultaneously. On the one hand, he emphasizes a certain kind of speech, where one speaks by *not saying*, or by avoiding saying something. On the other hand, he points to a psycho-linguistic structure ('I am myself') whose expressive signature is a form of language-use that objectifies its self-presence by way of a self-possession. This psychic structure can be described as one that articulates its being as an 'I am my-self' (*haumai*). The self affirms itself as an individuated unit or 'I' by possessing itself (*haumai*).

Step 4: Let ego stop saying 'I am myself'

How does one put such an imperative, which seems to be expressed as a negative statement, into actual practice? How does one avoid speaking in a way that avoids the self-possessive affirmation 'I am myself' (*tan haumai kahai na koi*)? How does this differ from the kind of auto-affection or self-enjoyment that characterizes mind in its immediate or primordial state? Is the call to avoid saying 'I am' an imperative to say silent? To stop speaking altogether? If so, why would Nanak, and other spiritual masters like him, actually say so much, as is evident by how much they wrote, composed and discoursed with others? As we noted in stanza 1, Nanak repudiates the idea that silence is an answer to this problem (*chupai chup na hovi je lae raha liv taar*).

What Guru Nanak seems to signal in this fourth crucial step is that there may be a different way of speaking\thinking\acting. To better comprehend this, it helps to rephrase the imperative as: 'let ego say "I am not"'. Instead of thinking about it as a doctrinal statement, it is more useful to consider it as an *invitation to experiment* with one's own consciousness (as it is expressed in one's thoughts\words\actions) with the aim of discovering the nature of reality for oneself as an experience. From this angle the imperative (*hukam*) 'let ego say "I am not"' is an injunction which basically states: speak\think\act in such a way that your life's basic instinct is to stop repeating, and therefore stop inscribing, the psychic formation 'I am myself'. Instead shift it towards a different psychic formation which says and thinks 'I am not'. To put this differently, the ego must become silent so that one desists from saying 'I am myself' even as ego continues to be formed.[11]

The crucial point for Nanak is that the silencing of the ego is not to be understood literally. Silencing – to not say, to not bring to mind or repeat *haumai* – refers to a process of egoloss, a self-enforced withdrawal of ego at the very moment that ego names itself as an 'I' and subsequently objectifies itself as *haumai*. By doing so ego constitutes itself as an origin or absolute centre in relation to all existing things.

Though not immediately obvious, this psycho-linguistic formation 'let ego not say I am myself' answers an earlier question as to how oneness can be experienced at all times and in all things. Oneness fails to be experienced when ego asserts 'I am myself'. But when it desists from such assertions, oneness can be experienced as life itself. If ego constructs itself by using language in a certain way (self-naming as 'I am'), Nanak's argument is that it is also possible for ego to *not* constitute itself. The ego can just as easily un-constitute itself.

A question immediately arises here. How does one actually go from ego to egoloss? From asserting a perfectly reasonable logic of 'I am myself' to the seemingly nihilistic (and irrational) logic of 'I might not be'? From the certainty of 'I exist' to the uncertainty of 'I might not exist'? Is it even useful or practical to ask such a question? Would it not lead to self-annihilation? One way to think about Nanak's entreaty to the self, that ego should not say 'I am', is that it points to an altogether different psychic formation whose primary function is not to accumulate a self-possessive autonomy, but rather whose functioning is centred around an innate capacity to let go of itself, one that is able to negate itself *without annihilating itself*, at the very moment that ego is formed. A formulaic operational logic for this alternative psychic structure might be something like: [I am + I am not . . .] or simply [I + not-I . . .].

The series of dots indicates a repetition in sequential time. The 'I am not' or 'not-I' signifies a silencing of the 'I am myself' at the very moment of its emergence. In this way, an otherwise identitarian self negates itself in the moment of its formation but without annihilating consciousness, so that a psychic formation not only survives but is repeated in and as a new and different state. In other words, in the process of negating itself, the self re-creates itself anew – which is to say that it repeats itself with an openness to its own difference.

From a common-sense standpoint, the idea of a self that is open to its own difference (a self-differentiating self) might sound absurd. This is because common sense operates in accordance with the law of non-contradiction which stipulates that identity is the condition for difference and not vice versa – 'the same subject "A" cannot at the same time have opposing attributes'[12] – which means that in order to exist as an identical subject (in time), time itself has to be negated, immobilized or transcended. Our common sense therefore finds the idea of a psychic structure or self characterized by [I + not-I . . .] to be absurd because we find the paradoxical nature of time unbearable: either the 'I' exists or time exists. In order for 'I' to continue to exist, time has to be immobilized and vice versa. Common-sense logic tries at all times and at all cost to remove the contradiction either by reconstructing the passage of time as an imitation of eternity or by assuming that the contradiction is simply a negation and therefore illusory.

A way to take the structural logic of [I + not-I . . .] seriously is to think of this formation as denoting an immanent power of self-differentiation, which in differentiating itself ceases to be what it is while continuing to survive as something new. Far from implying any negativity or nihilism, the structure I + not-I denotes an entirely positive mode of being that both ceases to be and continues to exist in the same moment. In other words the structure I + not-I is a structure of the self grounded in an ontology of becoming, and a structural logic grounded in pure consciousness, or immediacy, which entertains no distance between the knowing subject and object known. The structure [I + not-I . . .] therefore not only correlates Sikh ontology and epistemology; it ends up making epistemology (the logic of [I + not-I . . .]) the condition for any ontology.

In short, the particular mode of knowing (*giān*) that constitutes Sikh epistemology gives rise to a form of consciousness fundamentally attuned to the imperative *hukam*. If the modal logic of this form of consciousness (and of Sikh epistemology per se) can be represented by the formulaic logic [I + not-I . . .], the implication of this logic is that the subject who investigates as a knowledge seeker is codependent on the object being investigated. Subject as seeker and the object being sought (divine *hukam*) are never separate. Rather, they participate in a directness or immediacy of knowing. Thus, as a mode of knowing, *giān* operates in a radically different manner from the conventional way in which objectivity is synthesized.

From a theological standpoint we might think of this knowledge as recovery of the self's capacity for beholding the face of the Beloved with attention, thought and devout meditation. Another name for this mode of knowing might be contemplation. As B. Allan Wallace notes, such 'contemplation does not merely move towards its object: it already rests in it'.[13] To say, as Wallace does here, that contemplation rests in its object corresponds to what Guru Nanak means by *giān*. For Nanak *giān* is a participatory knowing, an event that co-implicates the lover (knower) in the object of her knowing (Beloved). Such co-implication does not merely annihilate the seeking self (as the term 'egoloss' or the formula [I + not-I . . .] might imply) but, rather, results in transformed states of consciousness, as we'll see in later chapters.

This raises a slightly different question. Is there a practical method which corresponds to this logic of egoloss, or to the formula [I + not-I . . .]? Or to put it differently, are there techniques one can put into practice for undergoing egoloss, both at the level of self/ego and at the level of thought? What kind of contemplative thought-practice might be conducive to the kind of knowledge as *giān* which Nanak himself is teaching about? It is here that the role of *śabda* (Word) becomes central to Sikh epistemology and ontology and therefore to *giān*.

What does *śabda* actually do?

Throughout the twentieth century, Sikh philosophers have consistently tried to push the boundaries of familiar theistic frameworks by highlighting the underlying nuances in the Sikh system of knowledge (*giān*), nuances that come into play due to the role of the concept of *śabda* (as *guru*) in opening up and expanding consciousness. This transformatory aspect of *śabda* is difficult to explain in the face of rigid adherence to an ontotheological model of the divine, where, for example, *śabda* is reduced to the Word of a personal deity, or where *hukam* represents the Will or fiat of a personal God.

Sikh philosophers wrestled with this issue – personal versus impersonal – though not always with great success. A good example is Sher Singh's *Philosophy of Sikhism* (1944), which sets the tone for such explanations by arguing that knowledge (*giān*) is attained directly through insight or intuition rather than coming through the senses or the intellect. For Sher Singh, the medium for knowledge is intuition (*anubhav*).[14] Almost half a century later Nirbhai Singh suggests that the Sikh system 'presents different kinds of knowledge as a continuous process which starts with perception and culminates in intuitively realizing the mystic unity in the *ik*'.[15]

This gives the impression that intuition (*anubhav*) can simply be picked up off the shelf and dropped into philosophical discussion about the nature of *giān* or knowledge. While neither scholar is wrong in suggesting that *anubhav*/intuition is the apex of knowing, what seems to have been overlooked is a crucial step explaining *how* intuition is obtained other than assuming that it is a supernatural process gifted by an eminent personal deity. The point here is that there might be a perfectly natural explanation for this, one that involves *śabda* – albeit an understanding of *śabda* that is markedly different from the traditional Indian system. A further clue is provided by Sher Singh who notes that if *giān* is indeed the conceptual cornerstone of Sikh epistemology, it has to consist in an active realization or 'living experience of unity of the One within, with the One without'.[16]

In other words the heart of Sikh epistemology is a *living consciousness*. What links the internal and external experiences of oneness is the dual nature of the self or ego. On the one hand, it is a self-limiting and individuating consciousness ('I am myself', or, ego), and on the other hand, it has the potential to lose its limitations and merge itself into unifying consciousness (*surati*). The shift from limited consciousness (= ego) to infinitely expanded consciousness (=egoloss) is precisely the living consciousness referred to as *anubhav*. But, just to repeat what was noted earlier, these expanded states of consciousness (*anubhav*) cannot be accessed directly by the overwhelming majority of people. Most people can only access it indirectly through a tool or vehicle, which in the Sikh philosophical system happens to be *śabda*. To recall what Nanak himself stated in his dialogue with the Siddhas: 'the Word is my Guru, the consciousness attuned to it is the disciple' (*śabda guru surat dhun chela*).

What needs to be further investigated, therefore, is the role of *śabda* in producing this living experience or living consciousness. We can begin by asking some relatively straightforward questions: What exactly is *śabda* (Word)? Is it simply an aspect of language? Is it perhaps a linguistic tool for communication?

In the *gurmat* system, objectively *śabda* refers to a 'revelatory' form of language expressed by the Sikh Gurus (*dhur ki bāṇī* – lit. words from the primordial source). But does this mean that there are two interpretations of *śabda* – on the one hand language as theological, on the other hand linguistic? And are these interpretations necessarily opposed?

One way of circumventing this opposition is to look more closely at the term *dhur* in *dhur ki bāṇī* as a way of thinking about 'revelation' in a more productive way. The word *dhur* literally means 'from the primordial source'.[17] Although its connotation is closer to an origin that's obscured from our everyday view, it is popularly believed to be evidence of divine revelation by a transcendent source. In this way, it is still possible to retain the idea of revelation, but with the difference that the latter term refers to a movement that happens within consciousness. From this perspective the term *dhur* can be more usefully understood as an utterance (*bāṇī*) that comes from a deeper aspect of the psyche normally hidden from view. In which case it is equally of-this-world, only obscured by a certain psychic formation, hence the need to reveal it through *bāṇī*.

Another way of getting past the worldly–otherworldly opposition is to accept that the actual words and meanings that constitute *bāṇī* (even in translation) are understandable and therefore shareable with ordinary humans in this world, and insofar, they create effects which are also in this world but work at the level of psyche. The only difference being that their source (*dhur*) is to be found in the depths of a perfected (human) consciousness that once lived in the world but attained perfection by attuning to *hukam*. In turn, this attunement to *hukam* transforms the function of ego by bringing into perfect harmony the measurable time of lived existence (*kāl*) and immeasurable 'aionic' time (*akāl*). Both of these times are equally real; they differ only in their ontology and epistemic status. Whereas *kāl*-time is generated by ego and is measurable, in the sense that every moment is the same as every other moment, *akāl*-time is not generated by ego but, rather, annihilates ego by taking time and difference into the heart of the ego. We can think of *akāl*-time as creative time; it cannot be measured, it can only be felt as the intensity of emotions, passions or affects. The important point here in regard to the function of *śabda* or *bani*, is not only that it effects a shift into one's consciousness from *kāl*-centrism to *akāl*-centrism, but that the shift towards *akāl*-centrism is an immeasurable, ineffable event that takes place first in the psyche before this shift is translated into external measurable changes in *this* world. To put it more bluntly, although the effects of *akāl* are prompted by changes that occur in the inner world of the psyche, they nevertheless have an impact in *this world*, in *this life*, rather than a world beyond this one. It is, therefore, possible to eradicate the opposition between the worldly and the divine, or between philosophical and theological connotations of *śabda* if we accept not only that *śabda* is intrinsically linked to consciousness but that the very same consciousness enables the opposites (*akāl/kāl* or 'divine'\worldly) to be associated.

If we recall Nanak's reply to the Siddhas (*śabda guru surat dhun chela*), the problem can be more helpfully posed as one of explaining the relationship between language (*śabda*) and consciousness (*surati*). In what ways, then, are the two spheres of language and consciousness associated by means of *śabda*? How does *śabda* mediate or effect a transformation from one state of consciousness mired in worldliness to the other state (*dhur*/origin) considered to be divine?

The following section examines the operative role of *śabda* at the level of consciousness in a way that is fully in tune with Nanak's concept of *hukam* rather than resorting to non-worldly metaphysics. From this angle, the work done by *śabda* can usefully be conceived as a psycho-linguistic performative consisting of two broad moves. First, *śabda* inverts the conventional relationship between language and self, thereby effecting radical alterations within everyday personalized consciousness. Second, the progressive deepening of one's experience with *śabda* culminates in what might be called a trans-personal state of consciousness.

In order to explain how these two moves take place, it is helpful to juxtapose it against the development of ordinary consciousness as it is broadly understood in contemporary Western psychology. To do this, I deploy a series of diagrams illustrating the role of *śabda* as a philosophical and psychological performative tool. Figure 3 depicts the relationship

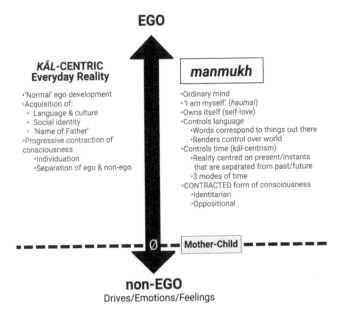

Figure 3 Development of everyday consciousness.

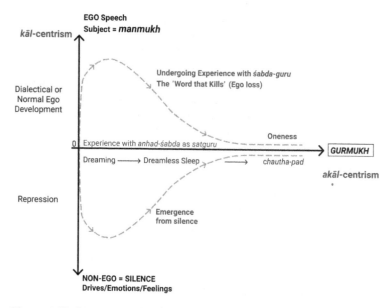

Figure 4 Undergoing egoloss: Transforming ordinary consciousness.

between ordinary everyday language (*śabda*) and the formation of ordinary consciousness. Figure 4 depicts *śabda* as *dhur ki bāṇī* which *reveals*, in the sense of uncovering, access to more expanded levels of consciousness and, in so doing, effects a transformation of ordinary consciousness.

Śabda and everyday contracted consciousness (*manmukh*)

If we piece together many of Guru Nanak's compositions on the nature of self, mind and consciousness, we can build a picture of the psyche and psychic development that has interesting overlaps with certain aspects of modern psychology, even though, as I argue later in the chapter, it differs in crucial ways. As a heuristic method[18] I'd like to assume a broad convergence between Nanak's implicit theory of human psychological development, which can be gleaned from his explication of ordinary everyday consciousness that he calls *manmukh*, and the modern Western theories of ego development (Lacanian, Kleinian and Freudian). For the sake of argument, therefore, let us call Nanak's implicit theory of human psychological development, the theory of *manmukh* (or ordinary) mind. As I note in the discussion later, wider comparisons eventually break down, not least because Nanak's understanding of the relationship between *śabda* and consciousness diverges radically from the standard Western approaches in terms of the moral value attributed to ego formation. Nevertheless, at a certain level, the convergence between Nanak's critique of the contracted consciousness of *manmukh* and Western psychology's eulogization of the same contracted consciousness serves a useful purpose in so far as they both describe a similar psychic apparatus corresponding to ordinary, everyday consciousness applicable to the contemporary world, even as they provide radically different valuations of it.

As shown in Figure 3 it is possible to adduce some minimal overlap between modern (Freudian) and *gurmat* explanations of early psychological development. In the early stages, both models suggest that the human psyche develops in several stages, the first being the child's attachment to the mother's psychic apparatus. In the next stage the child is able to acquire language by acceding to the rules and conventions of the social symbolic order in which the child is reared. With this accession, which takes place primarily through linguistic and cultural semiosis, begins a steady process of ego development which matures after adolescence. Driven by a certain kind of individuation (*haumai* – I am myself) the ego develops by actively repressing archaic layers of psychic material (*mn* and *chitta*) attuned to preverbal processes of sensing, feeling, drives, instincts and intuitions that are more in touch with the natural rhythms of the cosmos.[19] According to the rules of the dominant social order, these affective materials *mn/chitta* constitute non-ego (or not-I) and are deemed incompatible and detrimental to the normal, stable and self-possessive ego that can say *haumai* (I am myself). This development is synonymous with the progressive formation of boundaries between ego and non-ego. Failure to form such boundaries would result in a fusion of ego and non-ego, self and other, which society would deem a regression either to the mother–child dyad or to an extreme asceticism which altogether withdraws from the world and therefore from self-making.

Either of these alternatives would be considered detrimental to societal conventions that determine what a normal person should be. Protective boundaries manifest themselves when the ego enunciates its subjectivity by complying with the linguistic rules of the dominant symbolic order. To become an ego (*haumai*) it has to be able to speak in a manner that is understandable to other egos, who recognize others as similar, though numerically distinct, egos. This oneness and distinctness of each ego crystallize through (i) its distinctive mode of self-reflection which enables it to relate itself, first and foremost, to itself and (ii) in its everyday normal speech which accords to a conventional sense of reality. Indeed, the conventionality of this reality depends on maintaining an opposition between self and other in order to project itself as an individual.

Key to this normalizing function is the ability of the ego-subject to name itself as 'I', where 'I' denotes the self's possession of itself. The self-naming of ego as 'I' works by adopting an objectifying perspective towards language or words (*śabda*), such that language is reduced to a tool for communicating between similarly constituted egos. This forces the *mn/chitta* to be subjugated by social rules, particularly rules that determine patriarchy. Society considers this ego and its ability to speak, think and act normally as the pinnacle of human psychic development, one which must be maintained at all cost. We can see an instance of this in the PJS episode of Guru Nanak's struggle with conventional ego, which corresponds well with what is depicted in Figure 3.

This normalized social ego is what Guru Nanak calls *manmukh*. The term *manmukh* signifies one who is guided by his or her own mind, self-orientated, driven by egotistical desires. *Manmukh* refers to a debased psychic formation whose desire, speech, thought and actions can't go beyond social conventions or ingrained habits which block its own life force by building walls that shield it from the possibility of experiencing oneness directly. For Nanak, this psychic formation needs to be radically transformed. The *manmukh*, however, resists any attempt to transform its debased consciousness, striving to maintain separation in the form of dualistic oppositions between I and not-I, self and other, lover and Beloved. The result of such separation results is the withdrawal of the Beloved. It is this loss that causes Nanak to feel the pain of separation and the pain of craving for oneness in the depths of his soul.

Gurmukh

Although Nanak depicts the *manmukh* as a psychically debilitated state, he also provides a solution, as depicted by the dotted line in Figure 4. However, the solution does not involve simply debunking the *manmukh* state, whether through an ascetic renunciation of the world or by various material techniques to satisfy the cravings of ego, or by austerities to try and annihilate the ego. Rather, the solution, Nanak suggests, is to accept the *manmukh* state along with ego formation as a necessary precondition for any possible alteration of the state. In *Asa di Var* Guru Nanak gives a hint about the starting point for a solution. He says:

> *haumai diragh rog hai*
> *daru bhi isu mahi*

> *Haumai* (self-attraction) is a chronic disease
> But its cure is contained within (the self)

(GGS: p. 466)

Ego may well be the congenital disease (*diragh rog*) that afflicts humanity, but the remedy (*daru*) is contained within its very structural formation (*daru bhi isu mahi*). This statement resonates well with Nanak's statement in *Japji* where we noted that the way to become a realized self who knows the truth of reality (*sachiārā*) is to submit to *hukam* as it is found within the constitution of the self. And where is that imperative? It is located\written into our self-formation (*Nanak likhia nal*).

The solution, it seems, is to alter the way we form ego, and since we form ego by acceding to language, this entails simultaneously changing our relationship to ordinary, everyday language. And this in turn means acceding to a different order of language, one that is beyond the control of egoic processes of self-naming (*I am myself*). By different order of language, what I'm suggesting is that *sabda-guru* is qualitatively different from ordinary language. It means that while *sabda-guru* is materially constituted from the very words we use in everyday speech to refer to the real world (hence understandable by all), it is qualitatively different because this language emanates from a different source (*dhur ki bāṇī*) – namely the selfless self of a *gurmukh* who actively accepts and imbibes *hukam* (to not say 'I am') into the core of her self-formation. Moreover, insofar as this poesis is marked by a structural relation to egoloss, *it can be described as sovereign*. My use of the term sovereign is meant to suggest that this poesis is not derived from social language norms, but gifted by a *satguru*. Nanak's solution can therefore be expressed in a paradoxical formula: annihilate ego without annihilating it; kill ego, without killing it, whose structural formula might be [I+not-I.....].

This paradoxical formula is schematically depicted by the dotted line in Figure 4. Note what the dotted line is doing. For a certain period of time in human life, the self is ensnared in the kinds of desires that perpetuate ego attachment and lead to the degenerate consciousness of *manmukh*. At some point in one's life, however, triggered by events such as death, illness and old age, the *manmukh*'s false sense of reality comes crashing down. Those who come into contact with a *satguru* (*śabda-guru*) and are able to embark on a path of self-realization or praxis, begin to struggle against the conventional ego. This struggle is not a wild or uncontrolled process which would endanger the constitution of the self. Rather, as successive verses in the *Japji* indicate, it is channelled and controlled through contemplative practices which begin with something as simple as a deep and sustained form of listening (*sunniae*), which leads to a change of heart expressed as a mindful reflective thinking (*mannana*), which can culminate in a psychic state characterized by mindful focus which alters one's speech, thought and action in the world. This state is called *dhyana* (meditative focus).[20]

This practical side, which is instrumentally tied to *giān*, will be discussed later. For the time being, we need only note that this praxis is part of a controlled struggle against the ego, entailing a movement away from conventional or ordinary states of mind. Indicated by the different directions of the dotted line, this movement away from societal convention represents a violent internal struggle against one's own ego.

Guru Nanak describes this internal violence as a 'dying to the Word', meaning that the self painfully and traumatically tears itself from habitual control over language and undergoes a sacrificial death in which it sacrifices its old degenerate self to the word of the *satguru*. Through this self-sacrifice, a new self emerges, one which participates in the pluriverse of signs, not through a logic of representation but through a devotional or nonrepresentational logic of egoloss associated with poetic form, with musical melody and rhythm, with visual art and dance. While this logic of egoloss is closed to domination by rationality or reason, it nevertheless opens a more primordial 'threshold of sense' or affect. By primordial I mean that both sense and affect are ontologically prior to words, sounds, images that are grasped by the cognitive faculties and turned into mental representations whose primary function is to measure and compare the world. What governs such logic of sense or affect is not correctness of representation but the force or intensity of an idea, its affectivity, its ability to excite the body to produce sensations or affects which cannot be measured or compared but only felt intensively.[21]

In Figure 4, the dotted line corresponds to the process of death and rebirth of the self described earlier. The dotted line on the left-hand side, which is in the process of struggling with and tearing away from the ego, corresponds to what mystics call the 'dark night of the soul', a stage of uncertainty and chaos in which the ego's initial socially sanctioned form is dissolved into a formlessness, before coming through its tribulations and finding a new form – where self is beginning to be reborn as [I + not-I] indicated by the two dotted lines. These two forces – one towards formlessness, death, disconnection, the other towards form\life\reconnection – coexist in a tensional balance, a kind of unformed-form or formless-form which also describes the new composition of the self that is reborn or re-created out of the old one.

An important caveat needs to be noted here. The question may arise, for example, as to whether this explanation does not point to the problem of human freedom. Does it not imply that human beings are free to overcome their egotistical natures, to transform ego without the intervention of a mediator, divine or otherwise? The seeming circularity of this argument notwithstanding, the Sikh Gurus have a very clear answer to this conundrum. Self-effort, they suggest, takes the individual a long way towards 'liberation', but in the end it can only take you so far. By itself, by means of its own effort, the ego cannot effect final transformation or self-realization. The final 'act' that the ego needs to undertake is an existential realization that ultimately its self-power is not sufficient. It has to surrender belief in its self-power, which in effect is a form of self-sacrifice to a wholly other power. In the philosophy of *gurmat* that wholly other power is none other than *hukam*. It is at this point where paradox reigns supreme, when strictly conventional common-sense logic fails, that theistic concepts such as *nadar* (glance or grace) and *kirpa*, grace/mercy come into play as a way of personifying *hukam*. In other words theistic explanation merges seamlessly with non-theistic (psychological) explanations. This issue, and the question regarding human freedom, will be further discussed in Chapters 4 and 6.

Contraction-expansion of consciousness

If the solid vertical line in Figure 4 represents a contraction of consciousness into ego, resulting in a separation between the individual and the oneness from which s/he emerges, the dotted line's progressive spiritual struggle, or movement towards the horizontal axis, represents an expansion of consciousness. The end result of the spiritual movement is not a total dissolution into pure consciousness, which might be interpreted as the death of the subject. Quite the opposite is the case as individuality is never completely extinguished. The endpoint is a psychic state in which opposing forces of separation (pure individuation) and fusion are counterbalanced in a state called *sahaj avastha* (existing in equipoise).

In other words the endpoint is neither death, nor nothingness, nor any kind of metaphysical heaven, but a mode of creative life marked by a balance of opposing tendencies – life/death, personal/impersonal, material/ immaterial, and so on. This state of balance, known as *sahaj*, is marked not by quiescence but by a life overflowing with intensity. Although the personal-I is counterbalanced by an impersonal not-I in the very moment of its production, enough of the personal remains to continue the movement of life. Nanak refers to this excessive and intensive form of life as *gurmukh* (lit. facing the guru).

How *śabda* becomes *nām*

What's interesting about the disjunctive synthesis of personal/I and impersonal\not-I is that it is expressed as a fundamental change in the new individual's relationship to language. No longer bound to ego, the *gurmukh*'s speech, thought and action are also marked by egoloss; it is pure or unpulsed language (*anhad śabda*). This is language attuned to, and expressive of, pure consciousness (*surati*). Such language is still connected to the world, but it no longer begins and ends in self-naming (I am myself, family name, my name, etc.). Rather, this transformed order of language originates not from the place of ego but from the unnameable in-betweenness of ego and non-ego, I + not-I. Because its source is unnameable Nanak refers to this order of language as *nām* – the singular word that signifies the agency and imperative of creation. In this sense *nām* is closer to what might be understood as the force that impels language to do what it does: languag*ing*, or how words make things happen in the world.

In line with the way that *nām* was described earlier, I'd like to hazard a few more ways of depicting what is otherwise unnameable and indescribable. *Nām* is language/consciousness that cannot be objectified because it expresses only pure intensity or force. *Nām* speaks the inexplicable, unnameable thing of experience. In order to express its event-nature *nām* requires vehicles appropriate to its formless-form, its temporality of pure becoming. Appropriate vehicles are melody, song, rhythm, poetic form, visual art and dance. As the highest order of language *nām* corresponds to the central function of Nanak's concept of *śabda-guru* as sovereign authority. *Nām* is the expression-event of *śabda-guru*. Or to put it differently, *śabda* is *guru* when it expresses *nām*. Stated otherwise, *nām* is the expression of *śabda* when *śabda* becomes self-referential. *Śabda* as *nām* does not convey useful knowledge of actual things, objects or states of affairs. Rather, the knowledge that *nām* expresses, and *śabda* conveys, is direct or intuitive knowing (*anubhav prakash* or *anubhav giān*). It is knowledge that is immediate. It expresses or speaks about and speaks through states of intensity or affect. We can say that *śabda* as *nām* is not a mere vehicle for talking about experience. *Śabda*-as-*guru* equals *nām* equals experience itself.

We can now better see what is happening in Figure 3. The overall process depicted is the transformation of the human psyche from a *manmukh* state (unbalanced ego-centred consciousness) to a *gurmukh* state (balance of ego and non-ego). The shift to the *gurmukh* state (corresponding to the line going from vertical to horizontal axis) is enacted through a monumental struggle initiated within the ego, by the grace of a *satguru*, through listening or accepting or surrendering to *śabda-guru*, which in turn implies accepting *hukam*. This shift from *manmukh* to *gurmukh* is the unfolding of consciousness from a contracted state (*haumai*) to an expanded form (*surati*). One can see the horizontal axis as an unfolding of knowledge from mediated knowledge of things (or an attachment to thingness or objectification) to immediate or direct knowledge in which one's senses are awakened (*surati*), to the underlying force of *nām* that connects all things. So the end of knowledge itself is a state of consciousness (*surati*) marked by relationality. Knowledge or *giān* only begins when one's state of mind shifts from self-centred existence to a non-dualistic, non-oppositional being-in-the-world that is thoroughly relational.

GIĀN: How knowledge is synthesized

If *giān* is the basis of Sikh epistemology, how is knowledge actually synthesized? What are the various components of *giān* as a system for synthesizing the contents of our knowing? To simplify matters it is helpful to understand *giān* as operating at three different levels: (i) practice\discipline, (ii) thought and (iii) faculties. It is important to note that these three represent different levels of the operation of *giān*; otherwise, they are part of the same process. Let me briefly elaborate each in turn.

giān as practice or discipline

As practice or discipline *giān* works through processes that interiorize the contents of empirical cognition produced through encounters with the outside world. As outlined in the *Japji* and other compositions, the contents of empirical cognition are initially collected by sensory faculties before being synthesized by interiorizing faculties that comprise the mind (*mn*). These processes include *vēkhaṇā* (beholding or observation) *suṇaṇā* (hearing-listening of instruction or concept), *maṇaṇā* (reflection/thought) and *dhyāna* (contemplation as intuitive knowing). Through these processes, the practitioner's interaction with the world is progressively interiorized beginning with gross empirical percepts (*vēkhaṇā/suṇaṇā*), going through a deepening of reflection or thought (*maṇaṇā*) and ending with intuitive unity of being and knowing in *dhyāna*.

Cognizing	>	Minding/Contemplating	>	Becoming One

Empirical Cognition > Internalizing objects into subjective thought   >   Unity

vēkhaṇā / suṇaṇā > maṇaṇā > dhyāna

giān as refining of thought (*vichār*)

The term *vichār* has a variety of meanings at different levels and is intrinsically related to *maṇaṇā*. It begins with the process of mundane reasoning (*sōch*), hair-splitting forms of discursive reasoning (*tark, bādi*), from which one can progress to deeper internal searching (*khōj*), which in turn leads one to acquire practical wisdom (*aql, siāṇap*).[22]

All of these come broadly under *vichār* (thinking or thought), but *vichār* itself is progressively refined as one learns to discriminate and judge at increasingly deeper levels – pondering, deliberation, examination, reflection, all of which are essential. Thought (*vichār*) reaches its zenith when it becomes *bibēk vichār*: awakened or enlightened thinking, which is the kind of thought process associated with the *gurmukh*. There is a mistaken tendency to think that the *gurmukh* does not need to think, that she or he expresses merely poetic or aesthetic sensibility. In fact the Sikh Gurus use the word a great deal in their writings, and it is used almost always in a positive sense, indicating that the *gurmukh* does indeed indulge in thought, albeit with the difference that her speech/actions/desires do not emanate from ego, but from a different psychic structure. It is a thought process that is intrinsically imbued with aesthetic feeling, affect, and is therefore in tune with the cosmic processes of *hukam*.

Vichārana

tark/bādi/sōch	>	*khōj*	>	*aql/siāṇap*	>	*bibēk vichār*

Thought develops into awakened thinking →

Surat(i): Faculties for contracting consciousness

In the previous section we have seen that *giān* is not an objectivizable thing but a process involving three key elements. First, contracted or subjective consciousness (*haumai* or *mn*). Second, the crucial element which mediates all contraction between consciousness and materiality, namely *śabda* or *śabda-as-guru*. Third, the state of equipoise (*sahaj avasthā*) that results from this. What needs further elaboration, however, is how consciousness interacts with materiality, and in the process becomes contracted prior to undergoing expansion. In Sikh philosophy this is the role of three main faculties: *mat(i)* (practical wisdom), *mn* (mind) and *buddhī* (intellect or intelligence).

mat(i): although in Sanskrit context *mat(i)* carries connotations of a faculty for processing sensory information, in Sikh philosophy it signifies a faculty which receives empirical knowledge of the world through the five sense organs (*giān indrian*). On its own *mat(i)* is an unstable faculty and if left to the conventions of culture or society the sensory information is channelled into pure ego production (*haumai*). In the epilogue section of the *Japji* Guru Nanak suggests that *mat(i)* is an anvil (*ahṛunn*) which needs to be fashioned with the practical tools of wisdom (*vēdu hathiār*). The suggested tool is the *śabda* of a perfected master which mediates the contact between consciousness (*surat(i)*) and external objects in the world in such a way that the individual generates a practical or worldly wisdom, one that is neither detached nor attached and is not trapped in the fires of attachment and delusion.

mn (mind): an ubiquitous term in Sikh philosophy, *mn* represents the contracted or personalized form of the vastly more expansive or pure consciousness (*surati*) and can be usefully described as the faculty for synthesizing the stream of consciousness (*chitt*) into which humans are thrown at birth. The philosopher of Sikhism Nirbhai Singh describes mind or *mn* as an evolute (*jiu*) of the five gross elements (*panj tat*) (Singh: p. 188). As such it is a dynamic energy (*śakti*) with two opposing tendencies (*dhatu* and *liv*). The *dhatu* tendency attaches the mind towards the material world whereas the *liv* tendency pushes towards realizing oneness.[23] By contrast *mn* is described as fluctuating between two different tendencies. On the one hand, a tendency towards pure materiality, which begins with the objectification of things, setting them out in space, which leads to a form of subjectivity resulting in the contraction of consciousness into the personalized material form of an individual who can identify only, or primarily, with his or her body.

And on the other hand, a tendency towards pure consciousness exemplified by the realized person (*gurmukh*).

buddhī (intelligence): in the Sikh system *buddhī* is an aspect of *mn* or mind, specifically the faculty of mind's inner functioning, also known as *antahkaran*. As a faculty *buddhī* receives percepts through the five senses before immediately synthesizing the percepts into the contents of *chitt* or storehouse memory. *Buddhī* has the role of judging, discriminating and discerning contents presented to the mind in the form of concepts (*sankalap*) which are then used by the self for practical purposes, for example, in order to carry out an action and for thinking in general. By effectively formulating the individual's conceptual world view, *buddhī* comes close to determining the nature of our thought, speech and actions. As the faculty central to the self's day-to-day functioning, *buddhī* can potentially develop in different directions. On the one hand, it can become egocentric thought or action (*hau-buddhī*) which leads to the *manmukh* state. On the other hand, if guided by a *satguru*, it can help the psyche evolve in tune with cosmic laws. Such transformed intelligence is the *bibēk buddhī* or enlightened, self-aware intelligence. To realize this transformation, however, *buddhī* has to struggle with the so-called Five Thieves or Five Demons. We shall look at the struggle with the 'Five Thieves' more closely in Chapter 5 as it is closely associated with the themes of liberation and mental well-being. In short, however, the climax of *buddhī*'s development is its transformation into a self-luminous mode of knowing (*suddhi*), which is a psychic state of pure consciousness or oneness referred to as *sahaj avasthā* (Figure 5).

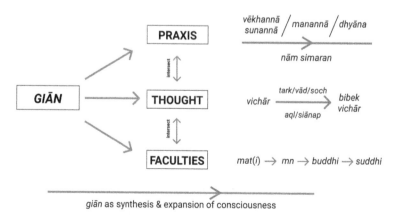

Figure 5 *Giān* as epistemic apparatus.

Discussion questions

(1) How does the Sikh philosophy of oneness reorient the conventional dualism between the material world and a transcendent realm?

(2) How does one alter their perspective or state of consciousness away from the *manmukh* and towards liberation?

(3) How does Sikh philosophy envisage the relationship between a personal 'Guru' (or 'guru') and the impersonal concept of Guru-as-*śabda*? What's the difference between the two? What are the implications of transmuting the figure of the 'personal Guru' into the impersonal *śabda* (Word)?

(4) How does Sikh philosophy of *śabda* challenge Western conceptions of language and its purpose? Can this impersonal principle of *śabda-guru* become a resource for thinking across cultures?

(5) Is there a specifically or uniquely Sikh epistemology or theory of knowledge? What are its basic constituent concepts?

(6) As long as we continue to utilize Anglo-Europhone languages (such as English) to do Sikh philosophy, will it ever be possible to truly decolonize Sikh thought from the influence of European ontology and epistemology?

(7) Systems of oppression often invent and reify identities of marginalized groups as part of their function. As such, social justice issues have historically utilized and embraced these identities as forms of ego to combat oppression. Are there alternative means, embracing the tenets of Sikh philosophy, that may also align with the mission of equity?

Consciousness

A common concern among modernist philosophers of Sikhism was the need to establish a definitive ontology of Sikhism. In many cases this concern translated into book-length works focused on trying to define the 'true nature of reality in Sikhism or ultimate reality'. From a decolonial perspective it seems almost as if the early treatises on Sikh philosophy were responding to an intellectual imperative which demanded of them: Tell us what is *really* real? How does Sikh thought separate reality from illusion? In other words what do Sikhs understand as the *ultimate* reality?

To try and address this question/demand a common practice among modernist scholars was to set out competing notions of reality in other traditions, especially Hinduism, Buddhism and Islam, before presenting Sikhism's own reality principle in a favourable light. One scholar went so far as to write an entire monograph attempting to establish an 'Ultimate Reality' dividing his book into three main sections: 'Reality in Sikhism', 'Reality and its Attributes' and 'Social Reality'.[1] Everything, it seems, led to reality as humanity's central concern. What this modernist strand of Sikh thought appears not to have realized is that the quest for 'ultimate' reality was more an issue for philosophers of the European Enlightenment than it was for Guru Nanak. European philosophers such as Descartes, Kant and Hegel needed to establish reality as a foundational principle in itself, for the purpose of grounding humanistic self-representation (giving priority to the 'I think') as the foundation of self, thought and all relations to the world. The result of the European Enlightenment's philosophical quest was an objectification of reality.

This was certainly not Guru Nanak's quest! As we have learnt from Chapter 2, Nanak's central concern was to liberate us from this extremely limiting and unhealthy preoccupation with centralizing thought and relations within the human mind or ego. His remedy was to break the self-constituted walls of ego – to annihilate ego – by opening the mind to the One-All, and thus to attain the liberating insight that *all is consciousness*, in such a way that the question is no longer about an objective reality 'out there' but about 'us' *realizing* oneness as the nature of all things, as that which is always already given, but from which we are constantly shielded by a wall of ego.

In this chapter I want to look more closely at the kind of ontology that emerges from Guru Nanak's own writings. Note that I say a *kind* of ontology rather than presupposing ontology to be universal. My point is that we should not simply assume that the category of ontology as it is understood in Western philosophy can be uncritically mapped onto Guru Nanak's teachings. This is not only because, as Walter Mignolo reminds us, 'ontology is an epistemological concept'[2] but because ontology in the singular is derived from a specifically Western sense of world-making which privileges entities and beings, by assuming a primary distinction between Being and beings-in-the-world. And this particular kind of ontology in turn derives from Christian creation cosmology, in which 'God' is the ultimate or true foundation of all existence because the same 'God' transcends all existence.

But this does not automatically mean that Euro-Christian ontology and its creation cosmology are universal. All it means is that Western Christian epistemology became hegemonic in the modern era due to the global spread of European imperialism. Having said that, I don't want to simply ditch categories such as ontology. As I show in this chapter, when we apply it to Guru Nanak's teachings, the sense of ontology itself is altered in such a way that it's difficult to separate it either from epistemology or ethics. So if I continue to use the term 'ontology', it is because it refers to a radically different sense of world-making which derives from Nanak's unique understanding of cosmology, on the one hand, as intrinsically related to consciousness, whose operative principle is a sense of oneness (*ēk*) in which opposites belong together (*ēk-anēk*), and on the other hand, as giving rise to a world-making that privileges relations between entities rather than distinct entities per se.

A useful entry point into the question of ontology can be found in two substantive and very different compositions by Nanak. The first is the *Rāg Mārū* composition, a long poem which at first sight seems to be a straightforward creation hymn expounding yet another cosmology based on God's movement from a state of un-creation (void, nothingness) to creation. What becomes evident in this hymn, however, is that Nanak's central concern is not necessarily with the theme of creation but with showing that the same cosmological processes are occurring in the human mind, or in the making of the human self during an individual's quest for self-realization. The second composition is Nanak's *Siddh Gosht* (or 'Dialogue with the Siddhas'), which was briefly examined in an earlier chapter. Between these two compositions, it is possible to discern the basic elements of Nanak's ontology, which not only provides a passage to the question 'What is Consciousness'? but converges with Guru Nanak's treatment of consciousness at the end of the *Japji*, where he explicates the nature of consciousness through his explication of the *khands* or planes of consciousness. In this way it also provides an entry point for exploring wider themes such as freedom, free will, the nature of God, individuation, nature and life, to name the more prominent ones.

Cosmology in Guru Nanak's *Rāg Mārū* hymn

In Guru Nanak's writings the most elaborate and sustained statement about creation cosmology can be found in a twelve-page section of a hymn recorded in the musical register of *Rāg Mārū*. These twelve pages contain two sets of poems which describe the cosmic state prior to creation when the One was latent rather than active. This is followed by verses that describe the unfolding of the universe into a multiplicity of forms, among which is the human form:[3]

Set 1 GGS p. 1026
For countless aeons, chaotic darkness reigned
As the Infinite One, remained seated in trance.
Alone and detached in the heart of chaos
The cosmic expanse was non-existent. [16-1-7]
In this manner aeons passed
Things worked as the One intended.
No Other existed, only the Absolute infinitely pervasive. [16-2-7]

Set 2 GGS p. 1035-7
(a) For countless aeons nothing but chaos
Neither earth, nor sky, only infinitely pervasive Will (*hukam*) [16-4-1]

(b) In seedless void/chaos, force remained latent
Unattached, infinite, yet One.
Exercising creative power
Inanimate nature sprang from primal chaos

Most modern translations and commentaries on the beautiful second trio of *Rāg Mārū* hymns (16-3-15 to 17-5-7) have suggested that Guru Nanak makes clear reference to an actual creation event, and before that to an age when the cosmos did not exist, thereby providing clear indication of creation *ex nihilo*.[4] By indicating that there was nothing *prior* to the act of creation modern Sikh philosophy has tended to mirror Christian apologetics by stressing the idea of creation *ex nihilo* as a symbol of man's absolute dependence on a unique and transcendent deity. That is, only God can make the transition from non-existence\non-time to existence\time.

The obvious problem with modernist interpretations, however, is that they contradict the opening lines of the hymn itself (*arbad narbad dhundhūkārā.* . . . For countless aeons, nothing but chaos) which signal the impossibility of conceiving anything like a pre-creation state. They spatialize the temporal act of transition from non-existence to existence (or from nothingness to creation). In doing so they effectively construct creation as an absolute origin, which then comes to dominate (transcendentally, patriarchically) whatever derives from it.

When examined more closely, however, the *Rāg Mārū* composition suggests a more complicated scenario. To appreciate this one needs to pay closer attention to the conceptual rhythms within each hymn, as well as the connection between concepts in the trio of verses (16-3-15) to (17-5-17). By conceptual rhythm I refer to subtle but important shifts in Guru Nanak's hymn from a preoccupation with the macrocosmic creation event to a preoccupation with microcosmic processes such as the nature of humanity, exemplified by two opposing states of mind: *manmukh* and *gurmukh*.

On the surface of it, such shifts might indicate that the *Rāg Mārū* hymns are as anthropocentric as they are theological in nature. However, the conceptual rhythms of the verses are too intricate to support either theocentric or anthropocentric interpretations. We can see this partly in the way that Guru Nanak's shift of emphasis from macro- to microcosm is mediated via two moves. First, a subtle but important differentiation in what is signified by *hukam*. Second, the linking of void/chaos directly to the qualitative state of the *gurmukh* as opposed to chaos\void being a state of the cosmos. But the question that arises here is whether this shift is simply a way to connect the outer (cosmic) with inner (human) without differentiating between them. If so, are the references to creation merely superfluous in Nanak's hymns? Are they basically metaphors for something more human? If not, how are we to interpret the connection between cosmic creation, void\chaos and the figure of *gurmukh*? A brief foray into intricacies of the *Rāg Mārū* verses will be helpful to understand what is going on.

Creative void – discussing time, again

The opening verse of (16-3-15) describes the state prior to any beginning as *dhundhūkārā*. Derived from the word *dhundh* for shapeless mist, *dhundhūkārā* signifies the spreading everywhere of a mist in which no shape or form can be discerned. It can be interpreted as a pervasive state of formlessness. But crucially, the nature of this formlessness is not presented negatively, in the sense of a state that is lacking. Rather, as Nanak tells us, the

One subsists in a state of formlessness that can be usefully envisaged as a state of infinite potential, which he refers to as *hukam apārā* – more specifically the infinite potential of a command (*hukam*) that remains unrealized, undifferentiated (*apārā*). The formlessness indicated by *dhundhūkārā* is not indicative of non-existence but of a state of endless, formless multiplicity without limits. As a state it can be expressed only from a subject position that is unconscious. It could be said that *hukam* permeated the chaos and that the state of this *hukam* is best described as a process of continual and limitless differentiation 'within' the One, and therefore describable as the self-differentiation that is proper to the One. The next twelve verses describe this infinite self-differentiation in seemingly negative terms:

> No day, no night, no moon, no sun, only Oneness in meditative void;
>> No sources of creation, no power of speech, . . .
> No births, no death, no coming and going, no transmigration:
>> No Brahma, no Vishnu, no Shiva:
> None to be seen but the One alone . . .

Yet despite the negation of qualities in these verses (*neither this, nor that . . .*), Guru Nanak is equally emphatic about avoiding an either/or logic to describe the state of formlessness. Thus, while the One does not *formally* exist at this 'pre-creation' stage, nevertheless, the same One is described as eternally subsisting as limitless all-pervasive Will (*hukam apārā*). The distinction between existence and subsistence is not a difference between non-time and time, or between non-existence and existence, but between two distinct forms of eternity. One form of eternity unfolds in spatial–temporal coordinates allowing for measurement; the other form of eternity repeats internally, an absolutely interior self-differentiation. Stated differently, the One expands infinitely without, but it also expands infinitely within as a process of self-differentiation. As Nanak states in verse 6, the state of *hukam apārā* entailed a process of continual, eternal differentiation which is equally a process of eternal self-creation to which the One is not only sole witness to its own processes (*apai aap upai vigsaii*) and therefore provides the measure of its own value (*appai kimat pai*) but abides in a state of absolute self-enjoyment.[5]

In the above verse the reference to self-witnessing (*vigsaii*) of one's own undifferentiation or unfolding (*upai*) is an indication that the state is measureless (*aappai kimat pai*), because there is no outside to it. The One gives itself its own value (*kimat*) through self-witnessing. Another way to describe this state might be to resort to the term 'immediacy', as I have done in previous chapters. This state of the One is unmediated, meaning that it can only be understood without distance, without external observation, which is to say, it cannot be witnessed by another. Hence the descriptive negations, which are actually negations of the possibility of an exterior self or subject position. But apparently, this eternal self-differentiation does not bear fruit, which is why it must be described through negation.

The negation of predicates continues until verse 14. After verse 14 a distinct change in emphasis can be detected. At this point we read that in accordance with the Will, desire or command of the One (*jā tis bhāṇā*), the current of cosmic creation comes into motion, that is, a world takes form (*ta jagat upāiā*). The question here is whether Nanak is describing a transition *from hukam apārā* (latent formlessness) *to jagat upāiā* (manifest form). If so, has he created a subject position that contradicts any 'original' state of the One?

The very next line of this particular verse makes clear that there is no external transition as such from one state to a different state – a transition that could be measured, in which case it would require an external subject. Nanak says that all along, the One remains suffused with its own formless power (*bhajun kala adarn rahaia*). And towards the end of the hymn Nanak expresses that *hukam* is eternally pervasive. The One was *hukam*, remains *hukam* and will be *hukam*. *All that has changed is the nature of this eternity.* If we continue to narrate this process in terms of change or transition, it is because ordinary words fail us. We need words, or a manner of narrating, able to address the contradiction that despite being perceived as two, the nature of this eternity is *always* One. Or as Nanak says: *kar kar dekhai hukam sabhaia* – the One remains *hukam* as it witnesses its own creation. There is no outside to the One. It is all-encompassing. Change occurs but the One remains One. Again, the key here is immediacy, which is also to say that this is a state of consciousness that brooks no mediation.

It is only in the next two major sets of verses, (16–4–16) and (17–5–17), that we get a better idea about how Nanak addresses the problem of transition. These two sets of verses consolidate the theme of *hukam*'s actualization, but this time by signalling an interminable link between the life of the cosmos and the psychic life of the individual. It is here that Nanak shifts the reader's gaze away from a cosmological speculation towards the human body, more specifically by alluding to a certain type of individuation vis-à-vis the figure of the *gurmukh*. In expounding this section my narrative will stay as close to the text as possible.

Cosmic creation *is* psychic individuation

Thus in (16–4–16) Nanak writes that while remaining detached, the One unfolds a creative process (*aape aap nirala*) by binding the cosmic elements into the body (*paun pani agni ka bandan, kayah kot rachaida*), which becomes the location for transacting all manner of worldly affairs (*garh meh haat patan vapārā . . .*). Of all the bodies that participate in the to-and-fro of worldly affairs, Nanak privileges a certain kind of individual, the *gurmukh*, who alone remains unaffected by material states of affairs (*gurmukh mail na laida*), for only the *gurmukh* recognizes that the body is the seat of our creative power (*sarab kāla le aap rahia gurmukh kisai buchaida*). But who or what is a *gurmukh*? Moreover, what is the *gurmukh*'s relationship to *hukam*?

> *gurmukh hoe su hukam pachanai mannia hukam samaida*
> The *gurmukh* is one who recognizes, meditates on, and merges with *hukam*.

Guru Nanak elaborates on the relationship between *hukam* and the *gurmukh* at length in stanzas [16-4-16], on the one hand equating the figure of *gurmukh* with an individual who recognizes, devotes herself to and merges with *hukam*, and on the other hand, describing *hukam* as the imperative immanent in the multidimensionality of the creative process. While the force of *hukam* maintains cosmic and psychic processes, its power is located in the fortress of the body. But in case we forget the absolutely univocal nature of the One, in verses (17-5-17), Nanak states in no uncertain terms that the source of the same power (*kala*) derives from a state of absolute detachment, for which the term used in the hymn is *sunnaṇ*. Though it bears a close resemblance to the Buddhist and Jain concept of *śunyā* (nothingness/emptiness/void), Nanak's explication of *sunnaṇ* further emphasizes the positive potential of void. It is an absolutely fertile void, a desert teeming with unactualized life, a nothingness full of potentiality. Or as Nanak states, the power of creativity emanates from the state of absolute detachment\void\nothingness (*sunn kalā apārāmpar dharī*). While remaining unattached and limitless, the same One in full awareness evolves nature, drawing creative power from absolute void (*aap niralam apar apari aape kudrat kar kar dekhai sunnaṇu sunn upaida*).[6]

From the potential of the absolute void (*sunnaṇu sunn*) come the dualities of light and dark, life and death, pleasure and pain (*sunnaṇu rati dinasu due kiai// upati khapti sach dukh diae*). The only true means for negotiating between finite and infinite states is the state of mind fostered by the *gurmukh* (*sukh dukh hi tea mar atita gurmukh nijh ghar paida*).

In the state of actualization, the primal void gives rise to the three modes of time, to all sources of creation and to the power of speech (verses 5-6). Additionally, the power of void brings into existence the *gunas*: *rajjas, sattva, tamas*. These are the three motions or rotary drives of the cosmos. And from these drives arise the modes of time – past, present, future (*rajo tamo satto kāl kri chaia*) which the human mind internalizes giving rise to the disease of ego

(*haumai*). Once ego's individuating impulses take hold, all beings suffer the pain
of death (*janam maran haumai dukh paia*). As with the previous composition,
the focus of the last few verses successively shifts towards the figure of the
gurmukh. By embodying the creative impulse of the primal void the *gurmukh*
is able to overcome the disease of human individuation (*haumai*) by cultivating
a state of mind that does not suffer the pain of birth and death and is able to
achieve the fourth state or *chautha pad* (verse 11). Because the *gurmukh* does
not suffer this disease of ego, s/he is liberated and liberates others.

Embodying void and creation freedom, consciousness and the figure of the *gurmukh*

What are some of the broader philosophical implications arising from Guru
Nanak's shift of focus away from metaphysical speculation on creation
cosmology towards the embodied experience of the enigmatic being that he
calls *gurmukh*?

Clearly, the move significantly complicates theistic and non-theistic
explanations which depict the act of creation as God's transition from
formlessness to form, or as a self-conscious assertion of divine Will, which
in turn becomes the foundation of divine sovereignty. The theistic model
is complicated by Nanak's refusal of any ontological separation between
formlessness (*nirgun*) and form (*sargun*). As we noted earlier, for Nanak,
states of formlessness and form are equally aspects of *hukam* and do not
change the nature of oneness as he further clarifies elsewhere in his writings:

> *nirgun aap sargun bhi ohi*
> The One is simultaneously existent (has form) and non-existent
>   (formless).

> *sargun nirgun nirankar*
> *sunn samadhi aap*
> *āpan kia Nānakā*
> *āpe hi phir jāp*

> With form and without form, the Absolute
> In trance-like void, maintains self-nature.
> From the same impulse, O Nanak,
> Creation happens, and is eternally repeated.

What the above verses suggest is that the One cannot be thought other than
through the simultaneous co-implication of transcendence and immanence,

which not only contradicts the transcendental logic of classical theism but, through reference to form (*sargun*) and immanence, shifts the work of thinking away from speculating on the origin and cause of cosmic creation towards contemplation on the processes of human individuation. The takeaway from this alternative perspective is that the processes of individuation at play in the workings of the cosmos are no different to those at work in the formation of the human psyche. The cosmic and the psychic are thoroughly and mutually imbricated. This absolute entanglement of the cosmic and psychic has implications for understanding the nature of consciousness (as co-implicating materiality and ideality), the nature of freedom and the figure who embodies them, namely, the *gurmukh*. Thus the possibility of human freedom depends paradoxically on a separation, *not* from *hukam* (which as we noted in the previous chapter can only be recognized via the 'I am not') but a separation from the opposed principle of *haumai* ('I am myself' or pure ego)! While the former would be a performance of atheism, the latter is the negation of the oppositional framework that gives rise to the atheism/theism duality.

What this means is that the process of *haumai* or ego production is more complex than meets the eye. *Haumai* is both the main impediment to and a necessity for freedom. This means that freedom is attained *not* by negating the 'I am' (which would be a pure asceticism in the worst sense) and the state of primal void, or chaotic self-differentiation. The void (*sunn*) is not to be envisaged as a thing or an entity in the sense of a vacuum or nothingness but as a *process* of negating the psychic formation 'I am myself' in the very moment in which the 'I' or self is produced. It is a self-emptying inscribed within the self. And if one is to recognize and name this self-emptying process, it would be none other than *hukam*. As a negation of the negative, the void (*sunn*) is purely generative. It is a self-voiding that produces newness by differentiating the self, as opposed to merely annihilating it. The individual who embodies this seemingly impossible process is the *gurmukh*.

The relationship between the state of void or detachment and the *gurmukh* can be seen in other compositions by Guru Nanak, a good example being *Siddh Gosht* ('Dialogue with the Siddhas'). This particular composition lends itself more directly to philosophical questioning and poses some interesting questions about the themes of creation and human freedom. This is not surprising since the entire composition is purportedly a dialogue between rival forms of contemplative thought-practice. The Siddhas were spiritual masters who had discovered ways of overcoming *āhamkāra* (the ego or I-making function) through rigorous philosophical and bodily training. *Siddh Gosht* indirectly raises questions such as how can we think detachment (or void) and creation simultaneously, that is, in a non-oppositional manner? What does it mean that the One remains detached in the very process of creating? Or that the One is always already absenting or withdrawing as s/he creates? As we see in the passage reproduced here, arguably with even greater directness than the *Rāg Mārū* hymns, Nanak juxtaposes the cosmological scene of creation onto the psycho-somatic scene of the body as the privileged site ('fortress' or 'palace') for the attainment of freedom:

Siddha's question:
What have you to say about the origin?
What was the abode of the void then? (V.21)
Where does the self come from? Where does it go?
Where does it stay when merged? (V.22)

Nanak's answer:
About the origin, we can only speak in terms of wonder
About the One absorbed in void. . . .(V.21)
Self comes and goes by nature's order,
By the same order it remains merged (V.23)

First, imperceptible form arises,
Then from unconditioned being arises conditioned being (V.24)

Void within, void without,
Emptiness grounds the three worlds.
Whoever knows the fourth state is beyond vice and virtue
Whoever knows the mystery of the voided-existence
Attains the primal immaculate state.
O Nanak, becoming imbued with immaculate *nām*
One becomes a creative being (V.51)

Everyone speaks of absolute void
From whom did you gain instruction about the nature of void?
What state of mind corresponds to absorption in undifferentiated void?
There, like the one from which they originated.
They're neither born, nor die, nor come and go.
Nanak, so the Guru instructs the mind. (V.52)

The question that resurfaces again is how to think of the relationship between what are normally considered to be opposed states: the cosmic and the psychic, the eternal and the finite, or between cosmic and human individuation?

The clue here resides in the figure of the *gurmukh* who harnesses the potential of the body and becomes able to straddle both cosmic and human time. In *Siddh Gosht*, after the initial metaphysical questions about the nature of the origin, void and the self (verses 21 to 23), approximately twenty stanzas (24–44) examine the nature of the *gurmukh* as one who destroys ego-sense, remains detached while living in the world, attends a blissful state of void, develops awareness within all creation, becomes a bridge between creator and created and thus embodies oneness within and without.

But even a cursory reading of these verses gives rise to some perplexing questions. How, for example, can the embodied, lived experience exemplified by the *gurmukh* in any way correspond to the cosmic process of creation? Is Nanak simply reducing the cosmic and the human to material processes? This would seem unlikely given the overt references to mind, self and experience. Or is he perhaps juxtaposing the material cosmological processes with immaterial psychological processes, in a way that presumes consciousness as im/material foundational?

I would like to suggest the latter interpretation as more viable and therefore more helpful for Sikh philosophy. The only impediment to realizing this is the dualistic belief that matter and consciousness are opposed, and that there must be a radical separation of mind and matter, or reduction of one to the other. Reading Guru Nanak closely, however, it becomes evident that mind and body, consciousness and matter, cosmos and psyche are intrinsically linked. More importantly, the entanglement or association between these apparent opposites is neither mediated nor created by human consciousness. Instead, the non-oppositional perspective derives from a principle of ontogenesis[7] as the condition for human consciousness. In Sikh philosophy ontogenesis is closer to the concept of *hukam*. Indeed, *hukam* can be better understood through ontogenesis than through reference to an eminent divine entity (monotheism). And, although space prevents me from following through with a discussion on the political implications of ontogenesis-as-*hukam*, for future reference I would like to register here that ontogenesis as *hukam* pluralizes the concept of sovereignty, in the sense that sovereignty cannot belong to, or be invested in, a person or personal consciousness. An important implication of this is that all forms of political monotheism are incompatible with the philosophy of *gurmat* and with the figure of the *gurmukh*.

A clue to understanding ontogenesis (indicated by *hukam*) as the link between cosmos and psyche can be found in what makes the *gurmukh*'s lived experience different from others. It is only possible to become *gurmukh* by realizing (i.e. actualizing through mind and body) the same *hukam* by which cosmic creation is continually becoming. By realizing this in one's actions, thoughts and desires, it is possible to attain the true sense of freedom. If we follow the logic in Nanak's hymns, the very source of cosmic creation is embodied in the actions of a *gurmukh* who actualizes the work of creation in the experience of life itself. In the same way that creation implies the continual production of newness, so the free actions of the *gurmukh* embrace the newness of continual self-differentiation as opposed to the ego production of the *manmukh*.

Consciousness: Cosmic and psychic

What does the cosmology of the *Rāg Mārū* and Siddh Gosht hymns tell us? First, whether we think of it at the cosmic level (encompassing the external spatial world of material objects that are interacting with each other according to fixed laws of nature) or at the psychic level (encompassing the inner non-spatial world of subjective conscious perceptions) the fundamental nature of consciousness conforms to a oneness describable as a dynamic flux of interwoven states of awareness (*surat(i)*), which remains eternally creative, fresh and new. As indicated by the middle sections of the *Rāg Mārū* and *Siddh Gosht* hymns, everything created participates in a continuum of consciousness that encompasses materiality and immateriality.

Second, psychic life emerges from the creative impulse of the cosmos, which actualizes into various orders of complexity – inorganic, organic, biological, animal, human, civilizational and so on. Not only is consciousness coextensive and entangled with materiality, more importantly, consciousness and the various forms of psychic life are coextensive with the forces of the pre-individual state which Nanak refers to as the power of the void through which all forms of identity, difference, interiority, exterior authority, becoming and so on emerge.

Third, consciousness emerges through different stages of individuation which at the level of the human psyche include (i) individuality as the personalizing self-identification characteristic of the *manmukh*, (ii) the 'never self-identical' form of the *gurmukh* whose individuation makes it trans-individual or trans-personal in nature. Whereas the *manmukh* in his self-identification refuses or cuts himself off from the void, the *gurmukh* surrenders to the power of the void's potential (*hukam*) and brings into social life, thought and practice, new orders of creativity that associate the processes of individuation with new ways of knowing. The *gurmukh* can therefore be considered something like a trans-personal individual intermittently in touch with his or her own potentiality for creating new kinds of psychic and collective life, as well as the creation of new kinds of ethics and aesthetics. If a schema can be teased out of this discussion, it would not support an evolution of life in linear time, but an eventful metastable coexistence of the cosmic and psychic processes as outlined in Figure 6.

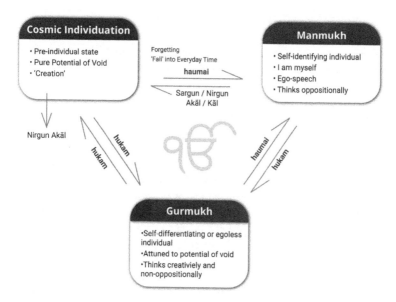

Figure 6 Schematic representation of relationship between cosmic and psychic individuation.

The *khands*: Planes of consciousness

If we can divest ourselves of misleading dualisms such as mind versus matter, or the distinction between a higher ultimate reality and a lower reality of the material world, and assume as axiomatic that All is One because it is Consciousness, and All is Consciousness because it is One, it becomes somewhat easier to explain how the cosmic/psychic, external/internal are ontologically entangled and co-implicated from the outset. Any explanation that associates conventional binaries such as materiality/ideality, outside/inside and time/eternity would be applying non-oppositional logic.

For Sikh philosophy the implications of this entanglement are significant. It would allow us to avoid the problems associated with normally opposed forms of explanation such as theology and historical materialism. While the former can only explain by resorting to a divine agent (eminent or otherwise) whose ultimate status devalues or ignores the world of materiality, resorting to materialist explanation is an equally reductive alternative.[8] This is where certain strands of neuroscience and neuropsychology are taking us today. A good example of the latter is the reduction of all consciousness, experience and thought to neurochemical processes in the brain, to physical laws of nature or to algorithms. This kind of reductionism not only reflects a poverty of imagination in scientific modelling but an impoverished understanding of what science is, or has the potential to be. Faced with such alternatives it becomes difficult, if not impossible, to address questions such as human freedom, or our relationship to the natural environment, or to adopt an ethical standpoint outside the alternatives of materialist humanism or theology. If matter is dead or unreal, why should we care? Is the body just a material object? Or can it be envisaged in terms of consciousness?

While Guru Nanak doesn't answer these questions directly, he does, nevertheless, bring into play a schema and a set of concepts that complicate how we think about the entanglement of opposites: mind\body, cosmic\ psychic, virtual\actual, *nirguṇ/sarguṇ* or spirituality\materiality. Nanak deploys this schema, and concepts associated with it, to explain the nature of consciousness in general and awareness at a human level (*surat(i)*) as a conceptual and practical aid for self-realization. To suggest that this schema is a practical aid means that it is inherently connected to the body vis-à-vis disciplinary techniques and is therefore capable of affecting our potential to act in the world. The specific schematic concept he introduces is the *khand*.

The term *khand* literally means region, dimension or plane. Although it seems to suggest spatiality, Guru Nanak's understanding and deployment of *khand* are grounded in an expanded temporality – a temporality that exceeds ordinary linear time to which our everyday consciousness is limited – in order to illustrate a trajectory of ethical–spiritual progress towards liberation in life (*jīvanmuktī*). The term *khand* can be more usefully envisaged as a plane of consciousness. The ethico-spiritual trajectory is attainable only by continual and arduous struggle of the self to unify the opposition between ideal\material, virtual/actual, outer/inner, cosmic/psychic and so on, through their continual interaction. In other words the *khand* is both a schema of spiritual movement and a concept that helps explain the absolute coincidence of the spiritual and the material localized in the experience of a body–mind complex that is always in the world.

As illustrated in Figure 7, there are five *khands* that Nanak refers to in *Japji*:

- **dharam khand** – the plane governed by societal laws and/or religious endeavour
- **giān khand** – the plane of cognition or perception
- **saram khand** – the plane of aesthetic or affective expansion
- **karam khand** – the plane of action and/or habit
- **sach khand** – the plane of truth.

The *khands:*
Planes of Consciousness

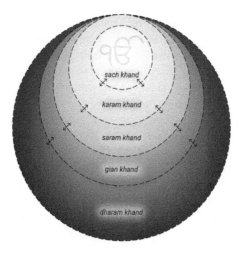

Figure 7 The *khands*: Planes of consciousness.

Each of these *khands* can be considered as distinct but interpenetrating and interconnecting planes of consciousness corresponding to the various dimensions of one's subjective experience in the world. Although a cursory reading of the stanzas dealing with the *khands* might lead us to conclude that the order in which the *khands* are listed and narrated (*dharam* > *giān* > *saram* > *karam* > *sach*) suggests a hierarchy of planes with *dharam khand* as the starting point and *sach khand* as the highest (the ideal), along with a distinctness of each *khand*, Sikh philosophers writing in the 1980s such as Avtar Singh have argued that this is not the case. For Avtar Singh, the five *khands* comprise a threefold interdimensional movement, but nothing like a strict hierarchical progress. Instead, the three dimensions of *giān, saram, karam* need to be seen as a vertical–horizontal synthesis of simultaneous processes of interiorization and externalization linked to the processes of cognition. Before elaborating on the individual characteristics of the five *khands* it will be helpful to present a brief summary of the dominant tendencies of each *khand* before discussing how they work to bring the cosmic and psychic aspects together.

dharam khand – The term *dharam* is derived from the Sanskrit root *dhr* which means to uphold, support or maintain. It refers to consciousness at the stage of customary or conventional morality where one's mind is governed by societal laws and obligations, which need to be observed to stabilize consciousness.

According to Avatar Singh *dharam khand* refers to a state of consciousness of an embodied being which acts and responds as if it were an object of nurture and therefore out of necessity to natural laws (days, nights, seasons) that work in a rhythmic capacity. In this state the person performs functions in accordance with socially approved conventions and moral contexts. It refers to the normative milieu in which one finds oneself, prior to making any attempt to progress beyond doing socially accepted duties.[9] However, *dharam khand* does not suggest a merely robotic or mechanical function, but involves a degree of voluntarism. One has to choose and assent to one's role, but this choice is constrained by social and cultural rules which predetermine the kind of morality involved: 'insofar as one accepts the social obligation in the role that he or she has chosen to play, s/he can transcend the ego to some extent'.[10] But more often than not, transcendence of personal or individual ego gives way to the kind of social ego determined by one's religion, caste or class.

Dharam khand can be viewed from two different perspectives. According to one perspective, the capacity to respond to the infinite flux of the cosmic One-All and make certain selections or choices can be regarded as a gift even though this gift of freedom contracts and limits the One-All into an individuated consciousness. So although it is a limitation or contraction from infinitely open consciousness to finite personalized ego-consciousness, it is still a gift\grace (*nadar/kirpa*) because the act of choosing unlocks and actualizes the virtual One-All. At the same time this limited–contracted consciousness (ego) is also a curse because it is also what prevents us from fusing with the One-All (the Beloved). Because we are prevented from moving beyond limitations imposed by the dominant symbolic order, the individual needs to undergo an arduous struggle within oneself. In short, the limited, contracted consciousness of *dharam khand* is both sickness and remedy. Struggling with this limitation can open us up to other *khands* or planes of consciousness.

giān khand/saram khand/karam khand

As noted earlier, there is a consensus among Sikh philosophers that these three *khands* should be considered together as part of a vertico-horizontal movement which is not a strict progression of consciousness, but rather a synthesis of different but intersecting forces. Basically, the three *khands* represent 'inseparable dimensions' – cognitive, aesthetic and conative – characterizable as a fused multiplicity that always retains its essential unity. Accordingly, if *giān* can be considered the cognitive dimension, *saram* as the aesthetic and *karam* as the conative or actional, then all are interwoven within the composition of the self. For the sake of discussion, however, it will be helpful to present each separately before we look at how they work together.

giān khand – Stanza 35 in the Japji is devoted to a description of *giān khand*, the plane of cognition and knowing. One thing that immediately stands out in the stanza is the prevalence of the theme of multiplicity. As Guru Nanak himself says: 'if you were to ask me now to describe the dimension of *giān*', one would have to speak in terms of infinite possibilities. In stanza 35 Nanak uses the word *kété* (many, how many, infinite, etc.) at least eleven times. From start to finish the stanza on *giān* impresses on the reader that there is no end to the expansive knowing – it is without limit. What seems to be suggested is that there are two sides to this expansiveness of knowledge, corresponding to two radically different ways of knowing and therefore two different kinds of knowledge.

On the one hand, knowledge is quantitative, and there is a positive aspect to acquiring quantitative knowledge of the cosmic elements (*paun* wind, *pani* water, *baisantar*), or processes of creation, destruction and ordering, of worlds, of cosmic spheres, of the deities, of life and language, of mystics and their devotees. Mere accumulation of such knowledge swells the ego. But since knowledge is infinite and the ego is limited, then finite quantitative knowledge is ultimately futile. If one realizes one's limitations in the face of such expansiveness of knowledge, ego is humbled, and the person's motives for gathering knowledge are transformed, such that quantitative knowledge gives way to qualitative knowledge, which is the opening of true wisdom. One thus comes to a realization that the accumulation of knowledge could only happen through an ego that was fundamentally distanced from everything else in the world.

In contradistinction, from the perspective of wisdom the ego realizes that all things, the infinite multiplicity of cosmic and psychic processes, are interrelated, interpenetrating and interwoven. Oneness runs through infinite multiplicity and vice versa. Once the egotistical person achieves this self-realization, s/he is filled with 'music, bliss and aesthetic self-enjoyment'. The reference to aesthetic self-enjoyment in the last line of stanza 35 connects to the theme of stanza 36, which focuses on the dimensional plane of aesthetic consciousness or *saram khand*.

saram khand – the term *saram* has meanings pertaining to the internal movement of consciousness in which the self struggles with and against itself, resulting in a spiritual orientation based on self-loss or surrender. In stanza 36 Guru Nanak opens his description of *saram khand* with the line:

> The aesthetic plane communicates to us through the beauty of form (*saram khand ki bani rup*). It is within this *khand* that the uniqueness of form is fashioned (*tithai ghariat ghariae bahut anup*), which is a clear reference to the process of individuation. However, its precise mechanism is impossible to describe. If one tries to define it, one would later regret it and be forced to alter the definitions. For it is here that the forms of perception and cognition that comprise our consciousness, intellect, memory and understanding are fashioned (*tithai ghariai surat(i) mat(i) mn buddh(i)*).

The words *ghariai* and *gharat*, indicating the fashioning aspect of form, appear three times in this stanza, suggesting that its central concern is the process of aesthetic subjectivity. Stanza 36 thus presents a different way to describe the process whereby knowledge (*giān*) is fashioned into an aesthetic form that governs the processes of selfing and de-selfing, that is to say, the processes involved in the making of subjectivity. Guru Nanak's stress on the difficulty of verbally describing such a process of selfing and de-selfing indicates that *saram khand* is realized primarily through affect or feeling. However, the fact that the stanza on *saram khand* opens with a reference to *giān khand* suggests that the two are intimately fused together. Knowledge gained through percepts is fashioned into affect (feeling) whose form can only be described as 'the beautiful' (*rūp*) because it is at the same time highly individuated and unique. Thus beauty or form (*rūp*) is itself a reference to the complexity of self-differentiation (*bahut anup*). Moreover, this self-differentiating form of consciousness is the mark of the perfected minds (*suddh*) of heroes (*sūrā*) and of spiritual adepts (*siddhas*). In short the Guru fuses perfection of cognition and perfection of intuition into a form of aesthetic realization grounded in affect and feeling. But neither cognitive nor affective realization is of any real use without being translated into action(s) or *karam*, which is treated in stanza 37.

karam khand – the language or medium in the plane of action is force, energy or power (*jōr*), and force alone (*karam khand kī bāṇī jōr . . .*). If we keep in mind that this is still a dimensional plane of consciousness, the central characteristic of force or power is exemplified by heroic figures such as the mythical Ram whose actions personify the unity of righteous *action* performed without desire for the fruit of their actions, or the *grace* of such figures as the mythical Sita whose actions were characterized by selfless devotion to her Beloved.[11] In short this stanza refers to modes of consciousness in which acts are done spontaneously, that is to say, without being motivated by passions, fears and egotism. From within this plane of consciousness actions do not give rise to ego. One acts in such a way that the self is not marked by the action, which is another way of describing a mode of subjectivity in which selfing and de-selfing are in harmony. One is able to kill the ego in the moment that it forms (a heroic act) but one retains enough of ego to allow it to survive (a graceful act: devotion to the Beloved).

Another way of understanding the balance between action and grace is that grace operates insofar as one harnesses the power to self-differentiate, that is to say, to lose ego in *hukam*. But it does so only on the condition that one's ego acknowledges to itself that it has no power to even lose this ego, that that power comes from a higher and more expansive source: the One. The ideal *karam* or action being referred to here is an act whose performance is marked by surrendering in love. To put it differently, *karam khand* is the mode of consciousness in which one's conatus is perfected – that is to say, one has perfected the self's inner impulse to continue to enhance one's power of existing.

sach khand – according to most Sikh philosophers *sach khand* can be considered a culminating plane, which integrates and harmonizes the three planes of consciousness previously described – *giān* (cognitive/conceptual), *saram* (affective) and *karam* (conative) – into a mode of existence characterized by the dynamic oneness of thought–feeling–action corresponding to the perfected self or, to use a term which we noted in earlier chapters, the *sachiārā*. The *sachiārā* is a person in whom the absolute or formless resides (*sach khand vasai nirankar*). Within this state of consciousness the cosmic and psychic are integrated into an intuition that connects external and internal dimensions within our consciousness. As Avtar Singh notes, in the state of *sach khand*, the self reaches the end of this expansion of consciousness and is able to directly intuit the world around us in such a way that the will of the *sachiārā* is perfectly synchronized within the cosmic Will (*hukam*).[12] It is this synthesis of inner and outer which enables the person to act in accordance with *hukam* (*jiv jiv hukam tivai tiv kār*). It is this integration that makes it possible to think of the *khands* as depicting a path of 'integral living consciousness' or 'integrated spiritual praxis'.[13]

How the *khands* provide an integral ontology

If we look at Guru Nanak's stanzas on the *khands* in conjunction with the more in-depth treatments of cosmology and psyche in the *Raga Mārū* and *Siddh Gosht* compositions, it is possible to discern the outlines of an integrative ontology, effectively a model of reality that integrates psychological and epistemological aspects with implications for wider themes that come under the purview of Sikh philosophy. These include (i) the idea of an embodied spirituality or embodied consciousness, (ii) the name 'God', (iii) the notion of human freedom, (iv) the question of discipline or praxis, (v) attitudes towards environment and ecology and (vi) pluralism, broadly conceived. The last two will be discussed in the chapter on ethics. The question of human freedom requires deeper discussion and is undertaken in Chapter 5. Here I focus on the first three, beginning with the notion of embodied spirituality or embodied consciousness.

Embodied spirituality-consciousness

'Embodied spirituality' is a term with deep roots in spiritual traditions. Jorge Ferrer defines it as a way of bringing all human dimensions – the body, the vital energies that make up our life, heart, mind, consciousness – into association with all cosmic dimensions 'as equal partners in bringing self, community and world into a fuller alignment with the mystery out of which everything arises'.[14] To illustrate how the cosmic and psychic dimensions are integrated into the *khand* model of consciousness, it will be helpful to map the various processes onto the same kind of diagram used in Chapter 2. The main difference is that the vertical and historical axes now map different ways of seeing reality (see Figures 8 and 9).

As before the whole process begins from the zero-point which depicts the creation of the cosmos from a state of void and/or the birth of an individual body in the world. Both axes represent reality but from entirely opposed perspectives. The vertical axes depict reality from the *manmukh* standpoint. Generated from an egocentric perspective this mode of reality is characterized by an objectification of primordial creative time (*akāl*), which becomes contracted and limited by the ego-apparatus into ordinary human time characterized by a linear succession of instants (*kāl*), with each instant being identical to the prior. This is uncreative secular time (*kāl*); it simply passes away. The result is an objectification of the cosmos and one's own body which it sees as pure matter and only 'for me'. This in turn generates

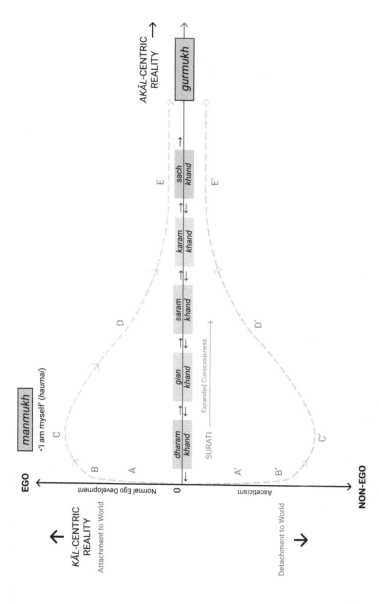

Figure 8 *Khands* and the transformational perfection of consciousness.

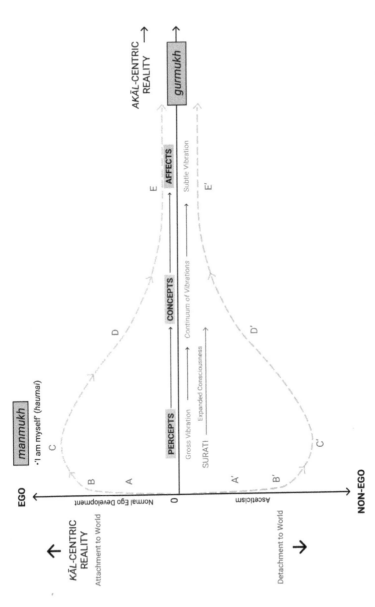

Figure 9 Progressive perfection of consciousness from percepts (gross vibrations) to affects (subtle vibrations).

an attachment to identity, which further separates the individual from the Beloved. The kind of 'reality' generated by this *kāl*-centric identitarian perspective regards the world outside of its own self as merely dead uncreative matter.

The horizontal axis is altogether different. At the simplest level it represents a rupture with egocentric processes. The horizontal movement from left to right depicts a gradual and progressive entry into a deeper reality, which is not limited by *kāl* or linear time but cultivates the more profound sense of time, *akāl*, signifying an eternity that constantly renews itself, and in renewing itself ontogenetically corresponds to an eternal differentiation of self and cosmos. *Akāl* is the underlying time of cosmic creation but is also the mode of time experienced by the self as it struggles to break with itself and produces a mode of individuation that can be described as a heterogenesis. The apparent progression of consciousness depicted in Guru Nanak's description of the five *khands* (Figure 6) not only illustrates the image of psychic life at each stage of this development but equally provides an image of the cosmic life.

What emerges from all of this is a model of reality that is neither ontology nor epistemology alone, but closer to an onto-ethics. That is to say, a model of reality that informs an ethical attitude towards oneself, towards other human beings and also towards every other living and non-living thing. In philosophical terms it gives rise to a form of thought that resists any kind of dualism. There is no materialism in itself, no idealism in itself. Whereas materialism has normally addressed the solid reality of things, objects, relations and events in the world, idealism, on the other hand, has tended to address things that supposedly exist only in the mind: significations, representations, thoughts, concepts and affects. But if the ideal and the material comprise opposing substances, then it is impossible to explain their interactions or effects as they occur in living bodies or in the life of the cosmos and world. And it becomes even more difficult to develop a value system or a theory of action – both of which pertain to ethics.

It is here that the *khand* theory provides a glimpse into how material\ ideal, matter\consciousness are thoroughly entangled, inform each other, interpenetrate and work through relations rather than oppositions. As Elizabeth Grosz reminds us: 'Ideality and materiality are therefore two ways in which the real is distributed. . . . Ideality informs materiality by enabling materiality to be in touch with itself, to be auto-affective, which is the condition under which materiality can complexify, give rise to life in various forms, to the technological and artistic inventions and transformations of matter that life enables'.[15]

'God' or *nām*?

Although these two concepts were introduced in Chapter 2 (on experience), their overarching importance to Sikh philosophy necessitates reiteration and expansion of the earlier discussion. Throughout the twentieth century modernist scholarship specializing in the study of Sikhism put a great deal of intellectual effort into describing the unity of God's existence, which for them was a condition for establishing the true or ultimate nature of reality. In ways that mirrored Christian philosophical theology, from which this intellectual effort derived, the preoccupation with the notion of ultimate reality led theologians and historians to rationalize notions of oneness as the unity *of an eminent divine entity*, such that unity is an attribute or quality that belongs to an entity 'God' whose existence is the ontological condition for thinking unity.

The result of this rationalizing logic was to bifurcate the concept of God into (i) a personal God that could be experienced, loved by humans, and (ii) an impersonal God, beyond the reach of human imagination. To back this up orientalists fabricated a conceptual opposition between the terms *nirgun* and *sargun* as descriptors for the impersonal–personal notions of God. *Nirgun* signifies the experience of an impersonal God whose qualities include ineffability, formlessness, detachment, which taken together implies a deity who is absolutely transcendent. The term *sargun*, on the other hand, is indicative of God as a personal entity, with infinite names and attributes, signifying a fullness or involvement with all things, therefore absolutely immanent.

In contradistinction to this dualistic approach, Guru Nanak, when he does occasionally use these opposing terms, regards them as the same, as opposites that coincide in the One: *nirgun aap, sargun bhī ohī* – being absent the same One is also fully present; or, the One detached from all things is the same One involved in all things.[16] Another way to explain this is to say that God actualizes all existence yet remains forever detached and formless, the same One: *sargun nirgun nirankar, sunn samadhi aap, aapan kia Nanaka aape hi phir jaap.*[17]

The question, of course, is what exactly is it that connects opposing attributes – transcendence\immanence, personal\impersonal, One\Many, form\formless, cosmos\psyche, existence\void, material\ideal, self\other, I\ not-I – yet retains oneness? Stated differently, is there a *name* for the function of consciousness that disjunctively synthesizes opposites yet remains one? What is this connective agency by means of which all existing things acknowledge their non-existent source?

Guru Nanak simply calls this associating agency *nām*, which is perhaps the most prevalent word in the lexicon of *gurmat*, the foundational principle of Sikh philosophy, alongside the words *guru* and *śabda*. A literal, theological translation of *nām* might simply be something like 'God's Name(s)'. But as Nanak and his successor Gurus use it, *nām* cannot be reduced to God's Name, or the names attributed to individual deities. In Sikh philosophy *nām* serves to replace what is named in other traditions as 'God', for the simple reason that the word 'God' itself is little more than a tool for calling this entity to mind at will. As Nanak uses it, *nām* renders the need for such an entity superfluous. If anything, *nām* is used paradoxically in *gurmat* philosophy serving, on the one hand, to dispense with the notion of *nām* as *belonging to* an eminent entity, while at the same time opening up *nām* as an active a/ theological concept.

So how best to understand *nām*? A helpful clue is provided by the third Nanak, Guru Amardas, who writes the following in a verse dedicated entirely to understanding the principle of individuation (or contraction) of consciousness as *haumai*. According to Guru Amardas:

> *haumai* acts in opposition to *nām*,
> these two cannot be in the same place or time. GGS p. 560

> *haumai navai naal virodh hai*
> *doe na vasai eko thae*

The suggestion here is that *nām* and *haumai* constitute two divergent and ultimately irreconcilable tendencies. *Haumai* is consciousness contracted by a human mind as it comes into contact with the material world through any social nexus, specifically through the mediation of language. However, the 'I' or self that is formed through social conventions has a tendency to forget its primal agentive source and thus forgets to primarily identify itself with its own image and the name given by society\family\father. Forgetting its inherently creative capacities, and in its quest to increase its power of existence, this self objectifies its relations to the world, in the process projecting everything as an identity, including itself. The tendency of *haumai* to forget the primal power from which it was created, sees the world as an obstacle to be mastered or controlled. By contrast, *nām* expresses precisely the opposite tendency – the conative tendency within all created things. The conative refers to a tendency within living things not merely to exist but to expand and realize its potential to the maximum by *connecting* across differences to everything in the world. As a tendency *nām* is therefore not something external to the world but its innermost principle of creative existence.

Keeping in mind the impossibility of defining *nām*, we can nevertheless suggest some of its attributes as follows. We could say that *nām* is that which inheres or subsists within each existing thing – sentient, organic, inorganic, cosmic, psychic – ensuring the continuity of a thing even as it undergoes change and becoming. *Nām* is the dynamic forming force, or form-giving power, which persists in the nature of each living and non-living thing, even as these things or beings are continually changing. For example, all things, living or otherwise, are never stable identities but constantly changing. Yet despite this change, something subsists in these changes, not as the same, nor as an identity, but as each thing's intrinsic power of self-differentiation. This paradoxical constancy-despite-change, its remaining One despite constantly becoming many different forms, is *nām*.

Stated differently, *nām* can be described as the underlying resonance, the 'mnemic theme' to use Raymond Ruyer's term, or melodic theme, that underpins all creation and created beings (Ruyer: 56–7).[18] *Nām* is the resonant unpulsed vibration that marks the working of every conscious subject: individual, societies, organs, cells, atoms, molecules – the entire cosmos. It is what gives the cosmos and the psyche a directionality, a tendency to expand, to live. In this sense, *nām* is that which links materiality to ideality. *Nām* is another name for consciousness understood as the capacity for immediate self-relation, self-proximity of an organism, self, individual, cosmos and so on.

The implication of *nām* as a concept or experience is that cosmos\ psyche are preceded by a primal force (*nām*) and a cohesive directionality, which is ontologically prior to anything that comes into being. As the *real*-izable name or form of all reality (*satnām*), *nām* is also the elusive the Name-of-the-Beloved, and therefore cannot be objectified. It is always that which is given as immediacy – pure consciousness, that which cannot be appropriated. Rather, it can only be re-called, remembered, by re-attuning one's individuated consciousness (*haumai*) to *nām* as melodic theme. In other words it cannot be known but only experienced through methods, through practices that re-attune us to its forming force. Hence the need for discipline and praxis.

nām as discipline\praxis

The idea of *nām* as a 'mnemic' or 'melodic theme' is a helpful one as it points to a form of consciousness as an inner orientation that is 'directed to a living engagement' with itself (psychically) and with its environment (cosmically).[19] Consciousness is this unending engagement between self\ other, lover\beloved and psyche\cosmos that renews itself constantly in each moment. As a oneness that eternally differentiates itself and yet remains One, it is like a 'harmonic melody', a kind of melodic theme which connects all materiality to ideology and vice versa. This 'mnemic theme' pervades all modes of time and everything that exists in the sense that it 'constitutes the melody, rhythm, through which each thing forms itself' and passes out of existence (Grosz: 216). The mnemic/melodic theme implies 'patterns of internal alignment', organization and directionality within individual psyches and within the cosmos. It is by means of such mnemic themes that 'values are imbued to organic and inorganic forms' (Grosz: 216). Most importantly the mnemic theme provides an 'enjoyable' form through which a being not only creates itself but inherits and transmits value to its individual self, its social collective and its broader environment (Grosz: 217).

As the fundamental resonance that connects cosmos and psyche, *nām* is also intrinsically connected to the *ways* in which we live, whether this is at the level of our body–mind or how this body–mind interacts with the world around it. The key here is the function of memory which can be of two types: (i) *habit memory* which is accrued through repetition of similar types of actions such as (for the sake of argument) operating a hand pump to provide water and hitting a tennis forehand stroke, where repeated actions are stored as muscle-memory, or perhaps learning a poem by heart; and (ii) *memory proper* by means of which we can access an event or image that has occurred and is stored in our individual consciousness. In Sikh philosophy both habit memory, which determines our bodily behaviour and actions, and memory proper are equally associated with mundane worldly and spiritual functions, and therefore have an intrinsic connection to *nām*. This becomes evident when our habits break down and become detrimental to our lives and the lives of others.

This is where Guru Nanak specifies a form of discipline called *nām simaran* – literally the constant remembrance or bringing to mind of *nām*. As a discipline it is meant to provide a mode of repetition for the body and mind, with the aim of reorienting our habits in accordance with *nām*. There are various levels of practical repetition that might begin with simply repeating a divine Name, for example, *vahiguru*, in accordance with prescribed techniques of breath control. Or it can involve *paaṭh* – the recitation of scriptural verses. A third method which practitioners perform individually and collectively is *kirtan* – the singing of the Gurus' hymns to prescribed musical melodies and rhythms (*rāga* and *taal*).

Many Sikhs practice all three of these to varying degrees. Ultimately, the idea is to begin with mechanical repetition by simply repeating the names in the manner of a mantric\tantric exercise. In the *gurmat* tradition this adoration of *nām*, attunes the body–mind into certain habits. Over time, as the body–mind complex masters the prescribed disciplines, these habits become ingrained and enter the deeper recesses of consciousness, so that one can draw upon *nām simaran* at will, at any time and in any situation as a way of calming body and mind. In this sense *nām simaran* is essential to the bodily and mental health of the practitioner.

But the end goal of *nām simaran* is not just physical or mental health but to achieve a spontaneous attunement of one's desires, actions, thought and speech. This is achieved when *nām simaran* effects spontaneous egoloss such that one's 'I' is naturally attuned to its not-I. This paradoxical dialectic between *nām* and ego should remind us of Guru Amardas's injunction that *nām* and ego (*haumai*) cannot be in the same place at the same time. It is also evident in the etymology of the word *simaran* (to remind\to repeat\ to remember constantly). Derived from the Indo-European root *smr* (to remember, to hold in mind) the term also resonates with the Sanskrit root *mr* and the word *marana*, to die or pass away, suggesting that *simran* is a form of remembrance–repetition that repeats the letting go or renunciation of one's ego. Stated differently, *simaran* is first of all remembrance of one's own mortality, of ego-death, and through remembering this, one's inner vibration comes into resonance with the underlying vibration of the cosmos. In *gurmat* philosophy this underlying vibration that links cosmos and psyche is called *anhad nad* or *anhad śabda* – the unpulsed vibration or unpulsed Word. Indeed, the unpulsed vibration par excellence is none other than *nām* itself. As a discipline *nām simran* is meant to creatively attune us to our immediate environment, and by doing so, to effect changes in society and the world around us.

Discussion questions

(1) In what way must we reorient our conceptions of ontology to include Sikh philosophy? What's the difference between ontology, ontogenesis and onto-epistemology in the context of Sikh philosophy?
(2) How is the concept of void conceptualized within Sikh philosophy?
(3) What is a *gurmukh*? What is a *manmukh*? Compare and contrast the notions of freedom pertinent to each of these states.
(4) What are the five *khands*? Describe the relationship between the *khands*.
(5) Western philosophy and theology's separation and evaluation of (positive) 'form' from (negative) 'formlessness' may be demonstrated in its prevalence as a common trope in films and stories. How do

reconsiderations of void from a negative 'emptiness' to a positive 'brimming with potential' realign our perceptions of reality?

(6) Memory often is defined in terms of contracted *kāl*-centric time, something that can only exist within particular living beings. How does a realignment back into expansive *akal*-centred time alter our conceptions of memory? What does memory mean? Who or what can have memory?

(7) Can you think of some practical and theoretical advantages of rendering *nām* as a 'melodic theme' or 'mnemic theme'?

(8) What does it mean to say that *nām* is a post-theological (or a/ theological) concept?

Death, rebirth and transmigration

Meanings of death

No matter what stage of life one is at, or whether one's inclinations are devotional, philosophical, scholarly or perhaps all three at once, anyone undertaking a close reading of Sikh scripture is immediately struck by a pervasive and persistent theme: the completely intertwined nature of life and death. It is the overall coherence and inseparability of life and death in verse after verse, page after page that makes the teaching worthy of philosophical investigation and inspiring at the same time.

In this chapter I ask the questions: What is death for the Sikh Gurus? How do they approach it in their writings? This will lead us into a discussion around the questions: Why do we fear death? How can we face death? Is death final? Or is there life after death? Do we have immortal souls? Can a philosophical understanding of death help us to live our lives in certain ways rather than others?

How, then, is the topic of death approached in Sikh scripture? Certainly, this literature never seems to convey a pessimism about death even when the subject of mortality is broached more or less directly or when, as Guru Nanak reminds us, death is simply inevitable because it is itself subject to *hukam* – the universal law of nature. Everything that comes into existence must pass away. This inevitability also affects the gods:

Death inevitably strikes
Even the likes of Indra.
Brahma's domain also is subject to death,
Likewise Shiva's world will ultimately come to nothing

(GGS: p. 287)

Each sentient and non-sentient being comes into existence
With death written as its fate

(GGS: p. 876)

Death doesn't wait for auspicious days, or
Ask whether it's the light or dark side of the month.

Some are treated harshly, others well cared for.
Some leave armies and palaces to the sound of drums
Nanak, this heap of dust returns to dust

(GGS: p. 1254)

Yet the inevitability of death need not induce a morbidity in one's attitude. Rather, it should serve as a constant reminder that one should cherish and value life instead of being swayed by false pretensions of immortality, which is nothing more than the play of ego. Mortality encompasses both life and death. Just as creation is unthinkable without void, so death is incomprehensible without life. Listen, for example, to Kabir who says that even a cursory glance at human habits and behaviour reveals a problematic duality that has embedded itself into our experience of reality: a duality between the desire for life and a fear of death. We desire more and more of life, even if it is of poor quality, but we shun death, as in the example he gives of a woman celebrating her child's first birth anniversary:

In celebration the woman exclaims: it's my child's birthday, he is
    growing up.
How little she realizes that he is growing towards his death.
The more she cuddles him saying he's mine! He's mine!
The more the angel of death laughs.
Lured by false attachment
This world is trapped in duality [life versus death]
Says Kabir: discard this poisonous love, it leads only to death

(GGS: p. 92)

Fear of death

Echoing these sentiments the Sikh thinker Giānī Sant Singh Maskin notes how interesting it is that 'we all ask for more life'. 'But why', he asks, 'does no one ask for more death?'[1] To most of us the answer might seem obvious. It is because we have a very natural and understandable fear of death. Which of course begets the question: Why? Why do we fear death? Clearly, it is because (i) no one escapes it, or (ii) as one philosopher aptly puts it, the 'fact that we die is perhaps the most important fact about us' (May: 4). In other words the fact of death simply outweighs every other fact about our lives for the simple reason that every other fact about us also comes to an end when death beckons.[2] There is no 'us' after death in the sense that our life-projects, our relationships with friends, with kith and kin, even with our enemies, our each and every involvement in the world, good or bad, come to an end.

These involvements and entanglements in the world with people, things, even beliefs create attachments, and these attachments give us a sense of who we are. We love life and ask for more of it, even if it happens to be a very third-rate life. This doesn't mean that we don't know about death, or that we're completely shielded from it – we do, and we aren't. Nor indeed that we don't experience something of the pain of others' death – we certainly do. But we do so in a way that constantly objectifies death, removes it from our sense of self. Death comes, we say to ourselves, but *not yet, there is still time*! The point being that our ordinary mind in its state of everyday attachment constructs an understanding of time as a buffer against my (present) time in which I experience myself and the world, and the time of my death. The mind does everything to prolong this buffer through a kind of *forgetfulness* of one's death.

Giānī Sant Singh Maskīn, an oral exegete who trained in the Nirmala tradition of Sikh thought, makes this point in the set of lectures transcribed in the volume *Guru Chintan* (*The Guru's Philosophy*):

> To fear death and to desire more life seems natural, but it is worth putting these opposing tendencies [fear versus desire] into perspective. To that end it is worth examining the relationship between death and sleep. In the esoteric traditions sleep is often considered akin to death in many ways. For example, in the state of deep sleep one's self loses connection to the things one has become attached to in waking life. With sleep we anticipate waking up and reconnecting to the things we love and are attached to, such as family, involvements in the world, projects . . . (*jaagan nal tutai sambhand jurr jandai hai*). This anticipation is due to memory which establishes a continuity of my past life and actions into a future, a continuous stream of consciousness. This continuity is established by the self which assumes that when I wake up, 'I' will still be my same self. Because of this assumed continuity we don't fear sleep.

> But death is a state where the connections I have formed to my-self and the world are deleted permanently. The stream of consciousness is not only broken, but forever wiped out. This is why we fear death. Thus, the point that Guru Nanak emphasizes is that we should focus less on fear of death than on our *tendency to forget death*. We should be more afraid of *forgetting* death than death itself.

For Guru Nanak this forgetting and objectification of death, even when we experience or objectify the death of others, boils down to a particular conception of time that becomes constituted as an existential orientation towards time. Not surprisingly the theme of time and death is an ubiquitous one in the philosophy of the Sikh Gurus, which can be gleaned from the fact that the word for time (*kāl*) is also routinely used for death. As argued in previous chapters, *kāl* represents our ordinary, everyday sense of time, in which we think and relate to time only as a static spatial grid, a screen on which objects in the world, including ourselves, appear to move between set coordinates, for example, from past to present to future. But this spatialization results, Nanak suggests, from an immersion into a form of consciousness that splits time into three distinct modes (*aadh*-beginning, *madh*-middle and *anth*-end). These three modes of time enable our self-consciousness to relate more easily to the continuous movement of time by generating the illusion that the self has control over the succession of time. By positioning the self as maker of its own time, we insert a sense of distance between subject and object, and it is this *di*-stance that gives rise to the dualisms we impose on life and world: inner and outer, life versus death, my-time versus death-time. It is precisely this sense of distance which buffers the sense of time created by ego, the time of one's own life, from death-time. In doing so it creates a delusional sense of duality and forgetting in which we are all immersed.

The effect of *kāl*-time emerges most poignantly in how we recount or remember the time of our life, which is almost always through sequential narrative-time.[3] The purpose of narrative-time is to keep us focused and immersed in the present, but in a way that separates us from the past and future. Thus the kind of memory based on narrative is, in reality, a forgetting. The past is that which is over and done with; the future is not yet here. In Nanak's philosophy, the cumulative sense of this 'not-yet' is precisely the problem that needs to be confronted existentially. Nanak's strategy is to collapse the dualism by shrinking the narration of the time of one's life into a single night, which he depicts as the four watches of the night corresponding to stages of infancy, childhood, youth, old age and death, as exemplified by the following hymn composed in the musical register of *Sri Rāg*:

In the night's first watch, my trader friend,
    You were despatched to the womb.
Hanging upside down in the womb, my trader friend,
    Your thoughts and prayers were fixed on the One.
Upside down you prayed,
    Your devotion was complete.
Free of convention you came into this world
    Naked you'll leave the world.
Each helpless creature must endure the written fate its forehead bears.

Says, Nanak: in the night's first watch my soul,
You'll be posted to the womb.

Engrossed in the night's second watch, my trader friend,
    The focus of your mind was lost.
They played with you, my trader friend,
    Like Krishna in Yashoda's house
Each took their turn to play with you:
    Your mother said, 'this child is mine'!
Remember, foolish mind,
    You'll have nothing in the end,
So let this wisdom fill your thoughts
    As you forget the One who fashioned you.
Says, Nanak: in the nights second watch, my soul,
    The focus of your mind was lost.

With the coming of night's third watch, my trader friend,
    Your thoughts were fixed on wealth and looks.
You quite forgot, my trader friend,
    The Name which saves you from your bonds.
Here all who forget the Name
    Must live distracted by the world.
Obsessed with wealth and drunk on looks,
    You've wasted the time of your life.
You neither traded in righteousness
    Nor made good deeds your friends.
Say, Nanak: in the nights third watch, my soul,
    Your thoughts were fixed on wealth and looks.

In the nights fourth watch, my trader friend,
    The reaper comes to the field.
No one knows, my trader friend
    When death comes to see them off.
Death's time is known to God and no one else.
    This lamentation is quite false
The dead one is their kin no more.
    And what you get is only that
On which you fastened so much love
    Says Nanak: in the nights fourth watch, my soul
The reaper harvested the field.

                                (GGS: p. 74)

As the previous composition indicates, to the person who refuses to confront the implications of time as radically impermanent – 'one dies of course, but not me, not yet!' – Nanak projects the true nature of time as *akāl*, a concept introduced and developed in Chapter 2. One of the most important terms in the Sikh lexicon, the literal reading of *akāl* conveys something akin to the death of ordinary time or *kāl*-time. *Akāl* signifies a non-time which cannot be conceptualized through linear narrative. In this sense it is also treated as a divine time. Signifying more than just a negation of ordinary time (*kāl*), the term *akāl* can be more usefully envisioned as an infinite expansion of time, a deepening or making-immanent of time. Unknowable by nature, *akāl* can only be realized through a radical reorientation of the self, a conversion of the self from its self-attachment to a sense of mortality that is in tune with the eternal becoming of creation, in tune with *hukam*. Whereas people who are immersed in *kāl*-time ordinarily lament the passing of time, grieving for things lost, suffering pain when attachments are broken, fearing and forgetting the onset of death, Nanak suggests that fear of death results ultimately from the ego's habitual obstruction, and forgetting of, a deeper and more natural sense of time *akāl*, one that is beyond the capacity of ego to comprehend. By renouncing self-attachment and accepting *akāl* as always already written within the self (*Nanak likhia nal*), it is possible to be released from the fear of death. By doing this one inculcates a psychological state of fearlessness (*nirbhau*).

So what Nanak does is actually shift the emphasis from fear of death to a more productive stance: *Why fear death?* The fear of death is due to anxiety generated by not understanding, or relating to, the true and more authentic nature of time, *not* as an end-time (*kāl*) but as *akāl*, the time of eternal ongoing creation and destruction, not in cycles which would still be the perspective of *kāl* but in the very nature of time as creative moments that don't simply succeed each other in an eternal becoming. In this eternal becoming time is born anew in the very moment that the previous moment passes away. *Akāl* is therefore time that remains ever-fresh, ever unaffected by the three modes of time.

Why, then, should we fear death? What this question demands of us, according to Nanak, is a fearless attitude to death (*nidar*). But where does this fearlessness come from? Apart from the perspectival shift which has already been noted, Sikh scripture gives us further useful hints, such as this one by Bhagat Kabir:

Kabir:
There's a kind of death which creates fear in men's hearts
The real nature of that death is revealed to me through the Word.

How can I die when I've already died to my self?
Only they die, again and again, who know not the One.
Everyone says: 'he dies, she dies' to themselves, but 'not me'.
But one becomes deathless when one dies to the self

(GGS: p. 327)

Facing death: The deathless state

At the end of the above verse Kabir opens up the tantalizing possibility that death, or certainly the kind of death that is feared, is not all there is. He asks us to confront the possibility that death may neither be final nor sufficient. '*One becomes deathless*', he says, '*when one dies to the self.*' For some this might be slightly confusing. For did we not say earlier that death is inevitable? How can this inevitability be squared with Kabir's assertion that it is also possible *not to die*? Either there is death or there isn't death? Right?

Maybe not, for as Kabir states elsewhere, we all grieve when others die, but he (Kabir) would only grieve *if he had to live forever* (Kabir GGS: p.325). Endless life, it seems, is even more unpalatable than death. So it is not death he fears so much as endless life which is to be feared. What's important, therefore, is the *kind of death* we ought to desire. I don't want to live forever, says Kabir, but at the same time, I don't want to die *as the world dies* (Kabir GGS: p. 325). In other words, there is a conventional death that everyone fears, but there is also an entirely different kind of death, a more authentic death that is triggered by dying to the self, or dying to the Word. And this authentic death results in states variously referred to as *akāl* (timeless), *amrita* (deathless), *amar* (undying) and *amarapad* (the state of non-death). It may be helpful to juxtapose these with their originating terms as follows:

kāl	>	*akāl*
linear time	>	nonlinear time
death/darkness		non-death
mritya	>	*amritya*
death		deathlessness
mar/maraṇā	>	*amar/amarapad*
to die		deathlessness
process of dying		state of non-death

At first sight the set of terms on the right-hand side appears to be simple negations of *kāl*, *mritya* and *maraṇā*. The impression given is that *kāl/akāl*, *mritya/amritya* and *mar/amar* are simply binary opposites, where the impulse of change and becoming associated with everyday time, conventional death and dying can be negated to give timelessness, eternity, immortality.

However, this confusion arises from modernist secularizing interpretations that import an ontotheological framework into readings of Sikh scripture. This ontotheological framework transplants a metaphysical binarism which has the effect of devaluing *akāl*-time at the expense of a more conventional form of time which simply inflates *kāl* into endless succession of identical time-moments – which is effectively the conventional understanding of eternity or immortality.

It is precisely this duality that both Kabir and Nanak are trying to dispel by offering us a more complex and authentic perspective on time and death grounded in egoloss, death of the ego, dying to the self. From this perspective, the self negates itself in the moment it is created, but only to be reborn or re-created anew in the very moment that it dies. So what we have is not the eternal repetition of the same, but an eternal creativity which encompasses time and impermanence without being reduced to this.

Dying to ego, or egoloss, is not a finality, and it does not happen *in* time. Rather, it is to be practised, to be lived, in the sense that one learns to live the art of dying in one's own life. The importance of this perspective is not only that it breaks with conventional understandings of *akāl/amrita/amarapad* as immortality or eternity of successive, linear time (=*kāl*). More importantly this rupture or breakage happens in the heart of the ego, generating egoloss and the birth of new ego at the same time but without accumulation or marking. As a perspective, therefore, it also fundamentally challenges secular notions of death as a once-and-for-all event. The conventional secular understanding arises from an egocentric individuality (*manmukh*) which engrosses the individual in conventional death characterized by fear of death and dying. As Guru Amardas writes:

> Egocentrics are born, only to die,
>   Yet even their deaths are a waste.
> Attached to duality they remain deluded.
>   Always crying 'it's mine, it's my own', they are ruined.
> Without self introspection, they drown in doubt.
>   True death is attained by those who die to the Word. (p. 363)

Thus, by dying to the ego, by learning how to lose one's own ego as what one delusionally considers to be one's ownmost, one can achieve a liberation in life – referred to as *jīvan-muktī* – that brings about the *death of conventional death*, or the death of everyday, linear time: *kāl kāle*. Such liberation is often spoken of as achieving a state or eternity, but it is neither an eternity in linear time (*kāl*) nor a time beyond or outside mortality. Paradoxically, this eternal state (*akāl, amritya, amarapad*) is accessible within mortality. In other words, although all existence is marked by mortality, there is access to a deathlessness in the sense that it gives access to a deeper more authentic form of time (*akāl*), and therefore a more authentic form of selfhood which is simultaneously in the world but detached from it at the same time.

Such states are by no means impossible. They are achievable in life. Those who managed to achieve them are known as *jīvan-mukta* (liberated-in-life). One who has learnt to die to the self or die to the word, and therefore lives as a *jīvan-mukta*, is also known as *gurmukh*. To die to the Word means that one has learnt to transform the nature of consciousness, language and thought from an everyday practice of language use which assumes '*these words are mine! I can name things because I command my own words*', towards a form of expression where one's speech, thought, desire resonates with the ever-fresh impulse of creation called *nām*:

> Few indeed know the Word (*nām*)
> Through which one kills the self\I to attain release.
> Such dying is not death as such
> But a merger into a blissful state of equipoise.

(GGS: p.120)

Is death final? Is there life after death?

The foregoing discussion might lead us to conclude that death has a finalist status in the teachings of the Sikh Gurus, that death is no more than an actual event in the world in which one's allotted time is up. The social attitudes and funerary practices of Sikhs in the event of death and dying, with its emphasis on calmness, emotional restraint and remaining buoyant and hopeful about the future (an attitude referred to as *chardi kalā*), would also lend credence to this sense of finality. The only difference here is that the Sikh Gurus complicate this apparent finality with many other compositions that seem to suggest an alternative: that death may be much more than the dissolution of the material body, that something or some aspect of consciousness survives the physical body. Listen to the following verses, for example, by Guru Nanak and Guru Arjan:

Coming together, we become separated.
    After separation we came together again
Many lifetimes we've lived, only to die again and again
    After each death we began to live again
Time and again we became fathers, sons, preceptors,
    Countless the species in which we took birth
Before coming to this body. . . .
    What we do now, or did in the past, is done
As our account is written, so we transmigrate over and again.
    Egocentrics die, but gurmukhs are saved.

(GGS: p. 156)

The central message in verses like these seems to be fairly clear. Death may not be the end of the story. Before we attained this body we've lived numerous lifetimes, coursing through countless species, through sentient and non-sentient life forms. And this may not be the end; we may have to live and die, countless more times. In Sikh philosophy this endless repetition of taking birth, living and dying is referred to as *āvāgavan* (or *āvanjān*) which has a variety of meanings: wandering, transmigration, coming and going, or the cycle of birth, death, rebirth.

At first glance *āvāgavan* seems to be a variant of classical Indian (Hindu/Jain/Buddhist) theories of rebirth and *karma* which form a cultural backdrop for the Sikh Gurus, a view that is supported by a fairly widespread acceptance of the idea of rebirth and afterlife in popular Sikh discourses. But as noted earlier, it does not seem to sit well with an even stronger emphasis in the Gurus' teachings about the finality of death and the possibility of being liberated. Moreover, the references to *āvāgavan* raise a number of other questions. Is it rational to believe in rebirth? How does *āvāgavan* mesh with theories of evolution? In the process of coming into existence and going out of existence, does the self as a repository of personal identity remain identical? What exactly is reborn and passed on? What governs the whole process of transmigration? If the notion of *āvāgavan* is simply a part of the theory of *karma* which in turn functions as a way of explaining the inequities present in human societies, why then, are some born with a silver spoon in their mouth while others are destined to suffer in this life even though they may live good lives? Is *karma* a fixed cosmic law which predestines our birth in a particular form? Can we change in this lifetime or is our character already predetermined? All of which leads to the question of freedom: Do *karma\āvāgavan* preclude any real sense of freedom?

In order to gauge a Sikh philosophical perspective on these issues, it may be instructive to take a detour through two short chapters about rebirth written by the Sikh philosopher-theologian Bhai Jodh Singh. These two chapters form part of the influential work of proto-philosophy *Gurmati Nirnai* (Discerning *Gurmat*) published in 1932. In what follows I have chosen to let Jodh Singh explain *āvāgavan* largely in his own words, not least because of its clarity and succinctness but also because of Jodh Singh's stature and influence as a spokesperson for modern Sikh thought. More importantly, his philosophical-theological explanations of rebirth and the karmic process in *gurmat* resonate with prevalent themes in the regnant discourse of psychology in the early decades of the twentieth century. Thus, themes such as consciousness and memory, championed by figures such as William James and Henri Bergson loom large in Jodh Singh's reflections. Especially noteworthy is the way in which his rendering of *gurmat* vis-à-vis the discourse of active and passive consciousness manages to avoid the body/mind or materiality/ideality dualism. I begin by presenting a partial translation followed by a commentary on these two chapters. This will allow me to return in the final sections of this chapter to the question of life and death with which my discussion opened.

Karma and transmigration in Jodh Singh's *Gurmat Nirnai*[4]

According to contemporary psychology, the human psyche consists of two major parts: the conscious (*suchēt* = active memory) and unconscious (*achēt* = passive memory). In the waking state the thread of consciousness (*chētanā*) continues to flow in the mind of every individual.

This thread of consciousness is the result of empirical experiences of the world collected and registered as impressions (*sanskāra*) which are mediated by the faculty of cognition\perception\thought (*giān*) to create a theatre of moving images in our minds. Impressions of things that have happened (speech\thought and desires\actions) are recorded and remain in the depths of our psyche. We are almost never aware of this recording\etching of memory in the normal flow of consciousness. This deeper level of consciousness is *achēt bhāg* (unconscious destiny), and it is where thoughts and desires that don't fit with our social conventions are repressed and stored. These repressed thoughts and desires therefore never escape the internalizing operation of the psyche (*antahkaran*) but remain trapped in the unconscious (*achēt bhāg*). Whenever we dream, these repressed thoughts and desires are able to surface in dream-works and take on all manner of forms including evil acts which shake us when we return to the waking state.

It is in the depths of the unconscious (*achēt bhāg*) that man's instinctive nature (*subhāv* = drives, feelings, affect) subsists and creates a psychic inheritance (*virsā/virāsat*) that determines self-character as purely material (i.e. genetic). Rejecting all immaterial theories such as the rebirth of the soul, they believed that human character is physically transmitted via genetic material and becomes part of the family lineage.

By contrast, Indian philosophers have had a long-standing interest in theories of rebirth and transmigration of the soul (*āvāgavan*). They regard a person's character to be the result of traces (*sanskāra*) of past deeds\thoughts\ desires that are imprinted on the soul as it migrates through different births.

But what exactly is *sanskāra*? How do they work?

One way to understand what a *sanskāra* is, or what it does, is to think of what happens when you walk through sand and leave physical traces in the sand. In the same way violations, thoughts, desires that pass through the mind similarly leave traces in it. The only difference is that the im/material substrate on which thoughts and volitions are imprinted is consciousness. If this were not the case, we would not be able to bring our past actions\ thoughts (*karam*) back into memory. If the mind repeatedly recalls (*chitvey*) the same thought\intention, over and again, the imprints left by that thought or volition becomes deeper and deeper such that the trace takes on the form of a habit.

No matter how many drives, motivations or impulses are generated by the body, these processes (*karam*) are the result of the mind's predispositions. For this reason if we repeat those physical acts and mental tendencies again and again, the same volition comes back – it is recalled to mind – again and again. The result being that we have formed a habit out of that act or tendency (*karam*). Over time, these habits come to define our character, and it is the nature of this character that it becomes the cause of our joys and sorrows. However many worldly activities we become attached to, they mostly happen in accordance with our nature, and that nature is the result of past actions. Likewise, through habitual disposition, past actions exert a force which becomes an effect in a future life. It is this coming and going, cause and effect, which creates a self-enclosure, a net from which the person finds it difficult to extricate oneself.

This prevalent theory of cause and effect has ancient roots. But philosophers who uncritically accept it also tend to forget that the perception of a direct link between cause and effect is itself a play of the conscious, waking state, the mind. But where is the supposedly inexorable link between cause and effect for those things that are not within the flow of consciousness\memory? Individualized consciousness also has the power to make any effect into a cause, creating an infinite loop. For example, the pot is an effect. The potter takes some clay and moulds it into the shape of a pot by rotating the wheel through physical effort. But if the potter does not already have an image of the pot in his memory in order to replicate it, he would be sitting idle, and nothing could be made. The link between cause and effect is itself motivated by the power of memory. In *gurmat* this doctrine is referred to as follows:

karaṇ kāraṇ samrath hai
kahu Nanak vichār
Cause is immanent in the doer (kartā)
Who postulates it in time.

The doctrine of *karma* is therefore a version of the cause–effect doctrine and is accepted by Jains, Buddhists and Sankhya philosophy in one form or another. But none of these philosophies believe in the existence of a personal divine. At the outset of the Purva Mimansa the Indian philosopher Jaimani writes that within the actions (*karam*) there is an ineffable force (*shaktī*) which, at the right time, spontaneously produces results of its own accord. Jaimani does not regard a personal God (*ishvar*) as the producer of effects.

According to *gurmat* philosophy, however, *karam* (actions) by themselves don't have innate power to produce results. Between human actions (*karam*), whether psychic or physical, there is the agency of the power of consciousness\ memory (*chētan satta*) which is pervasive everywhere, that is, immanent in all existence and non-existence. If the Sankhya, Jain and Buddhist theories are to be taken seriously, then we would have to accept that the result of one's actions (*karman*) could be attained while one was unconscious or asleep. How then do we make sense of the idea that the receiving of karmic traces even has an origin? (Why does one need to bother with the origin of the idea of karmic traces being etched on us? They would simply be 'authorless', as the Purva Mimansa theorists hold, which is why these Indian schools of thought put so much stock in the idea of an inexorable law of *karma*, the so-called iron law which is considered axiomatic.)[5] According to *gurmat*, just as you need the mediating agency of a magistrate or a judge to put a law into effect, for example, when an evil actor or evil intention (*mandh karni*) needs to receive its just punishment, so the Sikh Gurus regard an immanent or pervasive force of *hukam* to be the originating source of the effect:

hukami utam nich
hukam likh dukh such paieh (Japji)

But in addition to this, *gurmat* as a philosophy also states that the writ with the pen of *hukam* operates through our actions, in the sense that we ourselves are complicit in the operation of *hukam*.

It was previously argued that individuation (*haumai*) came into existence through formless or impersonal *hukam*. Once *haumai* becomes the building block of human consciousness and drives the formation of one's personality, then any mental or physical actions performed take on specific character traits of that personality. Whatever vices we have within us, these become our limitations chaining us to a particular character trait, and so we have to bear the consequences of our actions. What this effectively means is that vices that become embedded in our character keep returning to cause mental and physical pain and suffering. This notion can be corroborated from the Gurus' statements.[6]

If, as stated earlier, past actions (*karman*) are etched into our consciousness according to formless or impersonal *hukam*, it follows that the totality of all actions accumulated by one's consciousness over a lifetime cannot simply be erased by *hukam*. Each individual has to suffer the consequences of these actions, good or bad.[7] Now although vices are an innate result of *karam*, there are also those causes in which vice becomes prevalent and gives rise to suffering. And when conditions of suffering become intolerable, they affect our character. For this reason previous actions (*pichlai karam*), all previously imprinted by traces (*likhai lēkh*), constrain us to walk or act in ready-made grooves, that is, to behave in predictable and predestined ways (*dhur likhia*). And as long as we keep using our normative logic, we cannot get into another groove.

In short, there is an intrinsic link between (i) *hukam di kalam* – the operation or writ of *hukam* which is described as *sarab viāpak* (immanent or all pervasive) and (ii) *chētan satta* – the force of consciousness which is *also* described as *sarab viāpak* (immanence). All of which suggests in turn that *hukam* and *chētan satta* are two sides of the same coin, which is referred to either in terms of its operation (*hukam*) or its essence (*chētantā* = consciousness). We should not forget that *hukam* operates according to the actions of sentient beings, and that while there is indeed within sentient beings a power of discrimination to affirm or not affirm *hukam*, without devotional practice (surrender) one's body–mind remains either in the throes of addiction or in a state of mechanical subservience (p. 258).

In the face of this pre-written *karma* one cannot exert one's self-power to overcome it. It needs to be remembered that these accumulated traces (*lēkh*) determine the character or nature of our self. And that the way we act is in turn dependent on this character. Man's powers of wisdom and intellect are useless in the face of these instincts (p. 259).

Above it was stated that *maya* and *mōh* are generated by the creator (*kartā*). And that *hukam* which discerns our past actions is a formless and unknowable force. But keeping all these thoughts in mind can lead us to anxiously ask: What's left in man's control? Where is man's freedom or willpower? Are humans simply limited to what they're given? Does this mean that freedom is necessarily limited by some regulation in nature (*hukam* as 'I am not')? The meaning of freedom does not reside in the enjoyment of my selfishness (*mn manṇanā*) which is autonomy. The foundation of human life is the formless force of *hukam* which is also gifted to humanity as *satguru* instructs us. (p. 260).

The question ultimately arises: How to break this accumulated net of *karam* (actions)? Indian philosophers such as Patanjali, for example, believe that we have to suffer the consequences of previous actions, no matter what. In his Treatise-4, verse 45, Patanjali argues that yogic practitioners harness spiritual energies of mind and body (*kaya vyohu*) and the karmic chains and the cycle of *āvāgavan*. But in *gurmat* one's *karam* (actions) are not accorded such power in themselves. Rather, their effect is to create specific character and habit. As long as we walk or act according to these predispositions, we remain under the influence of previous actions. But if we decide to let go of ego-logic, we can slowly begin to change our previously accumulated habits and thoughts, and begin to take on habits and character traits designated by the Guru (p. 261).

Making sense of transmigration (*āvāgavan*)

What can be learnt from Jodh Singh's discussion of *āvāgavan*? In contrast to earlier chapters in the same book which refer all agency to a personal deity, Jodh Singh's chapters on *karma* and *āvāgavan* move the debate on rebirth onto the terrain of non-materialistic naturalism, that is to say, a naturalized *karma*, a philosophy of nature in which *hukam* and *haumai* are (i) interconnected and (ii) along with *chētan satta* are both aspects of consciousness. Basically, it centres discussion of *karma* and *āvāgavan* back into *this* time, and *this* world – albeit in relation to *akāl*, and recentres it in the body, thereby freeing up human choice or freedom. More importantly, consciousness (*chētantā / chētan satta*) becomes a central element as opposed to either an eminent monotheistic deity or pure secular materiality.

However, the discussion of *āvāgavan* is too short and inconclusive to make any substantive conclusions. For example, Jodh Singh doesn't probe *āvāgavan* any further or develop any overarching or underpinning theory. This might in turn suggest that the Gurus themselves did not wish to speculate on it, other than presenting it as a mythico-poetic backdrop providing signposts towards a deeper understanding of life and death as intertwined processes. In spite of this, what remains intriguing about the Gurus' repeated references to *āvāgavan* and *karma*, as well as Jodh Singh's attempt to naturalize these two concepts, is the directness of the Guru's statements about transmigration as a process in which consciousness moves through different life forms or takes birth in bodies. Clearly, though, the underlying premise for there to be any discussion of or about transmigration as a movement of consciousness is an originary interaction of (supposedly dead) matter and living consciousness. Matter and consciousness cannot be opposed. They are simply different aspects of the same One.

At the same time though, the Gurus are equally direct in saying that the coming and going of transmigration as such is not something to be desired or hoped for, for example, as a way of prolonging life after death. Instead, each individual should maximize their efforts to minimize or eliminate the *karmic* process. If this is indeed the case, it suggests that the root of the problem all along is the bi-polar perspective generated by our inherently limited and contracted consciousness which projects death primarily as a passage out of or ending of life (*jāṇ*) in opposition to the process of coming into life\time\ world (*āvaṇ*). It is precisely this oppositional consciousness that forces us to avoid confronting the reality of death by seeing *āvanjān* as a process of infinitely prolonging life after death, even if that life is full of misery, suffering and unrestricted to the human form.

Sikh philosophy therefore deals with death, but maybe not in such a way that death is the end of life, or life is the end of death, in the sense of being the final event of life. The clue here is in the word *āvaṇ-jāṇ* or *āvāgavan* itself, where coming\going signifies not so much an objectively datable event – for example, she, he or it dies on such and such a date, at such and such a time, and at such and such a place – but rather points to the structure of time itself, as that which cannot be objectified, but must remain subjective *and* objective, therefore an aporia or irresolvable contradiction. What if the problem all along is the sheer limitation of the understanding or the concept of time in which we try to frame the time of life *as* the time of death? Of course, the caveat here is that life and death are inseparable from time; for example, *kāl* equally signifies death, the time of a particular life within *kālijug* – the time of the world.

But this raises further questions. Is it possible to read *āvāgavan* as a radical opening of everyday worldly time (*kāl*), as the normative standpoint from which we frame life (*jīvan*) and death (*maut*)? How do we free *āvāgavan* from the framework of *kāl* itself? Does the very concept of *āvāgavan* force the mind, as individually contracted consciousness, to think beyond its contracted bubble? Is it this contracted bubble of consciousness (ego-mind) that leaves us stuck in a cycle of cause and effect? How can we snap out of ego-based *kāl*-time and embrace a different mode of time-consciousness, one that can in turn provide a more nuanced approach to life-death-rebirth?

I would like to offer two different approaches to understanding time, both of which seem to be consonant with Sikh philosophy's emphasis on seeing life and death as intrinsically related processes. The first locates *āvāgavan* within the mythic notion of time that Sikh thought inherits from Indian cultural frameworks. It is one that takes human finitude and expands it infinitely into the cyclical framework of the ages of the world. The second model opens up two entirely different modes of time and confronts the problem of death more directly, refusing to countenance any notion of death as negation or opposition.

Time after time: *āvaṇjāṇ* as infinite finitude

As noted in previous chapters the theme of time is one of the most pervasive in Sikh scripture insofar as it weaves together so many issues including self, world, cosmology and psychology. Nanak's refusal to treat time and finitude separately from an objective cosmology or from the subjectivity of human existence and psychology reflects the aporetic nature of time, the fact that it is a contradiction irresolvable by the limited–contracted consciousness from which we try to understand time and its effects. Given its aporetic nature, Nanak uses various strategies to depict the workings of time. For example, Nanak often alludes to the cosmological scheme embedded in Indian culture and spirituality which happens to be articulated in terms of grand cosmic cycles (*kalpas*) of creation and dissolution that follow each other endlessly, and much smaller cycles or ages of the world or *yugas*: *satyug, tretayug, dvapuryug* and *kāliyug*. Taken together these ages of the world depict a successive degeneration of moral order in the universe:

> *satyug sat treta juggi duapar pujachar*
> *tino jug dirai kāl keval nām adhar*

> In the first three ages of the world
> Truth, religion and piety prevailed
> But with the passing of these three
> Only in *kalijug* can one obtain the support of *nām*.

(Ravidas GGS: p. 346)

> *satyug treta duapar bhanijai*
> *kālijug uttamo jug mahi*

ahe karu kare su ahe karu paee
koi ne pakariai kisai thai

Of the four cosmic ages
Kalijug is the highest (for in it)
Our actions have consequences
Few seem to have grasped this truth.

(M5 GGS: p. 406)

jug charai nām uttam śabda bichare
kāli mai gurmukh uttarai par

In the four ages of the world
Contemplating *nām* is the highest virtue
In the *kaljug*
Gurmukhs have been saved.

(M3 GGS: p. 229)

A superficial reading of these verses might lead us to conclude that the conception of time in Sikh philosophy follows classical Indian thought, broadly speaking, in that it is merely cyclical, where all things are ruled over by an impersonal order (*dharam* or *hukam*), thereby introducing ambiguity into the meaning of history, or worse, a lack of historicity altogether. In this reading, Nanak would appear to subscribe to a mythic conception of time wherein time is recurrent and ahistorical.

However, two things are immediately evident throughout the Gurus' writings. First, *kālijug* is the only favoured cycle of time or age of the world, insofar as it brings time to an end by going back to the beginning. Second, all of the ages and systems of time (*satyug, tretayug, dvapuryug*) become seamlessly concurrent with and incorporated into *kāliyug*. What this highlights is the importance of *kāliyug* as the cycle of time irreducible either to mere impermanence (the succession of individual moments that are essentially the same and pass out of existence) or to infinite repetition of the same eternity, which is broken only when the world cycle itself comes to an end. Rather, the finitude exemplified by *kāliyug* is to be understood as the coming into existence of a moment immediately followed by its inexorable passing into a new moment. Hence the infinite production of difference which is also the ground of mortality.

With this emphasis on *kāliyug*, what we are effectively shown is the possibility of an openness within time itself. The seemingly cyclical, mythical nature of time (hence the depiction of the cycles of time as the ages of the world) is actually a metaphor for a finitude of a higher order, something like an infinite finitude, in the double sense that finitude repeats itself eternally, as well as the idea of an infinite openness within finitude. In other words *kāliyug* is favoured because it symbolizes the aporia of time insofar as it combines two contradictory characteristics. On the one hand, the forward movement of time producing something new *in time*. On the other hand, the impermanence of each new moment which becomes old and passes in that very instant.

As noted earlier, this combination of newness and impermanence is illustrated in the 'Four Watches' compositions individually composed by Guru Nanak, Ramdas and Arjan. Each of these hymns variously depicts the rise of individual self-consciousness which the Guru refers to as 'My nomadic-trader friend' (*vaṇjāriā mitarā*) within the four-stage drama of human life: (i) pre-birth in human form, (ii) the mind's loss of focus through conventions of childhood and acculturation, (iii) the unhealthy attachment to the world\youth\beauty\riches adulthood and (iv) old age and death.

The Four Watches hymns present the drama of human life on the static screen of our mind with subjects moving in relation to the passing of time from past to future, giving the impression of a constant newness with which the person or life becomes infatuated. Yet it is this very infatuation with conventions and norms that distances her from the existential effects of time – suffering, old age, death. To prevent this distancing and to make the person see the passing of time as an intrinsically subjective experience ('this is my life'), Nanak shrinks the entire drama of human life into a single night, presenting the night's progression as the inevitability of one's own death, the realization of one's own finitude, here and now. By reversing our everyday standpoint, one that is grounded in the secure optimism of daylight in the waking state, Nanak shows how the perspective of impermanence and night is a better indicator of what we call reality.

The kind of stark warnings given in the *vaṇjāriā mitarā* compositions presents the mortal plane of *kāliyug* in an optimistic, if not entirely positive, light as the opening of a temporal horizon wherein one develops one's self-consciousness. Within this temporal horizon each new moment presents the opening of chance, the opportunity to become self-aware, the opportunity for practical self-realization. Moreover, the radically open time characteristic of *kāliyug* allows us to see *āvaṇjāṇ*, the comings and goings of rebirth, not as something external to *kāl*-time of human life, but within it. In this sense, the coming and goings of birth, death and rebirth exist and burst out of each moment of time. Each moment, insofar as it is new, and never stops becoming new, presents an opportunity for the individual to take birth, to be reborn again and again, to die to one's old self, and be reborn again and again. A desirable consequence of this is that the mortal is able to weave this realization into his or her self-consciousness, in a way that allows *kāl*-time to open up, to be expanded into *akāl*-time. And as we have noted earlier, it is only within *akāl*-time that one can become truly self-realized.

This presents quite a contrast from the mythical time frames of *satyug/treta/dvapar jug*, which depict an eternity in which there is no newness, no change, no impermanence. According to the perspective of mythical time, *kālijug* represents a fall from eternal or divine time. From this perspective, *āvāgavan* represents a time without beginning or end, a time that is infinitely open in both directions.

Discussion questions

(1) How do Sikhs approach death? According to Sikh philosophy, how does death tend to factor into our everyday lives?
(2) Why does Sikh philosophy reintegrate conceptions of death and time into its central praxis?
(3) How would integrating the Sikh understanding of death challenge our contemporary perspectives on life? How would this fundamentally alter the societal structures we live within?
(4) Do the Sikh Gurus support the theory of transmigration as we find it in other traditions like Buddhism or classical Hinduism? If so, how do they differ? If not, why?
(5) How does the theory of transmigration fit into the theory of consciousness? Does it improve or embellish it?
(6) What other theories of time do Sikh concepts resonate with? Does this resonate with any 'Western' forms of thought such as Nietzsche's concept of eternal return'?

Self-realization

Life, liberation and health

This chapter returns the focus of our investigation from meditations on death, rebirth, mortality back towards the theme of life. More specifically, if life is a precious opportunity given to us, how does one make the most of it? What is the purpose of life? How to achieve that purpose to the best of our abilities? If, as we have seen from previous chapters, life involves both care of the self (the psychic) and care of the body (the somatic), what does such care involve? The focus on psychic and somatic health provides a glimpse into how the concepts of Sikh philosophy can be practically applied to actual lives.

I begin the chapter with a reflection on the theme of liberation before transitioning towards health, well-being and mindful living. Liberation may seem like an odd place to start given that it normally deals with topics of a metaphysical nature which assume, for example, a separation of matter and consciousness, or the dualism of body versus mind/self/soul. As we have noted in Chapters 2 and 3, however, Guru Nanak's philosophy provides a different guiding principle – one that assumes a fundamental inseparability of the material and the ideal, in a way that allows for the prospect that materiality is conscious or that consciousness is material. It may therefore be more helpful to adopt the stance of im/materiality, which refuses any absolute distinction between the material and the immaterial, instead pointing to a oneness in which body and mind are fundamentally interconnected, which in turn provides the basis for a different ethic of living. From this im/material perspective, liberation is not an escapism to something beyond life, death or time but a liberation from limiting ideas that constrict the ability to live life to its fullest potential.

What is liberation? (*muktī, mōkh, mōkh-duār*)

In Western philosophy and religion, scholarly treatments of the concept of liberation generally vacillate between religious and secular representations.

Religious representations, for example, attempt to make different kinds of affirmation about the varieties of salvation, redemption, absolution and freedom, how to attain these states and the kind of persona and forms that are necessary for such attainment.[1] Secular humanists use terms that have similar connotations but refer to a different goal – a goal that is more social\political than religious. Expressions such as freedom, enlightenment, emancipation usually come to mind.

As the philosopher Kenneth Surin reminds us, common to both secularists and religionists is something that the sociologist Max Weber noted in his classic studies on *The Sociology of Religion*. According to Weber the key aspiration in these various notions of liberation is 'to provide a solution to the "problem" of the world'.[2] Accordingly, the person seeking liberation has to find a way of freeing oneself from something in the world that is deemed unacceptable and incompatible with one's existence in the world. As Surin puts it, from this angle liberation can be seen as 'the name of a desire to overcome, circumvent, or ameliorate an unacceptable condition of being'.[3] In short liberation is intrinsically connected to a condition of the self's relationship to the world that one wishes to overcome. For certain, what is 'important for any thematic of liberation is the insight that there is a need for liberation only because something about the world is distorted, because the world is a place of catastrophes. . . . Whether big or little, potential or real'.[4]

One of Weber's main contributions was to classify and compare religious or ethical traditions that consider the basically 'distorted quality' of the world as a reality. From this classification Weber deduced what he believed to be an axiom: that individuals and groups engaged on a personal quest for liberation were driven by the desire to change the old and current states of affairs, and usher in a new world.[5] This '"desire for the new" is thus the primary, though not exclusive, defining characteristic of liberation'.[6] In this way Weber's theories about liberation implemented far-reaching conclusions about the basic attitudes of world religions and philosophical traditions towards the world and self. Thus Hinduism, Buddhism, Jainism, early Eastern Christianity and early Judaism were world-rejecting in attitude and were positioned on one side of the comparative scale. Islam and the ethical Chinese traditions such as Taoism and Confucianism were classified as relatively adjusted to the world and therefore positioned in the middle of the scale. And at the far end was Protestant Western Christianity whose desire was classified as 'world overcoming' or 'world mastery' inasmuch as it alone was able to overcome and master the older religious world and establish modernity with its unquenchable desire for the 'new'.

Where on this scale might a Sikh perspective on liberation be expected to fit in relation to the major world systems? Might it be possible to find similar expressions from a Sikh perspective in the work of modern Sikh philosophers? As I noted in Chapter 1, most if not all of these philosophers acquiesced to the philosophical narrative of Western modernity in their efforts to favourably position Sikh thought in the arena of world philosophies and ethical systems. Given that (i) there is a preponderance of terms in Sikh scripture exemplified by the concept cluster *muktī, mōkh, mōkh-duār, mōkh-padvī* and *jīvan-mukt*;[7] (ii) that terms such as *mōkh* and *muktī* refer to states of freedom obtained through release from worldly attachment and (iii) that these terms are also Punjabi cognates for the Sanskrit term *mōksha* which figures so centrally in Hindu philosophies and Western representations of the Indian world view, would it not be reasonable to expect that a theory of liberation is central to the Sikh philosophical perspective?

Surprisingly, however, there is minimal discussion of liberation as a concept even in the works of modern Sikh philosophy, with some authors not mentioning it at all. This lack of discussion could mean one of two things. Either *muktī* or *mōkh* has little or no importance in Sikh philosophy aside from being metaphorical references to an older world-negating system from which it needs to separate itself. Or, there is indeed a Sikh philosophical perspective on liberation (which the prevalence of the concept cluster *muktī/mōkh/jīvan mukt* clearly attests to), but it is one that does not fit within the Weberian schema that dominates modern representations of Indian philosophies. I am inclined towards the second opinion, albeit with a caveat, which is that it points to a third option: that the *gurmat* perspective on liberation is grounded in an epistemology which fits neither the modern Western nor the classical Indian models of liberation.

In order to properly investigate this third option, however, we need to examine more closely the image of the self in Sikh philosophy, building on what we have learnt in earlier chapters. Given that epistemologies are always rooted in understandings of the self, the nature and operations of the ego need to be considered in its own right in order to better understand the concept of liberation in Sikh philosophy. To do this I want to probe a little further into different depictions of self and ego articulated by the Sikh Gurus in their writings. I begin with the notion of affliction or sickness of the self.

Sickness of the self

In a set of hymns recorded in the musical measure of *Rāg Bhairon*, there are teachings that give direct insight into the image of self\mind\ego and how it relates to the theme of liberation. In the opening verse the Guru sets out an axiom:

> The atman (soul) and God (One-All) inhere within each other
> If one accepts this Oneness by killing one's ego (or sense of separation),
> Then all suffering disappears.
>
> (*Rāg Bhairon*)

Two things seem to be implied in this verse: (i) that *consciousness is all there is* and (ii) that consciousness is One and only One. Suffering arises when separation or distance is introduced into pure consciousness. In the next nine verses of this hymn, the nature of this suffering or affliction is further elaborated:

> Diseases of ego make
> A single pain seem everywhere,
> Relief's appointed through the Word.

> Water, air and fire are diseased,
> Diseased is this sensual world.
> Parents and body and wealth are afflicted,
> Afflicted is the family

> Brahma, Vishnu and Shiva are afflicted
> Afflicted is the universe.
> Only those whom the Guru shows God's rank
> Are free of this disease.

> The rivers, seven seas, nine domains of the earth
> And the underworlds are afflicted.
> Only those favored with the divine glance
> Live happy in the truth.

> Diseased are ascetics of all kinds
> Dressed in their orders' robes.
> No help can come from holy books
> Which don't teach that Consciousness is One.

> Afflicted are the wealthy as they feast on fine foods,
> As are those who live only on roots.
> All those separated from nām
> Must finally repent.

(This disease) is not cured by pilgrimage
Accumulating knowledge only makes things worse.
Duality is a formidable disease
Which ties us to the world.
Adoration of the Guru's Word
Removes this disease.
O Nanak, pure are such devotees
Kept safe through (the Lord's) mercy.

(GGS: p. 1153)

In these verses Nanak explains that the sense of separation (*haumai*) is a disease so deep and pervasive that it afflicts everything that exists in this world: the elements, water, fire, air, earth are diseased; society and its conventions are diseased, ascetics and holy people, the gods, materialists, all are afflicted. In short, all things that have come into existence, anything that society has made, whether physical, social or intellectual are afflicted with this disease (*rog*). The message here is forthright that the disease is ego (*haumai*).

But what exactly is *haumai*? Is it not specific to human nature and therefore to our psychic apparatus, as noted earlier in this book? If so, why does the Guru apply it also to nature, natural processes, society and social processes?

In a different composition recorded in *Rāg Āsā*, Guru Nanak probes the nature of ego in more detail and subtly shifts the emphasis towards the idea that *haumai* is not a thing that can simply be identified (hence its elusiveness), but rather that it arises from our actions, thoughts and desires.

In ego they come, in ego they go,
In ego they're born, in ego they die.
In ego they've given, in ego they've taken
In ego they've gained, in ego they've lost.
In ego they're truthful, in ego they lie,
In ego they ponder virtue or sin,
In ego, to heaven or hell they're despatched,
In ego they left, in ego they weep,
In ego they're soiled, in ego they're cleansed,
In ego they lose status of caste,
In ego they're fools, in ego they're smart,
Ignorant of salvation's value
The world is trapped in ego's spell,
Through individuating,[8] creatures are made.
Once the gate is opened, they grasp onto ego,
Without wisdom, all is idle talk.

O Nanak, our fate is set by *hukam*
As we see others, so we are seen.

(GGS: p. 466)

The nature of ego is this: that in it our actions are done,
The bondage of ego is this: that again and again we are born.
From where does ego arise, what is it that makes it depart?
The order of ego is this: that past actions decide where we roam.
Though we inherit ego as a disease, it also contains its own cure.
Says Nanak: O hear everyone, if one receives (the Lord's) grace,
Live by the Guru's Word, and all suffering will cease.

(GGS: p. 466)

In other words, it is generated and perpetuated through an attitude we adopt towards the world in general. Hence, it afflicts every aspect of our social world, from the moment we are born to the moment we die. Once it infects our social worlds through prevalent practices of ego, it casts its shadow everywhere infecting the world we live in, indeed, all of existence.

But what does it mean to say that the entire world, all existence, is afflicted by ego? At this point, it may be helpful to revist and reiterate part of our discussion of cosmic and psychic creation in Chapter 3, namely, the discussion of the *Rāg Marū* hymn. Here, a very similar issue came to light in regard to the creation of the cosmos. This composition showed how Guru Nanak connected the macrocosmic creation process with the microcosmic processes going on in human psycho-somatic experience. According to this composition, both cosmic creation and the formation of the human psyche are propelled by the process of individuation. After verse 14 in the *Rāg Marū* hymn, a distinct change in emphasis can be detected in the Guru's narration. At which point we read that in accordance with the will or the desire of the One (*jā tis bhāṇā*) infinite currents of cosmic creation are unleashed, such that the state of oneness appears to transition from a state of absolute void/ undifferentiation/formlessness to a state of infinite becoming, whereupon worlds upon worlds, universes upon universes come into being, pass away and continue coming into being over and again, in an infinite process of creativity.

However, the key take away in this narrative was that the *change in appearance* of oneness from undifferentiated Will (*hukam apārā*) to manifest-differentiated Will (*hukam* as *jagat upaia*) is a process driven by individuation. In other words, *hukam* changes its appearance from undifferentiated void to differentiated *hukam*. Moreover, this individuation, which can also be expressed as a self-differentiation or a differentiation within the self, indicating a willing separation of the self from itself, names exactly the same kind of processes going on in the formation of the human psyche from a state of pre-individual to a self-separating individual. Just as the cosmos is subject to individuation, so the human psyche is also subject to individuation. In other words, *individuation names the process and substance of affliction or disease.*

Clearly, this lands us in a bit of a conundrum. While it might make sense to think of the human psyche as afflicted with disease, does it make sense to say that everything, especially processes of cosmic creation, is also diseased, in the sense that they are empowered by individuation? This raises a further question: If disease or affliction is individuation, then what exactly is individuation?

Again we can answer this question in two ways depending on the perspective we wish to adopt: cosmic or psychic. At the cosmic level, in accordance with its absolutely detached state of self-enjoyment or joyful bliss, the primal One (*nirgun*) wills into manifest being an internal separation from its primal state of void, and this self-separation or primal individuation sets into motion the process of cosmic creation, or the becoming-multiple of One, which basically indicates the unfolding of time and becoming (*sargun*). But this willing remains immanent, or internal to its primal oneness (*nirankar*) in the sense that each thing that is created (whether the tiniest particle or the most expansive galactic system) is co-implicated with the primal One as it develops or undergoes individuation. Thus individuation as a process works by co-implicating or diversifying each thing. Each thing becomes different from itself in and as time, while simultaneously each thing expresses the oneness from which it unfolds. This coexistence and co-implication of things in their oneness and in their infinite multiplicity are expressed by *nām*. In short, while 'God' (to give the One a limiting name and form) afflicts each thing with its own individuation, this cosmic individuation nevertheless remains within the ambit of oneness because it is always already subject to *hukam*.

So, yes! Everything that comes into existence, everything that we regard as nature, is afflicted with, or suffers from, the disease of individuation. But at the same time, everything in nature also contains the cure to this affliction in the sense that it remains in obeisance to *hukam* and therefore remains One in nature. The movement of cosmic individuation is therefore always creative, always renewing, always producing freshness out of everything that passes away. In short: the cure for the affliction is *nām*.

So much for cosmic individuation. But something altogether different takes place in psychic individuation. Guru Nanak calls this peculiar form of individuation (*haumai*). The term *haumai* is a cognate of the Sanskrit *aham* ('I am'), for which the Punjabi equivalent would be *hau*, meaning both 'yes' and 'I am', and is often used as *ahankār* which refers to a sense of pride, or conceitedness deriving from a narcissistic preoccupation with one's own self. In Sikh philosophy *haumai* is mostly used as a compound word: *hau* and *mai*, where *mai* = me, myself (self as an object to itself). The resultant meaning of *haumai* is therefore something like: 'I am me', 'I am myself', 'this self is mine'. What these enunciations point to is a psychic apparatus, namely the ego, which individuates itself through a process of self-willing, better described as an innate tendency to will itself, or to possess itself absolutely.

The problem here is that two different tendencies seem to be at work in the psychic machinery of ego generated by *haumai*. On the one hand, there is the tendency to individuate from oneself, that is, a self-separation or splitting of the self from itself ('I am' versus the 'Me-myself'), through which the 'I' creates within itself the sense of its independent existence. On the other hand, we have the tendency of self-possession, where the objectified 'me' being split off is instantaneously claimed as mine, as *belonging* to the 'I' (*hau*).

How do we account for these dual tendencies? The simplest way into this conundrum is to remember that *haumai*, before it is expressed as an enunciation ('I am myself'), is actually a key component of human experience, and therefore intrinsically connected to our faculties of perception, cognition and judgement. Thus the first tendency (splitting\self-separation\individu ation) is an ontological operation in the sense that *haumai* begins its work as an awareness or consciousness of being separate from the primordial One-All. This contracted consciousness *is* the split or individuation, and therefore it has the quality of a derived ontology. Otherwise, if it were not conscious of its independence from the One, it would be unconscious and would remain absorbed within oneness. Another cause of this secondary consciousness, which is created because of an awareness of distance from the One, is time. To be more specific, the 'I' exists in time, with a beginning, middle and an end. Moreover this 'I' experiences its separation\individuation from the outset through a feeling of anxiety caused by the knowledge of its being flung into a world that it cannot control. Flung into the flow of time, it marches inevitably towards death, over which it has no control.

In the context of everyday life the ego's entire effort is exerted to control the flow of time, very often depicted as the coming and going of waves in the sea existence. To overcome the anxiety of being overwhelmed by this constant coming and going, the individuated 'I' brings into effect a second tendency. It tries to exert a measure of self-control over the flux of existence by imposing homogeneity and permanence into its forms of knowing and controlling the world. This is done by subjecting all interpretation of objects that cognition encounters in the world, to an *a priori* form of identity, that is, by making representations of all objects in thought conform, in advance, to the rule of identity, so that anything it encounters, all reality out there, is already recognized as a self-identical object.

A skeptic might say that it doesn't sound much like a disease! Surely it sounds more like the working of a healthy mind! The kind of mind that is able to distinguish and keep a safe distance between subject and object, inside and outside, light and dark.

Nothing could be further from the truth, however. On closer scrutiny Sikh philosophy suggests that although the ego gives the appearance of health (look how *normal* I am!), the seeming normality is actually part of the self-beguiling effect created by *haumai*. According to *gurmat*, this self-beguiling tendency is called *maya*. Common to many Indic traditions, the term *maya* signifies a powerful force inherent within human individuation for creating delusion. Its purpose is to obscure the true nature of what is really going on in the machinery of the mind and its relation to external reality. In Sikh philosophy *maya* can be regarded as a mechanism by which representation does its work in and through any thinking self which believes itself to be normal and healthy. *Maya* is a power which tricks the mind into believing it is self-identical. And on the basis of this self-identity the mind reproduces all things or objects in the world, including the image of the very self doing the representing, as identities. In short, in the very process of individuating, *maya* is the power that deludes the self into believing the world outside is stable, identical and under control, even as it constantly individuates and creates divisions and opposition into a perceived self (I) and its other (not-I). In other words, *maya* tries to veil the primal oneness, and it is this veiling that creates a deceitful duality (*dūjā bhau*) between self and other, between I and not-I. We can say that the veiling *conceals* the original ontological *relation* that ties one thing to another or all beings to every other being.

What specifically characterizes this delusional tendency within the individuating self is that it reinforces the image of its own oneness by producing an opposite. That is to say, the object becomes its own opposite; it becomes foreign to itself, effectively becoming its own enemy. It deludes itself into seeing its own not-I as foreign to itself. This is the delusion (*bharam*) of duality (*dūjā bhau*) while pretending to be one. Thus the illusion of a bond between self and other created by *maya* becomes the cause of a false relation. It is a false relation because instead of keeping joined the two separated aspects of the psyche (I + not-I, self + other, lover and Beloved), what human individuation does is to give the self the illusion of being free. But from the *gurmat* perspective this freedom is nothing more than the freedom to chain itself to an identity that does not admit difference within itself.

As illustrated in Figure 10, human individuation of this normative kind fetters the individuating self into its own cocoon, which continues to

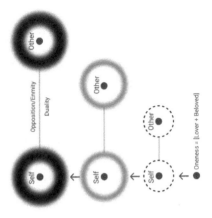

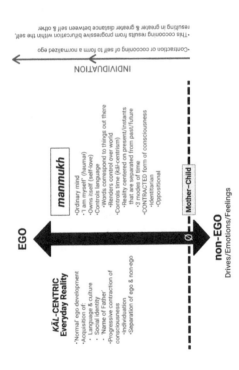

Figure 10 Development of ego or contracted consciousness (*manmukh*).

become more concrete and rigid as the self develops through life. In this way, not only does the power of *maya* conceal itself by disguising itself in the false appearance of what it believes to be its other (the not-I); it also projects the element of foreignness, enmity, opposition, onto the other. What the teachings of the Sikh Gurus allude to vis-à-vis the language of affliction is a process of self-enclosing or cocooning by which an individuating self creates a false unity, which our mind recognizes as identity. However, this identity, which our social acculturation designates as normal or healthy, is nothing more than a defensive shell separating the self from itself. This shell, in turn, is nothing more than the distance we introduce into pure consciousness, thereby limiting it. We then call this defensive limitation 'freedom'. In the modern period this highly limiting and limited freedom has given rise to 'worldviews' attributed to different cultures. Closely examined, however, these 'worldviews' are little more than a view onto world from within the bubble of a heavily contracted form of consciousness we know as nationalized identity. And today this nationalized identity has become the centre of all relations, and the master of the world which it objectifies and surveys at its pleasure.

From the perspective of *gurmat*, however, this is neither freedom nor the work of a healthy mind. Quite the opposite is the case, which is why Guru Nanak refers to *haumai* as a disease that afflicts human consciousness. From this perspective our sense of 'humanity' becomes a kind of viral agent which infects the rest of the world and tries to bring nature under our control. Thus to see *haumai* as a disease is to see it as a problem of the self, which in turn suggests that the *problem is also a practical one*. If it is a practical problem, it is one that can only be addressed by finding a treatment and therefore a possible cure for the disease. And to take this diagnostic logic a step further, the treatment and cure reside in *transforming the self* by transmuting the individuating power without completely annihilating it.

Contraction: Linking consciousness to the body

We're now in a position to begin talking about a treatment for the disease, and hopefully a cure. But before we move fully towards questions of a practical nature, we need to dispel one remaining issue which remains somewhat unclear. We can state the issue in the form of the following questions: In talking about disease or affliction as the Sikh Gurus have done, are they saying that all things are afflicted *because* they individuate? Or is individuation a purely human issue? In other words, is the nature of disease\affliction, and therefore the nature of individuation, ontological or epistemological? Is it rooted in the nature of all things, or is it rooted in human experience and therefore in our perception and cognition of a world that's given?

If it is purely epistemological – and the foregoing discussion might suggest this – then maybe we can just theorize our way out of it? Again *gurmat* suggests a more complicated answer which brings the ontological and epistemological together. Guru Nanak's verses about cosmic affliction of things in the world offer more than just epistemology, or a way of tweaking the human mind and its programming. This might be the case, for example, in Vedanta, where the aim is to return to a state of perfection by getting rid of nescience (*avidya*) and attaining enlightenment (*vidya*).

But if we consider Nanak's verses on cosmic and psychic aspects of individuation in toto, the notion of affliction really comes into its own when we see it in relation to the onset of creation where *hukam* undergoes a shift in emphasis from a state of unmanifest detachment (or void) to manifest attachment, but without losing its fundamental nature as oneness. This shift in self-nature is often presented as infinitely expansive consciousness undergoing a 'contraction' in the sense of willing itself (*hukam*) into manifest being. It is this contraction that gives rise to form out of formlessness.

A helpful way to visualize the nature of such contraction is to think of it as a primal or cosmic limitation such that the infinite One limits itself (by its own *hukam*) into finite forms: time\space\cause which are better known in the Indian philosophies as the three *gunas*: *rajjo gun*, *satto gun* and *tammo gun* or simply *rajas*, *tamas*, *sattva*). Another way to conceptualize contraction or limitation is to think of something like a primal vibration whose frequency is infinitely fast (infinitely expanded) to begin with but becomes contracted through self-willing, which in turn limits and slows down the vibrational frequency. This slowing down corresponds to the ongoing creative evolution of tangible form and matter including, eventually, the human body.

In many religious and philosophical traditions this transition from formlessness to form is depicted as a fall from a pure or higher eternal state of transcendence into a lower state of time as finitude. But this is not the case in *gurmat*. The two states remain One. They are simply different aspects of a heartbeat (systolic\diastolic), or like the rhythm of breathing (inhaling\exhaling), while the agent remains one. The important point here is that what Nanak refers to in his compositions as affliction or disease is more usefully seen as a contraction or a limitation, which is always already part of the nature of the One. Furthermore, to see contraction as an ontological limitation rather than ontological negativity (such as evil or sin) allows human psychic individuation to be more usefully perceived in terms of its material, mental and spiritual aspects. It is a way of bringing the body into consideration as

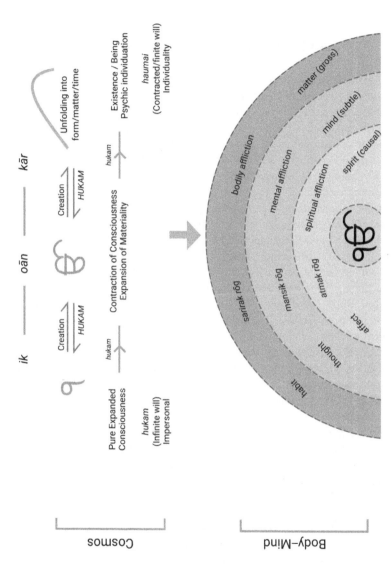

Figure 11 Interconnectedness of the cosmic with the psychic-somatic (body).

part and parcel of any overall treatment and cure of *haumai*. The body is part of a tripartite continuum which is depicted in Figure 11.

Pathways to liberation: *jīvanmuktī* and *jīvanmukta*

As we've noted at various points throughout this book, human individuation has both positive and negative aspects. On the positive side it is necessary for creating a defensive shell that allows us to help control the flux of the world and create a stable sense of identity that brings stability and order to oneself, to one's place in society. The negative aspect emerges when individuation goes too far, creating a separation from the underlying One-All in the form of an individual personhood, which it misperceives as the locus of freedom and as the centre of all reality. The end result is a sense of duality masquerading as personal unity. This sense of duality infiltrates and poisons every relation with things in the world. The self's default stance in relation to other individuals and societies is governed by a combination of fear (*bhau*) and enmity (*vair*). In psychological terms *haumai*, when taken too far, creates a self-constrained individual unable to touch or feel anything outside itself except through the window of its bubble. It is, in other words, a living psychotic individual pretending to be healthy as it spreads its poison and inflicts disease on the environment, on society and on other selves.

In philosophical terms, when self-individuation goes too far, it gives rise to an epistemological problem vis-à-vis the fundamental presupposition of an absolute separation between subjective and objective world, self and other, between the self and the world as 'independent, static entities'.[9]

Hence *haumai* is the root of all epistemological error, and Nanak was deeply aware of this, for it was the very problem he had struggled with since early adolescence and from which he had liberated himself through spiritual self-realization. It is awareness of *haumai*'s intractable nature that prompted Guru Nanak to state that all the processes of our lives – our comings, goings, death and birth, giving, taking, losses and profits, becoming truthful or deceptive, our notions of afterlife, our pleasures, our sufferings, our sense of purity and guilt – are filtered through and ultimately trapped in the mechanism of ego.[10] Indeed, the epistemological error arising from *haumai*/ego is so deep that we lose both knowledge and value of liberation, because we already believe we are free (*mōkh muktī ki sār na jaṇā* GGS: p. 466).

But, as noted earlier, precisely at the point when escape from ego seems impossible, Guru Angad raises the following questions:

What is the cause of *haumai*?
From where does it arise?
How can it be eradicated?

(GGS: p. 466)

To which he also provides an enigmatic answer:

Although the disease of ego is chronic and deeply rooted,
The cure lies within it.

So the key to eradicating *haumai*, the cure that can liberate us from the ego's trappings, lies within the nature of ego itself. What does this mean? How can the ego be the cause of affliction and at the same time the remedy to this problem? We get an inkling of what Nanak means by this when he says that *haumai* can be eradicated if, *first*, the individual is gifted with the grace (*kirpā*) to do so, and *second*, the same individual can make the effort to focus our consciousness on the Guru's Word (*śabda*):

kirpa kare je apaṇi
tān guru ka śabda kamāhe

(GGS: p. 466)

In a related verse Guru Amardas counsels the suffering mind that liberation is attainable if, instead of thinking in a self-referential manner, the self contemplates *nām* and thus aligns one's physical and psychic existence with *hukam*:

haumai navai nal virodh hai
doe na vasai ek thai

hari cetti man mere tu gur ka śabda kām ai.
hukam mannahi ta hari milai ta vich.

(GGS: p. 560)

Two things stand out in the Sikh Gurus' instruction about the battle with *haumai*. First, there has to be a level of self-effort if the individual is to battle with its own ego. This self-effort must involve a degree of individual and continuous volition to break free and attune oneself with *hukam*. Second, and perhaps surprisingly, on its own, self-willed volition will never be enough! To be released also requires grace (*kirpā*), which is an intervention that cannot arise from one's own self-power but from a power that is wholly other in nature to self-power. This wholly other power is *nām*. And this is precisely why Nanak stresses that *haumai* and *nām* are opposing forces – they are mutually exclusive and can never belong together in the same self.

A different way to say this is that the individual can negate or annihilate the separative tendency of *haumai* only through its own volition, but such annihilation alone does not release it. Final liberation requires that it ultimately surrenders its volition, its power of self-effort, to the One-All. This surrender is not a passive act of submission, but something about which the self comes to a realization at the very pinnacle of one's self-power by recognizing (*bujhai*) that this self-power is ultimately powerless, and that the true power comes not from within it but from *nām*. To realize this within the fabric of one's own being is to align with *hukam* and to become a self-realized person (*sachiārā*).

This brings us to the third point. What all of this instruction is telling us is that the path to liberation and becoming *sachiārā* (self-realized) consists in a progressive and practical self-effort, which we could also call the struggle with oneself, a battle of the ego with itself. In other words it is an internal struggle of the mind with its own nature. But, importantly, this struggle to be released (*muktī*) has to take place within the stream of life (*jīvan*).

What Guru Nanak has done is to redefine liberation as the self-struggle against *haumai* in terms of a path of practice within the parameters of a life that must be lived to the fullest. Liberation is now *jīvan-muktī*: liberation in the stream of life, and the person who can achieve such liberation is a *jīvan-mukta* – one who is released while living. The path of practice can be considered a seamless combination of psycho-philosophical theory and spiritual techniques for holistic attunement of mind, body and spirit.

In *gurmat* the idea of self-realization is meaningless without a psycho-somatic synthesis of all three of these elements into a state of oneness. Otherwise, it remains at the level of an idealistic goal that would remain ever out of reach in this life and would be projected into the next. Guru Nanak was anything but an idealist. Down to earth and practical to the core, his notion of *jīvan-muktī* cultivates the field of the body as an immaterial nexus of forces, the control of which becomes central to self-realization, and therefore to a model of health and well-being that weaves body, mind and spirit into a psycho-somatic unity. Before we get into a discussion about the path of practice it will be helpful to unpack the notion of *jīvan-muktī* in more detail.

jīvan-muktī: Self-realization in life

In Sikh philosophy self-realization has several interlinked aspects. First, *jīvan-muktī* or realization in life, which refers to an individual's struggle with the empirical form of the self or ego. Second, *avan-jan mitai* or *avan-jan chukai*, or release from the cycle of births and deaths. Third, in addition to these, terms such as *muktī, mōkh-duār, mōkh, nirbān, param pad, chauthā pad* and *sahaj avasthā* – all of which refer to a culminating state of consciousness – are also commonly used in Sikh scripture. In what follows I avoid the tendency to see these – especially (i) and (ii) – as different aspects, instead seeing them as part and parcel of a process of expanding consciousness from a contracted or limited state to one that is more attuned to oneness.

So how do the Sikh Gurus define a liberated or self-realized person (*jīvan-mukta*)? As noted earlier, the recurring definition of *jīvan-mukt* is a person who has struggled to eradicate the tendency to individuate or form ego traces that concretize over time into a psychic cocoon: 'a *jīvan-mukta* is one who has eradicated his ego' (*jīvan mukt so janiai jis vichon haumai jai* – GGS: M3 1010). Guru Amardas repeats this definition: 'A *jīvan-mukt* is not riddled with the disease of ego' (GGS: p. 1058). Similarly, Guru Arjan says that the *jīvan-mukt* has dispelled darkness and ignorance (GGS: p. 675).

Other noteworthy features of the *jīvan-mukta* include one's eradication of vices that plague the mind: *durmat parharai . . . . jīvan mukt gat antar pai*. In the Siddh Gosht composition: 'The *jīvan-mukta* is liberated because s/he eradicates vice and redeems her virtues.' Thus a characteristic of self-realization is achieving the level of control over one's mind and body and remaining undisturbed by imbalances (M1: p. 1343: *jap tap sanjam . . . jīvan mukta jo śabda sunahe*). The *jīvan mukt* should be able to regard pain and pleasure, poison and nectar, honour and dishonour, king and commoner alike (M5: p. 275: *jīvan mukt soi kahave, tesa harkh tesa ous sogh*). The implication here is that *jīvan-mukt* attains an ability to regulate her mind and is unphased by forces that sway, attract and repulse the self, so that one rises above the three modes (of space\time\cause):

jīvan mukta gurmukh ko hai, treh gun maite nirmal soi

(GGS: p. 232)

But what do these persistent references to imbalance within the mind and body, and the need to regulate the forces causing this imbalance, have to do with *jīvan-muktī* as self-realization or liberation? Is liberation or self-realization essentially epistemic in its orientation? Or does it have to do with the body–mind complex? Is liberation really about consciousness, or about the body or both?

In light of what we've already learnt, it is already a mistake to assume that there is any opposition between consciousness and the material body. They are both part of an im/material, in/corporeal continuum, which means that the self is also part of an im/material body–mind–consciousness. If this is the case, then liberation or self-realization is only meaningful if we assume that the internal life of the self is situated in the sea of external, everyday life processes. These processes are in turn constantly influenced by competing forces and valences which derive from the self's encounters with the outside world, whether social, natural or otherwise. The double implication here is that, first, the internal life of the self or mind cannot be separated from the life of the body which functions as a door of perception to the outside world. Second, that the life of the body must never be denied or subsumed under the practice of austerities, which is why the Sikh Gurus elevated the life of the householder – one who lives and negotiates life fully in all its worldliness, mortality and physicality – above any other form of life. In short, the life of the body is to be treated on par with the life of the mind, such that the two are inextricably connected aspects of the body–mind complex and therefore of the path of liberation or self-realization.

The obvious next question brings us back to those aspects of life that cause a mal-functioning of the body–mind complex. What are the propensities, forces or valences that cause imbalance to the body–mind complex (*tan-man*), and from which the self is to be liberated?

Before answering this question, however, it will be helpful to clarify what is meant by a state of imbalance or to be lacking in health. Clearly, the possibility of the body–mind complex becoming imbalanced, and therefore unhealthy, suggests that there is a prior state of balance as a state of health and well-being. What, then, is balance as the Sikh Gurus understand it? The term they usually use is *sahaj* (state of equipoise) which in colloquial Punjabi is normally associated with the process of bringing the mind-body complex to a calm and peaceful state. What the colloquial sense often tends to disregard, however, is that *sahaj avasthā* refers equally to a bodily process and perhaps even more importantly that it is connected to what neuroscientists such as Antonio Damasio have called the 'fundamental operations at the core of life'.[11] These operations which encompass the cosmic and the psychic are reflected in the 'dynamics of homeostasis' – a term normally associated with biological processes, but whose remit is far broader. In the following short excursus I'd like to redirect the question of balance\equipoise (*sahaj*) towards the relationship between life and homeostasis by briefly engaging with Damasio's ideas.

Excursus: Homeostasis and *sahaj*

According to the neurobiologist Antonio Damsio, 'homeostasis refers to the fundamental operations at the core of life' from its earliest biochemical origins to the immense complexity of human nervous systems that we have today. Damasio's definition of homeostasis is unconventional to say the least. He speaks of it as a 'powerful unthought, *unspoken imperative*, whose discharge implies, for every living organism, small or large, nothing less than *enduring and prevailing*'.[12]

The very idea of an 'unspoken imperative' sounds decidedly theological and reminds us of the definition of *hukam* in Guru Nanak's *Japji* (see Chapter 2), which suggested an unconscious regulatory order programmed into all existence and creation, that is to say, programmed into life itself.

This conception of homeostasis goes beyond the conventional biological sense of the body's need to reach and maintain a certain state of equilibrium by constantly monitoring internal states, as implied by Damasio's emphasis on 'enduring' and 'prevailing'. The term 'enduring' implies an organism's need to do what is necessary for survival. For example, any threats to an organism's survival from external circumstances (predators, disease, accidents, etc.) automatically produce alterations to the body's physiology vis-à-vis changing blood pressure or hormonal levels in addition to biochemical changes that may lead to cellular malfunction, breakdown and disease. 'Prevailing', however, indicates a more subtle aspect of homeostasis which ensures that 'life is regulated within a range that is not just compatible with survival but also *conducive to flourishing, to a projection of life into the future of an organism or a species*'.[13]

However, the more subtle aspect of homeostasis that Damasio is pointing us towards are feelings or affects. If to be 'conducive to flourishing' means that an organism possessing individuated mind is able to enhance its powers of existing, also known as *conatus*, then it is feelings and affects that enable this enhancement of one's power of existing. Feelings reveal the exact 'status of life' to an individual mind, a status that ranges from positive to negative. For example, if the body–mind complex happens to display 'deficient homeostasis', it does so via negative feelings such as sadness, fear, depression, anxiety and shame. Positive feelings express a correct level of homeostasis. Feelings are therefore intimately related to homeostasis. For Damasio, 'feelings are the subjective experiences of the state of life ... in all creatures endowed with a mind and a conscious point of view'.[14]

In a nutshell, the function of mind which governs our everyday existence has two aspects. First, it interacts with objects and events in the external world through the portals of our sense faculties (eyes, ears, skin, etc.), to form percepts and tactile images, which are subsequently translated into the symbolic medium of language. Second, there is a parallel interior world of affect which includes spontaneous homeostatic feelings necessary to an organism's survival and flourishing as noted earlier. Additionally, there are feelings in the form of emotive responses which result from engaging latent drives or instincts (hunger or thirst) or motivational propensities (lust, play, etc.). While most of these drives are necessary to enhance the quality of our existence, others produce negative emotions and bring disruption to the body–mind complex. These are 'provoked feelings' resulting from emotive responses which are in turn caused by the 'engagement of drives, instincts, motivations' that perturb the body–mind complex and result in 'major mental upheavals'.[15]

The machinery underlying emotive responses is not only biological but cultural. In fact drives, motivational propensities and conventional emotions originate and operate in social contexts as much as they do in individuals. For example, desire, lust, care, nurturing, attachment, love, even joy, sadness, fear, anger, compassion, jealousy and so on are all emotions that are socially activated. The key point here is that while sociality may have been an indispensable part of the emergence of human cultures, it is likely to have originated in the 'machinery of affect'. The affective and emotional response system in general is not only part of 'the toolkit of homeostasis';[16] it is also closely intertwined with the development of human consciousness and subjectivity. As Damasio tells us, 'feelings influence the mental processes from within and are compelling because of their obligate positivity or negativity, their origin in actions that are conducive to healthy or unhealthy existence or even death'.[17]

Emotive propensities and body–mind imbalance

Sikh philosophy implicitly recognizes the centrality of affect as can be seen in the organization of the Gurus' thought process, which is organized and articulated in such a way as to maximize affective\emotional impact. It can also be seen in their emphasis on the need to understand the inherent *quality* of the feeling that arises in the body's interior, for it is this quality which provides instantaneous reports of the organism's state of life, that is to say, the organism's health. This inherent quality of a feeling can be referred to as *valence*, which designates the experience as pleasant or happy, unpleasant or painful, or something in-between. In *gurmat* valence is designated as either *sukh* (experience of pleasantness, absence of pain, happiness, pleasure) or *dukh* (experience of pain, discomfort, suffering). The valences *sukh* and *dukh* evaluate the efficiency of the bodily and mental states and represent the valence as positive, negative or perhaps even neutral to the mind in the form of a specific feeling.

Our everyday lives abound within the duality of *sukh* (pleasure/comfort) and *dukh* (discomfort\suffering) in such a way that we normally seek out and eventually crave experiences that lead to *sukh*, and actively disavow experiences leading to *dukh*. For most of us this represents a perfectly normal response. After all, if *dukh* is an indication of pain\suffering, who would wish for more of it? As Guru Nanak states: 'everyone asks for more pleasure and happiness, but no one seems to ask for pain or suffering.' But what most people don't realize, he goes on to say, is that pain and pleasure, *dukh* and *sukh*, are intertwined.

> In the midst of pleasure, pain is always present
> > The only ones who don't realize this are the egotistical (*manmukh*).
> But those who see pain and pleasure as the same
> > Find true peace, and blissful states of mind.

> > > > > > > > (GGS: p. 57)

Both *sukh* and *dukh* are transitory states. Because the ordinary, egotistical mind wishes to prolong the state of pleasure\comfort permanently, it attaches itself to *sukh* by designating it 'good' and disavowing pain as 'bad'. Sikh philosophy, however, breaks this oppositional cycle by reversing the orientation of desire and by implication the valence accorded to *sukh* and *dukh*. He says that we should instead consider 'pain (*dukh*) as a medicine, and pleasure (*sukh*) as an affliction which causes our state of disease':

> *dukh daru, sukh rog bhaia*
> *ja sukh taam na hoi*

To consider pain/suffering as a remedy, and pleasure\happiness as a disease, is of course counter-intuitive to our everyday sense. Does it not reverse our normative perspective on health and well-being, which pushes us towards eradication of pain and suffering? If, as Guru Nanak suggests, the craving for pleasurable states and comfort is a disease leading to unhealthy states of body–mind, then what is it that pushes us to crave for *sukh* in the first place? What is it about human culture that seems to have reversed the very natural tendency to learn or respond to feelings of pain and suffering, rather than avert signals of pain and suffering – whereas all other creatures rely on pain and suffering to keep them and their homeostatic systems intact?[18]

The answer, clearly, has to do with human culture and its civilizing influence. Something in human social acculturation has turned against nature but, in doing so, ultimately causes self-harm by disrupting the homeostatic system. In fact Nanak identifies these culturally acquired tendencies such as craving, pleasure and the aversion of pain as a key set of psychological impulses or propensities that he calls *Panj Chor* or *Panj Dutt*, variously translated as the 'Five Enemies', the 'Five Demons' or 'Five Thieves'.

This brings us back to the question I raised prior to this digression: *What are the specific propensities or forces that cause unhealthy states leading to imbalance in the body–mind complex?*

According to *gurmat* the propensities of action, reaction and habit, which hinder progress towards liberation, are known as *kléshas* or unwholesome mental\psychological dispositions that are harmful to our overall mental and physical health and well-being. The term *klésha* means conflict or disturbance in the mind triggered by some fundamental motivational propensities or impulses which, if left unattended, afflict one's behavioural tendencies or habits. They do so by inciting unwholesome actions of the body, mind, speech and thought. *Kléshas* are motivational impulses that originate in the mind, but eventually take control of one's habits, ultimately causing conflict and disruption in one's everyday behaviour.

Sikh philosophy delineates the *kléshas* into five basic types which are variously referred to as Five Thieves (*panj chor*) or Five Demons (*panj dutt*) because they break into our house – the body–mind complex – robbing us of our blissful homeostatic state which should be the body–mind's desired natural state of existence. These five *kléshas* or conflictual tendencies are *kām*, *krōdh*, *lōbh*, *mōh* and *ahankār* which roughly correspond to craving, anger, covetousness, attachment and pride. My aim in emphasizing these fundamental impulses which distort our perception as well as our cognitive and affective capacities, is to show how they are capable of inciting and motivating actions\ thoughts\speech with potentially harmful consequences for body and mind. *Gurmat* effectively transmutes the discussion of liberation or *jīvan muktī* into the realm of health and well-being, albeit with the proviso that health is mental as much as it is physical. In the following section I analyse and examine the nature of these *kléshas* in more detail vis-à-vis a discussion of the five fundamental impulses: *kām*, *krōdh*, *lōbh*, *mōh* and *ahamkar*.

Health and well-being: Identifying and overcoming *klésha* (inner conflict)

In Sikh philosophy the *kléshas* are divided into two broad categories depending on whether the motivational impulse is characterized by a valence of attraction (*rāga*) or a valence of repulsion (*advesha*). The *rāga* valence is the tendency for thoughts, beliefs, feelings, perception and cognition to reinforce or congeal the sense of 'I'. It is an auto-attraction, a self-affection premised on the removal or distancing of the other (or not-I) away from what the mind considers as 'me' or 'myself'.

As we noted earlier in this chapter, creating a gap or separation between self and other (or between I and not-I) provides a false sense of independence, permanence and security to the ego complex. It also induces a deep-rooted craving to continue filling the gap between self and the exiled not-self. Because of this void that opens up between self and other, the ego complex craves more pleasure, more permanence, which in turn distorts one's perceptive and cognitive faculties and ultimately changes the basic direction of one's life and its projects. In this way the *kām*, *lōbh* and *mōh* impulses can be categorized as attractive or centripetal.

In contradistinction, the *dvesha* category of *kléshas* signifies motivating impulses that repel or avoid unpleasant experiences. Thus anger (*krōdh*) and pride (*ahankār*) are impulses that cause repulsion or rejection of things, persons, states that are likely to create any kind of unpleasantness or suffering to the ego complex. Instead of accepting them, one pushes them away; the result being a more fragile, less resilient state of mind or social existence. Taken together, *rāga* (attraction, positive valence) and *dvesha* (repulsion, negative valence) symbolize a fundamentally oppositional and dualistic manner in which the ego interacts with and reacts to the external world of things, persons, phenomena, events. This oppositional dualism is directly responsible for the arising and emergence of conflictual disturbances which manifest physiologically in the body and psychologically in the mind. However, since we are talking about a body–mind continuum, it is unhelpful to separate physiology and psychology. Nevertheless, we can treat each separately in order to aid a better understanding of the inner world.

The five psychological impulses (*Panj Dutt*)

Valence positive – *kām*, *lōbh* and *mōh* – craving, greed, attachment

kām is generally spoken of by the Sikh Gurus as a propensity that creates dis-equilibrium in the body–mind complex. Its broad meaning is lust or craving. Guru Nanak states that 'with *kām* advising the ego . . . the person becomes blind and dances to its tune like a zombie' (GGS: p. 568). Similarly, Guru Arjan, in a more detailed statement, addresses *kām* almost as if it had personal agency: 'Oh *kām*, you cheat the mind, leading people to hell and countless transmigrations; Shaking the three worlds, you defeat one's austerities, meditation and civilization; Through illusions of happiness, you weaken the mind's defenses and punish high and low alike' (GGS: p. 1358).

Basically, *kām* robs one's powers of discrimination and negates values. The satisfaction it brings is short-lived. No individual is immune to *kām* as its commanding impulse makes people oblivious to their own self-preservation and ultimately robs the mind of its authority.[19] Like the elephant (*kunchar*) or the deer (*mrig*) the person led by *kām* suffers from fickle, mercurial psychological states and constant restlessness.

lōbh can be described as the 'impulse to possess what belongs to others'.[20] Guru Arjan describes it in the following way: 'Oh *lōbh*, your tentacles sway even the best of men, making their minds waver, and run in all directions to possess more and yet more. You respect neither friendship nor kith and kin. You make one do what one should not, to eat what one should not, and to build what can't be built.' *Lōbh* is a tendency which creates a very specific force of attraction – the attraction between its object and the subject who is attracted towards it, thereby fostering a constant sense of dissatisfaction and restlessness.

mōh as a psychological impulse has two interrelated meanings: attachment and delusion. The sense of delusion refers to a warping of consciousness that leads to cognitive error about the nature of things, specifically the nature of oneness, believing them to be eternal and attracting oneself to them. As Guru Nanak explains, 'the whole world is mired in conventional values and attachment to it'.[21] *Mōh* can therefore be understood as the psychological propensity towards conventional identity which pervades one's entire perspective on individual and social reality. Guru Arjan regards the psychological charge of *mōh* as an almost unconquerable foe:

> Mōh, the mightiest of forces
>   whose power breaks even the strongest world.
> How you beguile gods and men,
>   demigods, even creatures of nature.

(GGS: p. 1358)

A person influenced by *mōh* is trapped in his or her circle of identification as manifested in his attachment to self-image, or to one's kith and kin. Consequently, *mōh* confuses the individual, creating hesitation, doubt and inhibition in one's actions. To break free from *mōh* one needs to make a heroic effort.

Valence negative – *krōdh*/anger and *ahankār*/pride

krōdh (anger): in contradistinction to *kām*, *lōbh* and *mōh* which are centrifugal or attractive propensities, *krōdh* has a centripetal valence which pushes the subject away from its object. A mind motivated by anger loses its powers of reflection and becomes open to suggestion like a monkey dancing to a particular tune. Guru Arjun states:

> O krōdh, you're the basis of all conflict and strife,
>   you know no compassion;
> Sinful creatures caught in your grasp act like monkeys dancing
>   to a tune.
> Your company debases the mind,
> subjecting us to punishments and death.

P.1358 M5

Though directed outward onto objects, individuals or society, it causes equal harm to the one projecting it. As the Gurus warn us, anger needs to be overcome before it 'destroys the body as fire melts gold' and generates kindred emotions out of itself, such as hatred and jealousy.

ahankār (pride or I-making): in Punjabi language the term *ahankār* means pride. In the Sankhya school of Indian philosophy *ahankār* appears as a metaphysical principle of individuation. The Sikh Gurus use *ahankār* primarily to signify pride or arrogance as a psychological impulse rather than a metaphysical principle, as can be noted in the everyday term *hankārī/ hankāranā* (one who is arrogant, or to arrogate oneself) to denote an arrogant person. Hence the subtle but unmistakable connection to the principle of individuation (I-making) is still there, as indicated by Guru Arjun who places *ahankār* last in his overview of the Five Thieves:

> *ahankār*, you're the root cause of birth and death,
>   the very essence of sin.
> betraying friendship you foster enmity,
>   as you extend the net of illusion.

P.1358 M5

As this verse indicates *ahankār* is regarded as a primary tendency in the double sense. On the one hand, it exerts centripetal force by spreading its effects outward. For example, 'betraying friendships\fostering enmity'. The key point here is the creation of enmity and hence the distance between oneself and others based on pride. On the other hand, though,

Table 1 'Five Thieves' and Their Central Characteristics

	Propensity/ Impulse	Action	Impact on Body–Mind Complex
Kām	craving	Pursues gratification	Activates excitement response system; Loss of discernment
Lōbh	greed	Pursuit of pleasure	Activates excitement or threat response system
Mōh	attachment	Seeks permanence via attachments	Activates excitement or threat response system
krōdh	anger	Avoidance of suffering	Activates response system
ahankār	pride	Self-assertion drives formation of normal 'I' or Ego	Self-attachment in face of external and internal threats

This table is an adapted and improvised version of the tabulation provided by Davinder S. Panesar, in his *Gurmat: Practical Self Realization (2018)*, p. 110.

the making of enemies directly 'afflicts the individual with incurable diseases'. Stated differently, *ahankār* becomes the cause of actions that directly impact one's sense of self or I-making, leading its victims into a vicious circle where the 'I' makes itself primarily in relation to an enemy. Such self-directedness is manifest through one's speech, thoughts and actions. In this sense *ahankār* as pride leads to a warped and unhealthy form of individuation, one that has become blind to the interrelatedness of life and things as a whole.

The impact and effects of these five psychological tendencies can be summarized in bullet points and tabular format showing the motivational impulses alongside the impact that each *klésha* has on the homeostatic system (Table 1).

What are the 'Five thieves'?

- The 'Five Thieves' are psychic impulses or emotive propensities that arise in the most highly evolved self-conscious organisms with complex nervous systems and 'minds'.
- Emotive forces that have evolved with human culture and are specifically part of human subjectivity.

What do the Five Thieves do?

- Once triggered, each psychological impulse enhances the mind's tendency to constantly seek pleasurable experiences (*sukh*) leading to a shallow and transitory happiness (*sukh*). But it does so only by repressing painful feelings such as sadness which serve to warn the body–mind complex of impending dangers. In this way the mind switches off painful experiences (*dukh*) which otherwise serve as a feedback mechanism for avoiding life-threatening collapses and serve to keep our homeostatic system in balance.
- This leads the mind to become addicted to constant happiness (*sukho sukh*), which becomes a form of self-gratification and ultimately afflicts our ability to balance feelings (*sukh rog bhaia*).
- Over time the Five Thieves interact to produce a preponderance of emotional states that hijack the homeostatic system of the body–mind complex and then drive 'the thinking process'. As these emotional states perpetuate themselves, they diverge our conscious mind away from the present dangers facing it, instead of connecting it to past memories.
- Ultimately the Five Thieves act in concert to reinforce the 'I am – Me/ Mine/Myself' into a psychological cocoon or a bubble, which enhances self-power, to make the ego complex into a relational centre of all existence. It cuts itself off from true or genuine relations to others because it has lost its ability to other itself.
- By separating from its Beloved, the person loses the ability to wonder (*vismad*) and experience the world as eternally renewing (*nām*)

Discussion questions

(1) What does liberation refer to in Sikh philosophy? Who may obtain it?
(2) Describe the relationship between the ego and health from the perspective of Sikh philosophy.
(3) What are the positive aspects of ego in Sikh philosophy? What are the negatives?
(4) How would you describe the typical relationship between the body and mind? How does Sikh philosophy suggest we shift this perspective?
(5) Health and well-being are defined either in terms of physical medicines or psychology aimed at enhancing and solidifying a sense

of self. How would the integration of Sikh philosophy complicate
fields of health and well-being? How does *gurmat* philosophy redefine
sickness and mental health?

(6) How does the Sikh philosophical view on happiness compare with
notions of self-optimization projected by the 'happiness industry'?
Discuss.

(7) Meditation and other 'eastern' practices have become commonplace
in the United States and Europe in recent decades. Meditation
apps and classes often advertise themselves as a means to 'get away
from the noise' of the world or increase productivity. Is this form
of meditation helpful or detrimental in achieving the goals of Sikh
philosophy?

(8) Sikh philosophy does not distinguish the body and mind as separate
objects but rather views them as an integrated body–mind complex.
How might we reform our views of mental health through this
reorientation?

Bioethics

If ethics is defined as the branch of philosophy that examines the moral principles and values governing a person's behaviour and activities in society and the world, then bioethics can be considered a more specialized version, which applies ethics to broader issues in healthcare, science, technology and medicine. By drawing from a variety of discursive traditions traversing the secular-religious divide, bioethicists contribute to debates on public policy and legislation on contentious moral issues and generate civic discourse aimed at understanding technological advances in medicine and how these can potentially change the way we understand questions of sickness, health and mortality.

The dominant stream of bioethics discourse has tended to work within universalizing philosophical frameworks which not only reflect the continuing dominance of Western thought but also the latter's proclivity to disregard the epistemologically and culturally diverse world we actually live in. In recent years, however, challenges to this monoculturalist tendency have emerged, arguing that bioethical principles can be derived from a variety of world philosophical traditions. In this chapter I show how some of Sikh philosophy's key concepts can provide a resource for bioethical reasoning, thereby demonstrating the importance of a conceptually pluralist approach towards bioethics. I begin by briefly outlining the cultural milieu in which the Sikh moral system arose before turning to the multiversal aspect of Sikh concepts that allows them to be mobilized for bioethical reasoning.

Cultural particulars

For guidance on ethics and morals Sikhs look to a variety of scriptural and other sources including the Guru Granth Sahib, accepted portions of the Dasam Granth, the *janamsakhis*, the writings of Bhai Gurdas, the Rahitnamas and a relatively recent document, the Sikh Rahit Maryada (Sikh Code of Conduct). These sources in turn fall into two qualitatively different categories. By far the most important are the scriptural sources, particularly the Guru Granth Sahib. However, the moral teachings contained in the Guru

Granth are non-normative and transcultural in their orientation. The Guru Granth provides guidance to humanity in general and not just to a specific community or ethnic group. On the other hand, while the Rahit texts provide basic life-rules, organizational duties or codes of conduct for how a Sikh ought to live, they were formulated in the context of Punjabi ethnicity and culture.

As scholars of Sikh history have noted, the Rahitnamas are essentially codes that were formulated after the creation of the Khalsa.[1] The compilers of these codes were faced with the need to consolidate differences and tensions within the early Sikh community by providing some form of internal discipline. Some of the codes came into being when the early Khalsa community was actively engaged in battles for survival during the early part of the eighteenth century. For Khalsa Sikhs the main ethical duty is a quest for justice on behalf of the weak, the needy or those whose basic rights have been disregarded by unscrupulous states or rulers. To maintain some elementary public form corresponding to certain ethical principles, Khalsa Sikhs pledged themselves to fulfil certain obligations such as wearing the 5K's, upholding prohibitions against cutting hair, shunning the use of tobacco or other intoxicants and avoiding marrying non-Sikhs. During the late nineteenth and early twentieth centuries, and particularly under the modernizing influence of the Singh Sabha, the Khalsa way of life regained and even surpassed its earlier hegemonic position. Considerable effort was put into consolidating the earlier Rahitnamas into a more coherent code of conduct applicable to Sikh society and more in line with the Guru Granth Sahib. These efforts culminated in the formulation and ratification of the Sikh Rahit Maryada (SRM) in 1954 by the Shiromani Gurdwara Parbandhak Committee.

Although the code outlined in the SRM continues to strongly influence the conduct of Sikhs, its limitations are becoming all too evident. The conceptual framing of the SRM belongs to the colonial period where the competition between religious identities took precedence over other considerations. Such a conceptual framing may have produced the desired effect in Punjab, but it is proving to be increasingly inadequate for contemporary life in the major metropolises of India and in the Western diasporas where Punjabi tradition and lifestyle directly encounter post-secular politics, technology, environmental concerns and pluralism on a scale not seen before.

To provide answers to increasingly complex ethical dilemmas, Sikhs are beginning to bypass the SRM and look at new ways of interpreting primary sources such as the Guru Granth Sahib.[2] The rest of this chapter proceeds by applying some of the concepts discussed in previous chapters of this book, such as *hukam* and *haumai*, to real-life ethical scenarios. It'll be helpful to begin by recontextualizing these key concepts within discourses on morals and ethics before turning to a consideration of a few commonly discussed topics in bioethics.

Is there a multiversal touchstone for morals and morality?

To the uninitiated reader the apparent lack of rigid ideology and categorical imperatives ('you *must* do this . . .') in the Guru Granth Sahib can be perplexing. But this does not necessarily mean the absence of a system of moral thinking in the teachings of the Sikh Gurus (*gurmat*). As indicated earlier in this book, Guru Nanak actually spells out something like a moral touchstone in the opening lines of the Japji, even though it cannot be made to coincide with societal norms of morality. Nanak identifies his moral standard in relation to a self-realized person (*sachiārā*), someone who has struggled to remain faithful to the truth of an experience of oneness whose manifestation is egoloss, and to one who acts and lives in accordance with a natural imperative (*hukam rajai chalana*) that undergirds any social law.

Thus the touchstone for morality is not grounded in any belief system or a standpoint. Rather, it is better understood as a general principle or sovereign imperative (*hukam*) which enjoins that whatever the duties or discipline entailed by one's station (*rajai/raza*), these ought to be performed in such a way that in each act performed or duty fulfilled, we actively imbibe the sovereign imperative (*hukam*) inscribed into life itself, indeed into all existence. Because *hukam* is immanent within life (*hukmai andar sab koe, bahar hukam na koe*), it replaces the need for a transcendental ground, be that a deity or otherwise. In other words, because of the immanence of *hukam*, life is revalued for itself and not as a supplement to 'the sacred'. Life itself is sovereign and cannot be captured within metaphysical distinctions such as sacred versus profane, sacred versus secular and so on.

This *hukam*, inscribed into all life, is the imperative to negate the ego which says 'I am'. If left unattended, the sense of 'I am'-ness becomes a disease engendered by the five propensities also referred to as the 'five enemies' or 'five thieves': (i) *kām* (concupiscence, lust or simply craving), (ii) *krōdh* (anger or wrath), (iii) *lōbh* (covetousness or the desire to possess what belongs to others), (iv) *mōh* (attachment or delusion) and (v) *ahankār* (egotistical pride). As noted in the previous chapter these 'five enemies' are psychic propensities of the self that either attract the person towards something (maybe an object or an action) or repel the person away from what is wholesome. They are not biological or primitive urges or instincts but learned dispositions or habitual frames of mind that can take on a life of their own. If left unchecked, these propensities keep the individual in a state of restlessness.

However, as Guru Nanak reminds us in the first stanzas of his Japji, the 'five enemies' cannot be controlled through ascetic practices, ritual cleansing or by reflection alone. Rather, they must be regulated by inculcating and actively practising virtues such as wisdom (*giān*), truthfulness (*sach*), justice (*niaon*), temperance (*sanjam*), courage (*niḍar*), humility (*garībī, nimarta*) and contentment (*santōkh*). Those who actively appropriate such virtues are able to inscribe *hukam* into their very being as egoloss. They actively resist saying 'I am' and instead balance this egotistical propensity by being able to say 'I am not', and thereby elevate themselves beyond the self-willed rationalist morality of societal norms (*manmukh*). Appropriating *hukam* (the sovereign imperative that resists being rationalized into a system of knowledge) forces the individual to think and act almost like an aesthete or artist. Such a person who is freed and empowered to challenge existing values, freed to create new values rather than blindly following social rules, is known as *gurmukh*.

Hence, Guru Nanak's moral standard of egoloss, the *gurmukh*, takes us beyond socially sanctioned oppositional norms such as good versus evil, wrong versus right and violence versus peace. It questions the very frameworks in which we operate even as it allows us to make deliberate, conscious choices in both mundane challenges of everyday life and the more extraordinary quandaries that face human beings today. Consequently, the Gurus' teachings are entirely practical and applicable to all life situations, actual or possible. They allow the person to determine how best to live from day to day in an ever-changing world.

To understand how this moral 'standard' of egoloss might work in actual practice, it will be helpful to pluck scenarios or questions from the stream of everyday life in order to engage the philosophical concepts presented in previous chapters. Some of the scenarios are real, some fictional, others based on dialogues with Sikh practitioners who have faced such issues, yet all of them involve real, often uncomfortable consequences. The scenarios will be organized around a set of questions that reflect the key moral and ethical issues.

Good and evil

Does it make sense to speak of good and evil, or 'good' or 'bad' persons in Sikhī? Does a gurmukh have to be a member of the Sikh community? Can someone be an atheist and still strive for the gurmukh stage? Why do bad things happen to good people?

The word 'good' has relatively little meaning in Sikh ethics unless it is understood in relation to the problem of self-centredness. Thus one might be deemed good in the sense that one diligently follows one's value or belief system which may or may not be associated with a particular code of conduct (*rahit*). And this may indeed involve respect or tolerance towards others. But according to *gurmat* (the Guru's philosophy) one might still be a *manmukh* (self-centred individual), whereas the aim in *sikhī* is to achieve the state of *gurmukh* consciousness – one who has experienced self-realization or oneness by shattering his or her ego. There is therefore no essential goodness or badness. It is more accurate to speak of good and bad actions. For a *gurmukh* dualities such as 'good' and bad' have only relative meaning. To become a *gurmukh* one has to undergo self-transformation by overcoming the five psychic vices: *kām* (lust), *krōdh* (anger), *lōbh* (greed), *mōh* (attachment) and *ahankār* (pride).

A *gurmukh* certainly does not have to belong to the Sikh community. The term *gurmukh* refers to a state of consciousness which can be achieved by anyone. Thus a Sikh can be fervently religious but still be no closer to overcoming the *manmukh* stage of existence. Overcoming the *manmukh* state involves a radical transformation of one's mind, and there is no reason why this could not be done by non-Sikhs as long as they remain focused on the desire to attain spiritual unity. Thus one can technically be an 'atheist' and still strive for a *gurmukh* state, since the basis of Sikhī has little or nothing to do with the artificial categories 'theism' or 'atheism' or with belief in a divine deity.

Bad things can certainly happen to good people. Again, the problem is with the terms 'good' and 'bad'. Sikhī teaches the equal acceptance of good and bad as part of the happening of *hukam* (the law of existence). Only a *manmukh* laments if bad things happen to him or her and celebrate if good things happen. As Guru Arjan reminds us, to a *gurmukh* who strives to attain a state of mental equipoise at all times, all that happens is acceptable as equally sweet (*terā kiā miṭhā lagai*).

Use of force

Can killing be justified? Can war be justified? To what extent is martyrdom acceptable? Is capital punishment acceptable?

In Sikh philosophy there is no metaphysical contradiction between violence and peace. These are relative terms. True violence is the self's

delusional sense of separateness from the world. True peace is attained
by violently struggling against the self's tendency towards individuation,
its tendency to believe that it exists outside of *hukam*. However, killing
can only be justified as a very last resort when all other means have been
exhausted, or when the lives of innocent people, including one's own life,
are threatened. There are examples in Sikh history when the taking of life
has been justified, for example, when it has been beneficial to a larger
number of people or to the survival of a way of life. So, if one is forced
to take the life of another, or that of an animal, in self-defence, it should
be done from a state of mind motivated by virtuous instincts such as
compassion and the intention to protect others, rather than anger or pride.
Thus one must not kill simply to protect one's possessions or for the sake
of revenge as these are tendencies motivated by egotism. Accordingly, war
can only ever be justified as a last resort when the innocent and defenceless
are under attack from oppressors. Under such circumstances, to not raise
the sword, to simply stand by and watch others persecuted amounts to
little more than self-preservation, a pretentious form of ego-indulgence,
which constitutes a greater evil. The opposite of this tendency is provided
by the figure of the martyr (*shahīd*) who is able to offer his or her own body
for the benefit of others in a pure and selfless action. From this perspective,
a martyr is one who has most struggled with his own self and is able to
imbibe the principle of *hukam*: to not inscribe ego on oneself, the one
who is most able to surrender the self. According to the paradoxical logic
of *hukam*, there is no consensus among Sikhs either for or against capital
punishment.

Behaviour, value, culture

*What is the value of marriage and family? Is sex outside marriage permissible?
Is it moral to have more than one spouse at one time? Is divorce acceptable? Is
the decline of marriage a good or bad thing?*

Although there is no religious or other imperative to 'go forth and multiply',
Sikhs are by and large family-orientated irrespective of their piety. Pious
Sikhs will often say that preference for family life, as opposed to, say, the path
of reclusive asceticism (*sanyāsa*), derives from the need to translate the three
central precepts of *nām japna*, *wand chakṇā* and *kirt karaṇā* into the practice
of everyday life. To properly imbibe these precepts and achieve the ultimate
goal of liberation through self-realization, Sikhs are strongly encouraged to
adopt the life of a householder (*grihasta*).

With the exception of the child-Guru, Harkrishan (who died at the age of nine), all of the Sikh Gurus took spouses, had children and lived lives that combined the roles of householder, warrior and spiritual preceptor. However, the Gurus were fully aware that this would also be the most demanding way to live. It was much easier to run away from social issues by renouncing family ties and becoming an ascetic.

In order to lead a life which allows full expression of one's emotional, psychological and biological impulses, Sikhism encourages and generally follows a heteronormative model of marriage. However, because the joint or extended family is still the prevalent norm within North Indian society and to a lesser extent in the Western Sikh diaspora, marriage is not a private affair between two individuals. Rather, it involves the joining of two families who become connected through the individuals. The concept of marriage in Sikhism is not based on a social contract but aims at the fusion of two souls into one. It is therefore analogous to the union of an individual with the divine, which is also the goal of Sikh spirituality. Marriage provides a socially sanctioned institution for consummating this relationship:

> They are not man and wife who have physical contact only.
> Only they are truly married who have one spirit in two bodies
>
> (GGS p. 788)

Physical consummation is therefore to be considered a necessary step towards a broader goal of awakening spiritual desire and longing for detachment within the very institution which joins two individuals. Such attachment, which is to be attained while being attached to another, is likened to the 'blissful state' in which the mind attains union with the beloved. Given this emphasis, it is not difficult to see why sex outside of marriage is forbidden. For the Gurus, while denial of the sexual instinct is certainly unhealthy, sexual activity should not be indulged in only for the purpose of procreation. Rather, it should be enjoyed between man and wife in a deeply committed relationship.

While monogamy is certainly the norm, there are occasions where taking more than one wife has been sanctioned. The obvious example are those of the sixth Guru, Hargobind, and the tenth Guru, Gobind Singh, who, under strong pressure from their parents and relatives, both remarried after the deaths of their first wives. Another circumstance that would allow a divergence from monogamy is where one's brother dies and the remaining brother takes the widow into his own household in order to protect her and her family. But the final decision in such cases is always with the woman.

Given the sentiment that the institution of marriage has to be entered into as a lifelong commitment, divorce is something to be avoided as far as it's reasonably possible. However, Sikhs also recognize that this ideal may be severely strained in certain cases, particularly when one partner or her/his children may be suffering unnecessarily due to domestic violence or related issues. In such cases, marriages can be dissolved and individuals allowed to remarry.

Gender: Equality and difference

Are the roles played by men and women a moral Issue? What value do Sikhs place on the notion of equality of the sexes?

The answer to this question has to be an emphatic yes! If the ultimate goal is to attain the *gurmukh* state, irrespective of one's gender, then the roles played by men and women should never become a moral issue. This is because the problem all along has been the role of societal conventions in defining maleness as normative. The result of this normativity is a conflation of maleness with divinity in such a way that patriarchy has been embedded into language, thought, desire and behaviour.[3] From this perspective it could be argued that whereas society's preoccupation with maleness hinders spiritual attainment – seen as one's ability to tap the reservoir of emotions and moods necessary for achieving a balanced state of mind, Femininity, however, because of its proximity to nature, may have greater potential for spiritual attainment or 'becoming divine', to use Grace Jantzen's term. This is partly because the central obstacle in spiritual attainment is not simply the ego but the conflation of the ego with the attributes of maleness. Moreover, ways of imagining the divine in the teachings of the Sikh Gurus are neither exclusively male nor female. The One, as conceived in Sikh philosophy, cannot be reduced to gender. However, the One becomes gendered when it is inflected through the cultural schemas which impose a gender normativity that is missing in authoritative sources of Sikh philosophy such as the Guru Granth Sahib.

Having said this, some might argue that if the moral standard is not biological but spiritual, there is nothing, scripturally or otherwise, to stop a simple reversal of these societal roles. The question of 'equality' is more complex, however, and to answer it we need to look at historical and contemporary examples.

In their writings the Sikh Gurus gave women an exalted place within society echoing the strong emphasis on practising spirituality within a worldly setting. In a much quoted verse Guru Nanak castigates medieval Indian society for looking down on women because they menstruated or bore children. Even more vehement was the Guru's condemnation of *sati*, the self-immolation of women at the funeral pyres of their husbands.

> We are born from a woman, and in a woman we grow.
> We're engaged to and wed a woman.
> We take a woman as lifelong partner, and from the woman comes
> family.
> If one woman dies we seek another.
> Without woman there is no social bond.
> So why denigrate woman when she gives birth to kings?
> Woman herself is born of woman, none comes into the world without
> her.

(A. G. p. 473)

Other Sikh Gurus further emphasized the status of women. Guru Amar Das forbade women to veil their faces while Guru Gobind Singh invited his spouse to become part of the ceremony for initiating Sikhs into the order of the Khalsa.[4] In keeping with this, monogamy is the preferred and predominant model. Widow remarriage is a relatively prevalent occurrence in contemporary Sikh society, although many other Sikh women choose not to remarry and remain single.

The hypermasculinized representation of Sikhs in contemporary media – bearded-turbaned men carrying swords, cases of female infanticide, combined with a growing chorus of voices advocating more women's equality – has given the impression that Sikh society is fundamentally patriarchal. Closer scrutiny of Sikh society, however, suggests that the role and status of women are more diverse and influential than is suggested by the media imagery. If the somewhat simplistic Western feminist notions of 'equality' with men is the goal being sought, then Sikhism does not fare all that badly. Women have exactly the same access to religious teachings and practices as men. In fact the task of transmitting basic spiritual and moral precepts to the next generation usually begins with women in their role as mothers.

Historically, women have risen to the highest positions in Sikh society. The tenth Guru's spouse, Mata Sundari, not only played a key role in the creation of a new spiritual-cum-military order (the Khalsa), but after the Guru's death led the Sikh community in spiritual and political matters, far longer than any male Sikh Guru. Other women such as Rani Jindan (the spouse of the Sikh ruler, Maharajah Ranjit Singh) wielded enormous power in the Sikh kingdom prior to British rule. In recent years, Bibi Jagir Kaur was elected the *jathedar* of the Akāl Takht, the highest ecclesiastical position in Sikhism. In short, there is no teaching in the scriptures or anywhere else that prevents women from receiving access to education or achieving social, political or spiritual ascendancy. Nor are the roles played by men and women a moral issue. Factors that prevent women from doing so are primarily ingrained in the social and patriarchal fabric of North Indian society. These include caste, kinship ties, and related to these, the notion of *izzat* or family honor. Contrary to what is often thought, Westernization has had an ambivalent effect on women's status in Sikh society. Although women have found and taken advantage of greater access to education and professions, colonialism also helped to foster a certain hyper-masculinity, thus further entrenching the notion that masculinity is normative, and all because of the erroneous belief that God is male.

Sexuality

Basic Questions: Is transgendering immoral? Is homosexuality immoral? Should gay marriages be recognized by the State?

According to the value system of modern Sikhism as prescribed by the Sikh Code of Conduct (1954), Sikhs are expected to live in a family environment in order to properly nurture their children. Most Sikhs interpret the family structure to be based on a heteronormative model of sexuality. Because the heteronormative model has gained a moral sanction, alternative models of family have been discouraged. Many Sikhs have interpreted this to mean that homosexuality cannot result in procreation and is therefore unnatural. However, such a judgement bears a strong Christian, and especially Catholic, imprint, which believes in natural law: 'what is natural is what is moral.' This can be seen in recent statements by Sikh religious leaders who not only openly condemned homosexuality as unnatural but seemed to justify their stance either by reference to 'other major world religions' or by suggesting that homosexuality is 'lustful'.[5]

As a result of these strictures many Sikhs with homosexual orientations have tried to enforce upon themselves a 'normalization' of their sexuality by believing that what they experience is merely lust, and as a remedy marrying a member of the opposite sex and having children. Such a process of forcing homosexuals to go underground, as it were, has led to a belief among many Sikhs that there are no homosexual Sikhs. This belief can, in turn, cause distress to those Sikhs who happen to find themselves attracted to members of the same sex.

However, a closer look at the primary source of Sikh ethics, the Guru Granth Sahib, shows that while the question of homosexuality has not been explicitly discussed, there is no justification whatsoever for castigating and banning homosexuality. In fact homosexuality need not even be regarded as a moral issue given the fact that Indic culture has by and large been far more diverse and open towards questions of homosexuality seeing it as a manifestation of ecstatic and erotic mysticism. Trans-sexuality and gender crossing is a well-known aspect of mystical enunciation particularly in those movements influenced by *bhakti* and Sufism. More recently many Sikhs have called for new ways of interpreting Sikh scripture on the question of gender and sexuality, which give greater credence to the transgendered 'standpoint' of devotional love that is central to the Sikh Gurus' teachings. Recent research suggests that such new interpretations are likely to complicate the issue considerably as the Sikh Guru's writings on love and eroticism may challenge the peculiarly modern perceptions of sexuality.

Diet, drugs, alcohol, tobacco

What is the Sikh stance on eating meat? Is the food a person eats a moral concern? Is there anything inherently wrong with drug use? Is the use of substances to produce an altered state desirable and/or part of common human experience, or does it defile the natural state of the body?

Despite the fact that communal eating and the sharing of food has been and continues to be so central to the Sikh way of life, the current Sikh Code of Conduct has left the question of dietary rules unresolved or ambiguous at best. This is perhaps not surprising when we consider that the primary source of Sikh ethics, the Guru Granth Sahib, does not provide hard and fast rules concerning diet. Instead, it offers more philosophical and pragmatic advice about avoiding or eating in moderation such foods that could potentially harm the body and mind.

Nevertheless, Sikh communities throughout the world have adopted a fairly pragmatic and consistent attitude towards certain kinds of food. As a rule, no meat or intoxicants are served in Sikh gurdwaras, all of which have a communal kitchen attached to them. Foods prepared within the gurdwara have to use wholesome natural products, primarily milk, wheat/corn flour and vegetables. A variety of Punjabi tea is also served in many Western gurdwaras, but this is not the norm. Sikhs initiated into certain Khalsa orders tend to adhere to a vegetarian diet with the exception of sects like the Nihangs. The Sikh Code of Conduct does not prohibit meat eating, but it does state that animals should be slaughtered as humanely as possible with a single blow. Only beef is strictly avoided as many Sikhs come from a rural background in which the cow, buffalo and ox were central to the livelihoods of many Sikhs. Cattle are therefore treated with respect and never slaughtered for consumption.

As far as drug, tobacco and alcohol use is concerned, the Sikh stance is fairly straightforward. Tobacco and drug use are strictly forbidden. The Gurus encouraged their disciples to practice natural methods to control and cultivate the potential of the senses. Each of the senses provides a particular pathway to states of consciousness that leads to the experience of oneness. But to achieve this state the senses also have to be directed by the primary virtues such as truthful living, wisdom, temperance, justice, humility and contentment which lead to egoloss and *sahaj*. At the same time one must avoid being directed by the primary vices of *kām, krōdh, lob, mōh* and *ahankār*, which redirect the senses towards worldly things, leading to craving, addiction and ultimately an increase in the egocentric state of *manmukhta*. The vices simply add fuel to the fire. Drugs taken for so-called 'recreational' uses may lead to fleeting experiences of ecstasy, but in as much as these drug-induced states are accompanied by hallucinatory and delusional states of mind, they also run the risk of long-term damage to the body through long-term addiction. Drug use is therefore to be avoided except where they are prescribed by competent physicians for treatment of a specific illness. That being said, there are sectarian orders such as the Nihangs, or followers of the Sant *deras* who use opium variants to treat illness or alter and enhance certain mental states. In so far as alcohol dulls the senses, its use is also to be avoided as far as possible. However, in practice the strictures on alcohol are less strictly observed by many Sikhs.

Life and death

What are the Sikh teachings on Life and Death? How do these determine Sikh attitudes towards issues such as abortion, pre-natal testing, suicide and euthanasia? Are contraception and reproductive technologies compatible with Sikh principles?

We have looked at death and life in Chapters 5 and 6. To reiterate the broad argument of Chapter 5, death is a powerful and abiding theme in the teachings of the Sikh Gurus and more broadly within South Asian spirituality. Despite saying much about the fact and phenomenon of death, however, the Sikh Gurus also acknowledge that death is and will remain a constant mystery, an irresolvable contradiction, not least because death is intrinsically connected to life and existence rather than being opposed to it. Death and life are often mentioned and discussed in the same verse and often in the same line. In this sense the Sikh Gurus perceive death differently from modern science which defines death as 'the permanent cessation of the vital function in the bodies of animals and plants' or, simply, as the end of life caused by stoppage of the means of sustenance to body cells. Far from being expressions of morbidity and nihilism, Sikh teachings on death and life remind us of their attachment to worldly things and to their own self-centred natures, and that the unavoidable event of death marks the end not of the body but of the very self and identity that one has so carefully nourished throughout one's life. Contemplating both together, one truly comprehends the phenomenon of life and death (*maran jīvan ki sojhi pae*).

Suicide and euthanasia

Sikhs believe that human birth is a precious gift, an opportunity with which to harness the body's potential for adoring *nām* and serving others. Life is a field upon which the self can properly experience the twin registers of *sukh* (pleasure/enjoyment/happiness) and *dukh* (pain or suffering) as thoroughly intertwined. Although one's existence may be imbued with pain, Sikh teaching emphasizes that one should not reject pain by labelling it bad, but rather accept it with the same demeanour that one accepts pleasure. From such a perspective, many Sikhs argue that taking one's own life is ethically wrong because the impulse to annihilate oneself emanates primarily and paradoxically from a deep-seated self-attachment, the desire to cling to one's own life as if it were one's own to begin with.[6] Moreover, suicide far from solving anything only creates more pain for those left behind.

The case of euthanasia is more complex, however. To begin with, it is necessary to differentiate between active and passive euthanasia. Whereas active euthanasia implies the intentional hastening of death by a deliberate act, passive euthanasia can refer to the intentional hastening of death through a deliberate omission or withdrawal of things that might otherwise sustain life, for example, food, medical treatment and an artificial life-support mechanism. Furthermore, euthanasia can be carried out against the wishes of the patient or actually be requested by the patient and undertaken by a third party who might be a physician or other accomplice. The modern and conventional Sikh response to euthanasia is to say that the decision to kill or ascribe death to a person in pain or undergoing other forms of suffering is based on delusion. The causal root of delusion can be traced to one or another of the five vices spoken of in Sikh scripture (*kām* (lust), *krōdh* (anger), *lōbh* (coveteousness), *mōh* (attachment) and *ahamkar* (pride)).[7] In such cases, the argument goes, the dying person and/or the person assisting the dying person should use the process of dying as an opportunity to reflect on the nature of self-attachment and other psychological charges associated with the five vices. The idea here is that as long as there is life, there is always hope. Sikhs contemplating euthanasia should look at the whole picture, as it were, and try to make the appropriate distinctions between ending life and not artificially prolonging a terminal state. For those who contemplate assisting the death of another, the emphasis of this argument is to provide greater care and service for others who are less fortunate.

While this theory works perfectly well in the cases where the motive for hastening death is bodily pain or a similar type of suffering, complications can arise when we broaden the motives for hastening death – for example, if we take into account historically important cases of Sikhs refusing to live in order to serve a 'higher' or nobler cause. The obvious example is the person who hastens his or her own death in order to save others from a fate that they themselves may not have contemplated – for example, the possibility of an entire community being enslaved or becoming subservient to more powerful external sociopolitical forces. Two of the Sikh Gurus (Arjan and Tegh Bahadur) willingly chose to be tortured and die rather than prolong their own lives and comforts, and in so doing condemn their fellow men and women to subservience and misery. Their deaths had a powerful emancipatory force on the community. There are numerous other examples in early and modern Sikh history. Of course, such death is normally classified as martyrdom. But how distinct, philosophically and spiritually, is the concept of martyrdom from other types of death, especially when the idea of a good or proper death is so strong in Sikh scripture? The point here is that health practitioners may need to be aware, on the one hand, of the psychological motivations for an individual's hastening death and, on the other, of the deeply spiritual and often ambivalent nature of Sikh teachings on death.

Abortion

The modern Sikh Code of Conduct and related historical sources are silent about the question of abortion. As a result, individual Sikhs and Sikh communities in Punjab and in the Western diaspora have had to work out relevant responses based on their interpretation of the teachings of the Sikh Gurus or by resorting to existing Punjabi cultural norms and shared traditions.

When one turns to Sikh scripture, however, the issue of abortion is not specifically mentioned although there are many references to the conception of life, the nature of sentient beings and the transmigration of the soul. In consonance with prevalent North Indian cultural beliefs and practices, many

Sikhs share a culture and world view that includes ideas of *karma*, rebirth and collective as opposed to individual identity. Unlike the linear notion of time held by Judaism, Christianity and Islam, many Sikhs (like Hindus, Jains and Buddhists) believe that time is nonlinear and consequently birth and death are repeated for each person in a continuous cycle. The desires, thoughts and actions one does in a particular lifetime leave their traces in the memory of an individual. These traces influence the circumstances and predispositions experienced in future lives. Accordingly, there is no absolute beginning or end. More importantly, from such a perspective, the moment of conception is the rebirth of a fully developed person who has lived in previous lifetimes. To terminate a birth through abortion would be tantamount to refusing a soul entry into a particular body and sending it back into the cycle of birth and death – a choice that is not ours to make.

As we have seen in Chapter 5, Sikh philosophy does indeed make reference to *karmic* theory. Consequently, those Sikhs who interpret the Gurus' teachings as inseparable from the broader North Indian cultural world view tend to take a firm position that abortion is wrong as it interferes in the divine play of things. If conception has taken place, the argument goes, it would be wrong to deliberately induce miscarriage and abortion. Based as it is on a purely metaphysical standpoint, however, such a view is increasingly recognized by Sikhs today as idealistic, and unable to provide suitable answers to instances such as (i) a threat to the mother's physical health if continuing pregnancy were to lead to her death, or if it were to physically harm the mother but not cause her death; (ii) a threat to the mother's psychological health, if, for example, the pregnancy is due to rape or incest, or if there is an adverse medical condition; (iii) problems with the foetus' health, for example, if the foetus is malformed or has contracted a disease such as HIV; (iv) when a woman simply wishes to exercise the 'right to choose' as to whether or not to abort the foetus.

Because the vast majority of scriptural teachings avoid such metaphysical standpoints as at the very least unhelpful, most Sikhs influenced by the modern reformist tradition tend to interpret the Guru's teachings in a more pragmatic fashion. Thus, if one follows the above-mentioned hymn through to completion, it becomes obvious that the Gurus had a more pragmatic and existential notion of nature of time rooted in an acceptance of impermanence. Consequently, neither modern Sikh society nor its ecclesiastical structure is concerned to lay down hard and fast rules in regard to issues such as abortion. Nevertheless, if there are strictures regarding abortion which would be binding on all Sikhs, it would be that abortion should not be linked to any kind of personal gain, economic or otherwise, nor driven by selfish motives or by the five vices.

A poignant example of the way that the doctrinal ambiguity can have negative social consequences can be seen in the continuing prevalence of female foeticide in many Sikh (and North Indian) couples.[8] This bias stems from the patriarchal nature of North Indian society in which women are viewed as economic liabilities, resulting in a social preference for male heirs. As a result, when they are married, sons receive a dowry along with their wives, which adds to the family prestige and wealth. For daughters the case is reversed. One result of this cultural belief/practice has been a slight decrease in the female population, especially in Punjab. As a social practice it has reached alarming proportions in the diaspora, where large numbers of Punjabi-Sikh women especially in Canada and Britain have succumbed either to greed or to the pressures of extended family and seek early termination of the pregnancy. There are increasing signs, however, that the political, social and spiritual empowerment of women in Sikhism may help to curb this unhealthy trend.

Contraception and reproductive technologies

Although contraception and abortion are often linked together, they are two rather different issues. In the case of contraception, birth control takes place before pregnancy begins. So, until the sperm fertilizes the egg there is no form of life that can be killed. However, the issue becomes a little more complicated when we consider forms of birth control that come into play after the egg has been fertilized but prior to pregnancy becoming established. A good example is the 'morning-after pill'. These birth control pills work by stopping eggs being released, inhibiting sperm or preventing the implantation of a fertilized egg.[9]

For Sikhs there are a number of interlinked issues to consider. How is life defined, particularly in Sikh scripture? If one could define life as such, at what point does life actually begin in the reproductive timetable? And is there is a moral difference between not starting a life (contraception) and ending one (abortion)? As we have seen, although the scriptures are non-committal on this topic, there are hints that the definition of life is relatively fluid and would incorporate a continuum that includes non-sentient and sentient forms. According to the writings of the Sikh Gurus, then, a proper moral issue can only arise when the new life-form becomes sentient. Even though sentience includes both unconscious and conscious states of existence, the crucial point of origin may not necessarily be the physical joining of sperm and ovum but happens at a later stage, that is, when the foetus becomes sentient. The difficulty of pinning this process down might explain why Sikhs are not unnecessarily concerned about contraception unless it becomes a process that is both driven by and leads to an increase in the five vices. In addition, it is also helpful to remember that women in rural India have long used alternative methods, techniques and traditional remedies to prevent contraception and carry out abortions. Thus, contraception and abortion are not linked strongly to religious concerns as they are in other cultures.

Nevertheless, the problem of female foeticide in many Sikh and Punjabi households highlights the way in which reproductive technologies, such as those that enable parents to predict the sex of the foetus, can and have been routinely used for unethical purposes. Given the strong emphasis in Sikhism on the family, the use of research and technology is generally considered an asset and has rarely, if ever, raised ethical issues. With the Sikh Code of Conduct being generally silent on the issue of technology, Sikhs by and large are likely to be open towards technologies such as in vitro fertilization which can give a woman the chance to bear children. Although issues such as genetic engineering have not been routinely discussed in the community, given the non-dogmatic nature of Sikh philosophy, Sikhs are unlikely to be opposed to such research given its potential to predict and eradicate cases of chronic disease such as Parkinson's, MS, Down's syndrome and certain types of cancer.

Mental illness

Disease according to its modern conception is an unhealthy condition, an illness or sickness of the body and mind. Such a definition presupposes that the body has a normal condition which is health and wholeness. Health, in turn, has been defined by the World Health Organization as a 'state of complete physical, mental and social well-being and not merely the absence of disease or infirmity' but is more narrowly conceived by many practising physicians as the body's physical display of vital statistics determined by medical science.[10]

While such definitions are perfectly acceptable to Sikh philosophy, as we've learnt from our discussion in the previous chapter, they're also far too narrow. Their narrowness results, on the one hand, from having reduced the idea of health only to what can be seen, measured and replicated according to scientific criteria and, on the other hand, from having determined health as opposed to disease. Health is the condition of the self and, by definition, that which must remain healthy in order to be self. And it does this by constantly staving off disease of body and mind. In the teachings of the Sikh Gurus, however, health and disease are ontologically connected. This is because body and mind are considered to be part of a continuum rather than opposed as matter versus spirit. Health is therefore imaginary if only because it is temporary. The real state of our being is dis-ease. In this sense, disease is not episodic but chronic. Dis-ease is a condition of existing in time and the world but without being in tune with its ebbs and flows, and without realizing its transitory nature. Therefore, loss of self and the collapse of the body are normative conditions.

In Sikh scripture disease is 'causally' connected, not to a bodily mis-function but to the way in which man fundamentally exists in the world – namely, the state of ego. In its wider ontological sense disease takes root when a person asserts 'I am myself' (*haumai*) and turns this enunciation of his state of being into a defensive posture resistant to the flows of nature that is the root cause of all disease, bodily and mental. Thus Guru Nanak says:

> Ego is given to man as his disease.
> Disease affects all creatures that arise in the world
> Except those who remain detached'.
> We're born into sickness
> Birth after birth we wander.
> Afflicted by sickness one finds no rest,
> Without the Guru sickness never ceases.

>   (GGS: p. 1140)

In a sense this may seem to suggest that disease is incurable, or, that it is not ultimately important to cure disease since any cure will be temporary. To the modern sensibility such a standpoint may seem overly resignatory, perhaps even nihilistic. A better way to look at this teaching is to refrain from automatically objectifying disease and sickness and consider it in the first place as an ontological and epistemological conditioning of the mind. From this expanded perspective it is possible to think of disease not simply as a person 'X' marked with disease 'Y', and therefore not as a terrifying other that must be stigmatized and isolated, but rather as something that is already part of my-self. Does this mean, then, that disease is simply illusory? If so, what would be the idea of a cure and of medicine?

A closer look at Sikh practices and attitudes towards health practices, however, suggests a very reasoned approach to the question of disease. The Sikh Gurus, for example, brush aside superstitious practices prevalent in South Asian culture such as the belief that disease is caused by the 'evil eye' (*buri nazar*), black magic (*jadu-tuna*) or possession by evil spirits (*bhut–preta*), or that it is the result of divine punishment.[11] Indeed, the Gurus built sanctuaries in which they along with their followers worked to heal the sick, particularly those afflicted by leprosy and smallpox. This can be seen in the Sikh practice of donating money for building hospitals and schools. The theory and practice of the Sikh Gurus are particularly evident in contemporary trends in Sikh philanthropy, a notable example of this being Sikh openness towards organ donation. Organ donation is also a common trend among Sikhs and is considered to be a good example of selfless giving as taught by the Sikh Gurus.

As we have noted Sikh philosophy cultivates a relatively holistic view of the body as continuous with immaterial consciousness. A consequence of this is a perspective where the accumulation of memory traces not only affects the character of the self and one's access to the soul (*atman*) but equally impacts the body. According to Sikh belief, the body is considered perishable and not needed in the cycle of rebirth. The real essence is the accumulation of memory traces that comprises one's soul: 'The dead sustain their bond with the living through virtuous deeds'. The final act of giving and helping others through organ donation is both consistent with and in the spirit of Sikh teachings.[12]

While the medical and nursing professions are highly regarded by Sikhs, health practitioners should nevertheless be aware that attitudes among Sikhs may vary depending on the individual's level of education and social background. Also, many Sikhs are increasingly turning away from the industrial drug-based approach of modern medicine towards a more holistic view of disease. This is partly the result of a resurgence of interest in alternative modes of therapy. Reliance on homeopathic medicine is becoming increasingly common as patients become more aware of the side effects of modern chemical treatments. This resurgence has been aided by ethnic TV channels which routinely teach yoga, Ayurvedic medicine and other techniques to combat a large variety of ailments.

Mental illness in the Sikh community poses a different kind of challenge to health professionals from somatic illnesses. For one thing, the stigmatizing view of mental illness that exists today in the Sikh and Punjabi communities is of relatively recent origin. It is now recognized that prior to its extended period of contact with the Western world in the nineteenth century, South Asian communities did not stigmatize many of the symptoms that we commonly associate with mental illness with the label of abnormality or disorder. In pre-colonial South Asian culture signs of madness and eccentricity were commonly connected to the spiritual quest and specifically to the attainment of ecstatic, erotic and emotional mysticism and related meditative states of mind. As the Indian psychologist Sudhir Kakar argues,

the mystic undergoes a creative immersion in the deepest layers of his or her psyche, with its potential risk of chaos and lack of integration.

The mystical regression is akin to that of the analysand, an absorbing and at times painful process at the service of psychic transformation. . . . the potential mystic may be better placed than the analysand to connect with – and perhaps correct – the depressive core at the base of human life which lies beyond language. (Kakar, p. 129)

In Chapter 2 of this book we discussed Guru Nanak's struggle with his own family regarding this issue. After he had shown physical and other signs of depression for several months, Nanak's family sent for the village physician to remedy his apparent illness. When the physician arrived and took Nanak's arm to check his pulse, Nanak refused the treatment:

The physician was sent to prescribe a remedy;
    Taking my hand he feels my pulse,
But the ignorant fool knows not that the pain is in my mind.
    Physician, go home; take not my curse with you.
What use is this medicine when my sickness is my state of love?
    When there's pain, the physician stands ready with his store of pills.
My body weeps, the soul cries out to remove this medicine.
    Go home, physician, few understand the source of my pain.
The One who gave me this pain, will remove it.

(GGS: p. 1156)

At the heart of this broadly South Asian perspective was a theory and practice of transforming the ego which was seen as a means of achieving a well-balanced and healthy state of being. With the rise of secularized Western ego-centred psychology in the twentieth century – a process that re-centres the person's psychic framework within and in reference to a strong normative ego, the indigenous perspective came to be thoroughly marginalized. This has had a profound effect on South Asians, Sikhs included, as they have been more or less deprived of an outlet for dealing with psychological problems of all sorts.

The problem is acute for those who migrated to and settled in Western countries but perhaps even more so for second-generation Sikhs and South Asians who are caught between two or more cultures and languages and often have to work their way through the proverbial 'identity crisis'. More often than not such psychological crises can be triggered by any number of events including most commonly for first-generation migrants: economic failures, or marital problems due to changing roles of Sikh men and women trying to balance a culturally conservative 'home' culture with a more 'liberal' culture outside, or the problems associated with children who demand a greater cross-over between the two cultures. More common these days are the problems stemming from racial and religious non-acceptance, addictions of various kinds, or failure to live up to the social ideals of one culture which often express themselves in the early years of marriage or inability to find appropriate partners, or simply being torn between conflicting cultural requirements, experienced by second- and third-generation Sikhs.[13]

These problems may be compounded by the fact that there is often no social, spiritual or other support mechanisms for second-generation Sikhs. So when Sikh and South Asian patients suffering from a psychological crisis are given counselling along with Western models – usually in the form of a 'talking therapy' – these patients have tended to terminate the counselling after one or two sessions.[14] This may be because psychologists and counsellors lacking exposure to non-Western traditions work within a monocultural perspective and are usually unaware of the complexities of the patient's world view. Very often this results in the South Asians being stereotyped as inappropriate patients for talking therapy. At the very least health practitioners need to be aware of their biases and value assumptions when treating Sikh and South Asian patients for mental 'disorders'.[15] By understanding the Sikh world view, for example, it may be possible to develop very different intervention techniques and strategies, which recognize that different cultures can offer equally valid and often more appropriate cures even though their theory and practice may be diametrically opposed to Western-based methods and therapies.

In recent years more and more Sikh doctors, psychologists and counsellors have begun to experiment with and incorporate therapies based on Sikh spirituality. Many of these models adapt traditional Sikh teachings about spiritual liberation to modern Western models. Central to these models is learning how to make the transition from a *manmukh* (self- or ego-centred personality) to a *gurmukh* (personality that incorporates egoloss into his or her every thought, word and deed). The passage from *manmukh* to *gurmukh* goes through several steps: (i) learning to identify the work of the ego in one's psyche; (ii) to understand the nature of ego; (iii) to undertake a path of self-realization through theory and devoted practice or meditation based on *nām simaran* (remembrance of the Name); (iv) to understand the 'five vices' (basic weaknesses of human nature manifest as: concupiscence, covetousness, delusion/attachment, anger, pride) and to identify the psychological charge associated with each 'vice' that specifically affects the personality concerned; (v) to supplant the 'vices' with the opposing virtues (strengths or qualities): wisdom, truthful existence, temperance, justice, courage and humility; (vi) ending with the achievement of a state of psychological and social balance (*sahaj*).

Genetic engineering and stem cell research

Is genetic engineering permissible? Should stem cell research be allowed?

Genetic engineering refers to technologies used to change the genetic makeup of cells and move genes across species boundaries to produce novel organisms. Genes are the chemical blueprints that determine an organism's traits. Moving genes from one organism to another transfers those traits. Through genetic engineering, organisms are given new combinations of genes – and therefore new combinations of traits – that neither occur in nature nor can be developed by natural means. Such artificial technology is radically different from traditional forms of plant and animal breeding.

As far as a Sikh position is concerned, there is as yet no clear consensus on genetic engineering. The natural evolution of organisms is understood as encompassed by the principle of *hukam* (life is ever changing by its very nature). So as long as it is therapeutic in intent and motive, there seems to be no clear reason for a Sikh position against it. On the other hand, its use for eugenic purposes, the creation of chimera, human clones or cosmetic purposes is much more problematic. For example, while gene therapy for preventing or curing illness is acceptable, tampering with the design of human (or animal) species to increase certain abilities, to select a child's characteristics might be construed as going against the principle of *hukam*.

Stem cell research (SCR) is a new technology that can extract primitive human cells and develop them into 220 different cell types found in the human body. Some scientists have argued that SCR may hold the key to uncover treatments and cures for some of the worst diseases such as diabetes, neurodegenerative diseases such as Alzheimer's and Parkinson's. Stem cells can be extracted from three sources: adult tissue, the umbilical cord and embryos. The first two sources present difficulties for extraction. While embryonic stem cells are much easier to extract and have greater uses than their adult counterparts, much of the ethical controversy surrounding SCR is also centred around the use of embryos because of questions about when life begins.

The actual debate involves two key ethical concerns: (i) the potential of SCR for human cloning and (ii) whether these embryos actually constitute human life. The pro-life lobby, which is particularly strong in the United States and in Catholic countries like Poland and Italy, argues that since the extraction process requires the destruction of the blastocyst, it is tantamount to murder. Against this, advocates of SCR argue, first, that the embryo at the blastocyst stage has no human features, and second, that the process involving removal and implantation of nuclear material has already existed for several decades in the common practice of in vitro fertilization which has helped many childless couples to conceive. Religious arguments that assume certainty regarding exactly when human life begins and arguments regarding the sanctity of life might not sound too convincing to many Sikh philosophers. For them questions such as 'when does life begin?' are problematic since we are confusing our role and ability to begin life with the fact that life is simply ongoing. It was there before us and will be there after us. In their writings the Gurus ask: Who can know when life will end or when it begins? Or how many myriads of streams of life there may be? Life is life. The force that propels life is outside our comprehension. It is arrogant to think of ourselves as guardians of life. We should simply live it. It is neither sacred nor profane, neither good nor evil.

Environment and ecology

Are environmental concerns part of the Sikh ethos? Do animals have a moral standing in Sikh philosophy?

There is simply no ethical issue more important right now, and in the foreseeable future, than the environmental crisis. In the manner of their initial response to this crisis, Sikhs have tended to follow other major religious traditions of the world. Practitioners, activists, NGOs and leaders from the Sikh community have developed greater sensitivity to the climate crisis, approaching it in ways that broadly correspond to the threefold schema: interpretation, practical engagement and transformation.[16]

Thus, activists have developed interpretations of Sikh scriptural sources with increased emphasis on recovering the spiritual wisdom from the writings of the Sikh Gurus, and using its philosophy as a resource to inspire and justify ecological activism. Much of this interpretive activity so far has been at a basic level and consists mostly of pulling relevant quotes from authoritative sources like *Japji*, *Aarti* and *Baramaha* compositions which provide intricate descriptions of nature's workings in different months and seasons, and juxtaposes them with the separation of the individual soul from its Beloved source. While these are rich and important resources which, at the very least, demonstrate *gurmat*'s deep eco-orientation, that is, the orientation of Sikh concepts towards, on the one hand, the earth as mother and physical home (*mata dharat mahat*), and on the other hand, its spiritual home, by way of reference to the relationship between soul and its primordial source. Second, numerous activists and organizations have not only applied Sikh philosophical concepts to engage wider issues in the world; they have also *applied themselves* as vehicles of engagement to enact real changes to their immediate environment; and here what comes to mind are the very practical concepts of *seva* (service) and *sarbhat da bhalla* (serving with a view to helping the wider world) thereby fostering a culture of care.

Despite this level of engagement, the sheer scope of the environmental crisis is forcing many Sikh eco activists to re-evaluate *gurmat's* epistemological counterpart to the activism, which we might call 'Sikh Eco-Philosophy'. Any potential Sikh Eco-Philosophy must significantly recalibrate and expand its intellectual scope above its current level to meet the sheer complexity of environmental issues and their relationship to life. This need for elevation-expansion brings me to the third aspect of the threefold schema mentioned above, namely transformation.

As individuals and organizations interpret and engage, this has fed into a growing realization that the existing social/intellectual vehicles through which Sikh practitioners have been working are inadequate to the current task. They require a radical expansion of their epistemic capacities – the need to combine knowledge of Sikh concepts with a clear-eyed reassessment of the intellectual frameworks and contexts in which interpreters are operating; frameworks which very often reproduce the very same oppositionalities and binaries that prevent Sikh concepts being applied to real-life problems. The scope of the ecological crisis means that activists need to maximize the connectivity of Sikh philosophical concepts to other traditions, to other movements and to realms as different as the theological, the secular, scientific, economic, the social and the political. Only by fostering such connectivity, will Sikh concepts be able to foster change in these realms.

To give a concrete example, by revisioning Sikh concepts in Guru Nanak's compositions (such as the *Rāg Mārū* hymn) in earlier chapters, I showed how reflections on the cosmic and the psychic were signalling towards the broader theme of *individuation*, or, more accurately, the double-bind of individuation as a medium of ongoing cosmic creativity, and as a disease associated with the limiting function of human ego. In short, the revisioning of Sikh concepts exudes an uncompromising demand to comprehend reality (ontology) in terms of absolute interconnection/relationality between the material and the immaterial. It's the absolute nature of this interconnection that makes it incumbent on us to connect spiritual ideas to ostensibly secular realms in ways that explode the understanding of what can be encompassed within the term 'ecology'. From this interconnected perspective, ecology must include economy, politics, health, society, technology – all of which challenges our understanding of what an ecosystem is. In other words, what we think of as planetary ecology (restoring planetary health) cannot be separated either from psychic ecology or from social or political ecology. And just to push this argument a little further, it is not only the case that the root cause of climate crisis is what numerous sages, including the Sikh Gurus, have called 'the disease of ego', which manifests today as the kind of human Exceptionalism underpinning neo-liberal capitalism and the politics of Un-caring spawned by it.[17] It is also the case that definitions of ecology need to be extended beyond merely environmental concerns to include human subjectivity and sociality, or to put it bluntly, to ask how societies can work together, collectively, in a unified struggle against neo-Liberal Exceptionalism's ongoing planetary ecocide.

On the question of animals and their standing, the simple answer is yes! Animals are sentient beings and part of an interconnected web of existence (*sargun*) and non-existence (*nirgun*) in which any particular being has as much right to exist as any other. In other words, in as much as every being (elemental, plant, mineral, animal and human) is imbued with *nām*, then each being is sovereign, not in its own right (as though beings exist independently), but only in their expression of *nām*, here envisioned as the interdependent being-with-others that is the natural organic intelligence of life itself.

In Sikh philosophy *nirgun* and *sargun* are envisioned as aspects of a single process that Guru Nanak calls *hukam* which equally encompasses the timeless infinite (or transcendent) and temporally finite (immanent) as absolutely inseparable. Thus the term 'moral' here cannot originate from human comprehension and calculation. Morality is therefore tied to *hukam* – the organic law of intelligence that supports life's ever-freshness, its perpetual renewal. That which supports all life forms in their increasing diversity is in tune with *hukam* – this is moral standing. And for life forms to sustain themselves may mean that they eat each other but in balance. Although they eat each other, animals do not take this to extinction as they live within *hukam*. Killing is therefore not against sovereignty or this kind of *hukam*-tied-morality. Human killing is a different matter – its net effect is the destruction of all life forms and putting an increasing number out of existence. The loss of species and the rate of that loss suggest that humanity's mode of being-in-the-world has tipped over into a form that is addicted to enhancing its self-preservation without regard for the cost. It's a reverse economy that many mystics speak of. Hence *gurbāṇī's* emphasis on constantly losing oneself (to know *hukam* let not the ego say 'I am' – *hukamai je bujhai ta haumai kahe na koi* as Guru Nanak says in his Japji).

Moral standing is thus measured by one's capacity to live by negating the 'I am', to live beyond the 'I am' so that everything else in the world can flourish. It could be argued that animals live life in a similar state – and hence (whether they do or not) – they have become part of the mystic's grammar across cultures – as exemplars of beings that can live beyond ego, 'I', etc., that is without fear, without hate, in co-existential spontaneity or *sahaj*.

Discussion questions

(1) What foundation does Sikh philosophy rely on to ground its ethical principles?

(2) Can Sikh ethics be separated from its cultural background? Discuss the implications of doing so.

(3) Can Sikh ethical concepts and practices be applicable to contemporary social justice movements?

(4) Are the notions of 'immanence' and 'transcendence' relevant to Sikh ethics? To what extent do 'immanence' or 'transcendence' succeed or fail in addressing issues such as wealth equity and global warming?

(5) How does *gurmat* philosophy justify the use of force?

(6) How is it possible to challenge oppressive systems of power through philosophy of egoloss?

(7) Sikh philosophy views all as consciousness. How would integrating this axiom affect our view of resource exploitation systems? How might this play into environmental justice movements?

Epilogue

Although this book opened with the question: 'What is Sikh philosophy?', it should be clear to anyone who has worked through each of the chapters that the question itself has been transformed over the course of our investigation. In view of what I have shown and argued, more fitting questions might be: What is Sikh philosophy *for*? What can it *do*? The nature of these questions signals a clear departure from the conventional notion of philosophical inquiry as a transcendental mode of knowing about the essence of things from a 'disinterested', 'impartial' or 'neutral' stance, which in turn is supposed to be 'achieved through a separation of oneself and the world in the act of knowing'. As Kirloskar-Steinbach and Kalmanson remind us, crucial to such separation is 'the view that philosophical inquiry is driven by an historical, culturally invariant, and universal self'.[1]

However, as each chapter in this book has tried to demonstrate in different ways, the epistemic stance proper to Sikh philosophy is one which co-implicates the self in a deep entanglement with other selves and with the world as we attempt to understand it. In other words, Sikh philosophy's epistemic stance, it's basic mode of knowing, is not only imbricated in social practice but in making connections to the outside world – and it does this through the event-nature of its key concepts, that is to say, the performative capacity of its concepts, their capacity to make things happen in the world, to change our world in positive ways.

To state this differently, the fundamental concepts of Sikh philosophy operate in such a way that they not only represent objects, propositions or facts about Sikh tradition but are practically involved with the world. In doing so, Sikh philosophy deals with 'embodied aspects of experience' which involve changes in the knowing subject itself. By making the knowing subject central to its epistemic stance, Sikh philosophy involves a 'sustained attentiveness' to transformations in one's self-understanding. As a field of inquiry it is able to simultaneously associate subjective and objective dimensions of knowledge, or, to use a term that's characteristic of more recent approaches in the field of world philosophies, Sikh philosophy engages in a 'relational knowing' through which one's sense of self is automatically decentred in relation to other selves, and to the world as such. To apply an insight from Helen Verran for our context, Sikh philosophy operationalizes the capacity for producing 'transformative encounters for deliberate pedagogical self reflection'.

Through such moments of transformation it may be possible to experience the 'insidious tentacles of the institutions and unacknowledged beliefs within which we negotiate our existential positioning as knowers' (Verran: p. 44). Verran's remarks are directed towards 'knowledge traditions that have been hitherto excluded from conventional knowledge frameworks' – a good example being the thought-practices of Australian Aboriginals. But they apply equally well to the contemporary Sikh world whose younger generations are not only becoming increasingly aware of the racialized, gendered and exclusionary ways that knowledge of their heritage traditions is positioned in the arena of global thought vis-à-vis the 'insidious tentacles of its institutions' but are also deeply embroiled in quests for epistemic justice.

My point here is that the philosophical explorations of *gurmat* as a knowledge tradition presented in this book have a counterpart in the contemporary Sikh public sphere. Notwithstanding the fact that books such as this one are written in the institutional context of an elite research university, the kind of 'relational knowing' I have tried to put into play throughout these chapters has a direct counterpart in the interpretive activities of a younger and technologically savvy generation of Sikhs who are trying to apply Sikh concepts to their daily lives and the world they live in, albeit in very different ways. This interpretive activity, which might simply be regarded as a diasporic version of *gurmat vichār* (philosophical reflection or contemplation on self & world inspired by *gurmat*), albeit one that no longer takes place solely in the Punjabi language as it did for first-generation migrant Sikhs, appears to have been triggered by something akin to a diasporic and postcolonial consciousness of living and thinking-between different languages, cultures and worlds.

Over the past decade or so this diasporic postcolonial sensibility has become prevalent, if not entirely pervasive, within academic and popular discourses about Sikhism. The burgeoning of this diasporic *gurmat vichār* in such a short span of time can be attributed to the availability of internet forums, social media and the recent rise of ethnic Sikh and Punjabi TV channels. These new forums have enabled complex ideas arising in academic texts to be translated (though just as often mistranslated) into popular language and vigorously debated in the public sphere at a speed that was unthinkable barely a decade ago. The interesting aspect of this phenomenon is how, in their attempts to imbibe and internalize these ideas, younger generations of Sikhs in India and the diaspora haven't simply been passively imbibing and internalizing ideas and debates originating in the academic sphere but managed to trigger processes of cultural, spiritual, philosophical, psychological and political introspection enabling them to uninherit debilitating frameworks and rehabilitate foundational concepts of Sikh thought.[2]

An important consequence of this un/inheriting is the rise of a critical awareness in younger generations of Sikhs motivating them to productively transgress limitations on their subjectivity imposed, on the one hand, by Sikh religious ethno-nationalism and, on the other hand, by the secular humanism of state discourses in India and the West. Such constructive transgressions are especially evident in the work of visual artists, musicians, feminist writers but also in the organizational efforts of social media and internet 'influencers' experimenting with forms of *gurmat vichār*. These 'influencers' are enabling younger generations of Sikhs to more effectively intervene in and influence the wider world they live in by bringing concepts and categories found in Sikh literatures and traditional texts – scriptural, commentarial, hagiographical *sakhī*, performative, musical and poetic – into contact with global flows of thought and practice.[3] In this way they are able to enhance their capacity to enact forms of agency that escape both the narrow ideological confines of religious ethno-nationalist identity and the objectifying secular humanism of the modern state.

More specifically, as younger Sikhs clamour for a more nuanced and meaningful engagement with the worlds in which they live, on the one hand, by improving the ability to make connections to non-Sikh cultures, ideas and institutions and, on the other hand, by widening the interpretative frameworks for understanding Sikh concepts beyond the religio-secular, the discursive sphere they are consistently drawn to, certainly in the last decade or so, is the sphere variously known as 'Sikh *chintan*' (thought or philosophy), *gurbānī vichār* (reflection on the Guru's utterances) or simply *gurmat* (lit. the Guru's logic). As I noted in this book's Introduction, this discursive sphere corresponds to the strand of scholarly activity by colonial elites which broadly equated *gurmat* with philosophical thinking and included within its ambit such activities as *chintan* (thought), *viākhiā* (commentary), *vichār* (reflection) and *kathā* (oral exegesis) all of which refer to the process of reflective thought based on modes of exegesis connecting Sikh concepts to the outside world, and in a sense provides a measure of the pulse of the Sikh life-world.

The broad shift of interest on the part of younger Sikh generations towards the philosophical strand of *gurmat*, combined with the fact that it now corresponds to an actual intellectual formation known as 'Sikh philosophy', can be regarded as the second phase of the decolonial turn mentioned earlier. If the first phase of genuine decolonization began with an awareness of the debilitating effects of religio-secular consciousness and a concomitant break with the revivalist neo-colonial identification of *gurmat* = religion = Sikhism,

the emerging second phase can be witnessed in the desire to re-appropriate
the processes of thought and self-reflexivity necessary for genuine agency, and
also in their attempts to experiment with new thought processes and forms
of identification situated at the intersections of the Sikh life-world and global
thought. The broad aims of such experimentation can be described as follows:
(i) to re-channel desire as a productive force for widening connections by first
unblocking the flows of meaning-making which have locked the Sikh life-
world within an ethno-nationalist frame since the late nineteenth century;
(ii) to actualize an agency capable of making and remaking Sikh concepts in
conjunction with processes of selfing and de-selfing, which results in (iii) a
radical re-orientation and expansion of the contemporary Sikh world view.

In this way, Sikh philosophy serves at least two very specific purposes.
First, it provides an entry point into, as well as a key for unlocking and
analysing the plane on which any thinking is occurring. Second, it provides
a vehicle for epistemically reconstituting key Sikh concepts. Such a vehicle
would allow them to interact with and potentially influence the flows of
global thought, while simultaneously allowing these same concepts to be
'molded and modelled according to the praxis of living of those who engage
in doing it'.[4]

In this vein I would like to point out two tasks towards which Sikh
philosophy may become an indispensable vehicle for interacting with and, at
some stage, possibly influencing global and local knowledge systems.

Arguably the most urgent task facing Sikhs is the question of sovereignty
which has political and epistemic ramifications.[5] If we accept a definition
of sovereignty as the 'power to authorize', which is first of all the power to
authorize the self, many Sikhs would argue that *gurmat* itself provides an
understanding of sovereignty that challenges modern Western notions of
territorialized state-centric sovereignty. In mainstream Sikh tradition the
'power to authorize' is vested in the living memory and practice of a very
particular phenomenon – the successive transformation of 'Guru' from
a living person to a central authoritative text (Adi Granth), and from this
text to an incorporeal concept of the Word (*śabda*), and from here to a
sovereign community (*Khalsa*). Underpinning the fluid movement between
corporeality and incorporeality is the authority of the name 'Nanak', who is
both the founding figure of the Sikh movement and the authorizing name
under which his successor Gurus signed their poetry.

Since the late nineteenth century, however, as various forms of modern
state-centric governance have redefined the nature of sovereignty in India and
elsewhere (British colonial, Indian secularist, Euro-American multiculturalist,
Hindu nationalist), Sikh life-worlds have been divested of access to their own
knowledge systems and thus to a sovereign consciousness. The question that

arises here is whether the role of modern government is so hegemonic, and the transformations wrought by colonialism and modernization so deeply internalized by Sikh elites, that indigenous sovereign modes of existence have become little more than a faint echo of what they were. However, as I have alluded to in the Introduction and elsewhere, the earlier forms of sovereign consciousness were never eradicated but simply *interdicted* – which is to say, their ability to manifest publicly in everyday speech has been privatized but not destroyed. So the answer to the above-mentioned question, and an important challenge for Sikh philosophy, depends on whether Sikhs in the twenty-first century can learn to 'un-inherit' the conceptual structures of colonial (European-white) supremacy in which *Sikhī*-sm is deeply entangled. The field of Sikh philosophy has an important role to play here, not only for decolonizing the dogmatic image of global thought but in helping Sikh concepts to negotiate new relations to the world without jettisoning what has been inherited.

Related to the above is the challenge of pluralism. Sikh thought, even the system of *gurmat* and its concepts, did not arise in a cultural or intellectual vacuum. Modern historians and scholars of religion have tried to demarcate the antecedents of *Sikhī* and *gurmat*. While some have attributed them to the prevailing Punjabi spirituality and cultural ethos, others have pointed to loose lineages of pan-Indian spiritual masters, or some have more crudely seen it as a synthesis of Hinduism and Islam, or as derived from Nath Yogic and Sufi systems. One thing is clear: *gurmat* and Sikh philosophy are not sui generis. Instead, they can be described as arising from the lived experiences of pluralism and its manifold expressions: spiritual, cultural, linguistic, political, ethical, intellectual to name the most obvious. The challenge for Sikh philosophy is to rediscover its internal multiplicity, to learn to be comfortable with its own difference in the manner of self-differentiation, to redefine its own identity in terms of its innately pluralist ethos, and then channel this same ethos into building relations with all expressions of difference: different peoples, genders, ethnicities, thought systems, religions, spiritualities, political systems, to mention a few.

Glossary

achēt: non-conscious; passive memory

achēt bhāg: state of non-consciousness; the unconscious; passive memory

Ādi Granth: lit. the first or original text, that is, the sacred scripture of the Sikhs; also known as the Guru Granth Sahib.

āhankār: pride; the 'I'-making function of the ego.

akāl: a key term in the Sikh lexicon which in theological parlance signifies 'divine-time' and has been misleadingly interpreted as the 'One beyond time' or simply as 'God'; conventional theology, however, not only introduces duality into the meaning of *akāl* but also diminishes its ontological significance by suggesting it refers to something ideal, metaphysical, that does not belong to *this* world; from a philosophical perspective, *akāl* signifies a time that is equally if not more real than *kāl* (human or historical time); it refers to a mode of time that can be accessed only via expansion of one's consciousness; *akāl* is the creative time, it cannot be measured, but it can only be felt as the intensity of emotions, passions or affects.

akāl purakh: often simply translated as the 'Timeless Being' or simply as 'God', a more suitable rendering would make reference to the agentive aspect of *akāl* (see above), in which case *akāl purakh* appears to signify something akin to the what is known as 'spirit' in Western philosophical theology.

Akāl Takht: the principal centre of Sikh temporal authority, this institution is located immediately adjacent to the Harimander Sahib or Golden Temple.

akhāṛā: wrestling arena; a monastic–militant order with its own centre that provides facilities for board, education and practice for a particular sect. It can either refer to a training hall used by martial artists or a monastery for religious renunciates.

amrit: immortal; undying in Sikh philosophy; in Sikh ritual it refers to the 'nectar of immortality' or sweetened water used in Sikh initiation ceremony.

anhad (anahat) śabda: 'unstruck' sound or word; poetic language in which ego traces are erased.

aql: everyday practical reason; common sense

anubhav: intuition

anubhav giān: wisdom or knowledge attained directly through intuition.

antahkaran: faculty for processing raw sensuous data of perception by interiorizing it.

ardās: formal prayer or supplication recited at the conclusion of many Sikh rituals.

artha: the meaning of a word or sentence

āvāgavan / āvanjāṇ: transmigration; coming and going; rebirth *avatār:* a 'descent' or incarnation of deity, usually Vishnu.

bādi: reasoning based on preconceived standpoints, beliefs or ideas; fallacious reasoning.

bhagat (bhaktā): exponent of devotional spirituality

bhaktī: form of loving devotion directed towards a personal or impersonal divine.

Bhaī: 'brother'; honorific applied to Sikhs of learning or piety.

brahman: the absolute as described in the Upanīsads; self-appointed highest caste in Hindu caste hierarchy.

buddhī: higher intellect related to *giān*

bibēk: awakened, enlightened

bibēk buddhī: awakened intellect

bibēk vichār: enlightened reasoning

birahā: psycho-somatic state in which the soul pines or longs for its Beloved; characterized by the inseparability of ecstasy and pain induced by separation from one's Beloved

chētanā: thread or stream of consciousness; memory

chētantā: process that brings something to consciousness

chētan satta: force of consciousness

chitt(a): mind, self-consciousness

chintan: thought

chintā: anxiety

darśan: the act of seeing or having an audience with the divine.

Dasam Granth: A Sikh scripture parts of which are attributed to the authorship of the tenth Sikh Guru, Gobind Singh.

dharam (Skt. dharma): philosophical teachings, doctrines, ethical obligations and practices associated with *gurmat* and *sikhī.*

dharam khand: plane of consciousness associated with conventional social obligations and ethical duties

dhyana: meditation; focused concentration

dukh: pain; suffering

fakīr (faqir): a Muslim ascetic loosely used to designate Sufis.

giān (Skt. jñāna): wisdom or knowledge.

giānī: knowledgeable one; in Sikhism individuals formally trained in scriptural interpretation and exegesis

gōshti: dialogue

Granth: lit. text referring to the Guru Granth Sahib or central Sikh scripture

guṇa: attribute or quality

gurbāṇī: 'utterance of the Guru'; compositions of the Sikh Gurus

gurdwara: a Sikh temple

gurmat: teachings of the Sikh Gurus

gurmat sangeet: Sikh musicology; sacred music of the Sikhs

gurmukh: one who lives according to the guru's teaching; one who has overcome ego

gurmukhi: 'From the Guru's mouth'; the Punjabi script

guru: a spiritual master; either a person or a mystical inner principle which aids emancipation of the disciple

Guru Granth Sahib: the Ādi Granth in its role as Guru

gurumata: 'Intention of the Guru'; a resolution passed by the Sarbat Khalsa (wider community of Khalsa Sikhs) in the presence of the Guru Granth Sahib

haṭha-yoga: yoga of physical exercises practised by adherents of the Nath tradition

haumai: 'I am myself'; self-centredness

hukam: order

ik oankar: One, manifest as the Word or command which sustains and unfolds creation; the opening words of Sikh scripture

janamsākhī: hagiographical narratives based on the life of Guru Nanak

jivanmukti/jivanmukt: liberation in the stream of life; one who is liberated while living.jap: the act of repeating the divine name, mantras or sacred texts

kāl: time or death

kāljug: the final and degenerate cosmic age in which human ego reigns supreme; age of human history; era of strife

kām: lust, craving

karam: one's deeds or acts

kirpā: grace

kartā: creator; agent, doer

kartā purakh: creative spirit

kathā: homily; exegetical narrative

Khalsa: A spiritual-cum-military order of Sikhs established by Guru Gobind Singh in 1699

khōj: seeking knowledge; research

kīrtan: singing of hymns (see *gurmat sangeet*)

klēsha: conflict, strife

Krishna: Hindu god; narrator of the *Bhāgvada Gita*

krōdh: wrath, anger

mn (pronounced 'mun'): mind; a common Indian term for mind, self, heart

manmukh: one who acts according to egotistical desires; contracted consciousness of ego

mantar (Skt. mantra): a verse, phrase or syllable invested with spiritual efficacy that is repeated by sounding

mat(i): intellect

maya: the illusory status of reality

mīrī-pīrī: doctrine of combined temporal (*mīrī*) and spiritual (*pīrī*) authority attributed initially to the living Sikh Guru but later adopted by the Khalsā

mōkh: free, liberated

mōkh duār: state of liberation

muktī (mokṣha): ultimate freedom; liberation from the cycle of transmigration

mūrtī: form or image of a deity in Hinduism

nām: often translated theologically as 'divine Name'; philosophically it refers to the creative impulse, a term expressing the central attribute of a paradoxical divine that is existent and non-existent at the same time

nād(a): sound

nadar: sight; divine grace

nām japaṇā: repetition of the divine Name

nām simaraṇ: devotional practice of meditating on the Name initially through vocalized repetition and eventually through interiorized repetition

Nath tradition: practitioners of hatha yoga; yogic sect influential in Punjab prior to and during the time of the Sikh Gurus

nirbāṇ (nirvana): extinction of suffering; without form

nirguṇ (Skt. nirguṇa): without qualities or attributes, not incarnated

Nirmala: A sect of celibate Sikhs influential in the nineteenth century

nirbhau: state of fearlessness; attribute of the One

nirvair: without enmity; no enemy; attribute of the One

nitnēm: daily rituals; Sikh liturgy

ōm (aum): the primal syllable said to contain the entire Sanskrit alphabet in seed form

ōankār: the primal Word or command that sustains and unfolds creation

Panth: lit. the way; the Sikh community

pāṭh: Recitations or readings from Sikh scriptures

prāṇa: life force, breath

Prnālī: lit. stream; traditions of Sikh thought-practice-commentary from which Sikh philosophy emerged

Puratan janamsākhī: one of the oldest extant collections of biographies of Guru Nanak

rāg: a traditional melodic type in Hindustani music, consisting of a theme that expresses an aspect of spiritual feeling and sets forth a tonal system on which variations are improvised within a prescribed framework of typical progressions, melodic formulas and rhythmic patterns

śabda: Word, language; verse or hymn of the Guru Granth Sahib

śabda-guru: the Word-as-Guru; Guru-as-Word

sabha: society or association

sādhan: method or technique of spiritual achievement

sādhū: a renunciate, mendicant or ascetic

sarguṇ (Skt. saguṇa): 'with qualities', possessing form or attributes

Śaiva (Śaivism/Śaivite): worshipper of the god Śiva

sahaj: naturally achieved condition of equipoise or bliss resulting especially from the practice of nam simaran Sahajdhari: A non-Khalsa Sikh

samadhī: state of deep absorption and concentration, especially in yoga

sampradaya: sect holding certain beliefs; traditional doctrine; a school of thought

sanātan dharma: perennial tradition of Vedic-Brahmanical heritage governed by the theological paradigm of 'eternal Sanskrit' and centrality of the Veda

sansāra: the material world; cycle of rebirth

sanskāra: trace; memory-trace; sacrament

Sant: person who has discovered the truth of existence and non-existence; teacher of gurmat

sat(i) *(Skt. satya):* reality, truth of existence

sati: practice of burning widows or concubines on the husband's funeral pyre

satnām reality is *nām*; or in theological parlance, truth is (your) Name

satsang: gathering of seekers after truth; Sikh congregation

sēvā: service

SGPC: Shiromani Gurdwara Prabandhak Committee – a committee that controls the Sikh places of worship

siddhā: individuals who have mastered techniques of yogic practice and believed to have attained immortality through it

Siddh Goṣṭ: composition in Guru Granth Sahib representing a dialogue between Guru Nanak and adepts of yoga named Siddhas

Singh Sabha: Sikh reform movement initiated in 1873 which split into two factions in response to stigmatization from Hindu reformist and traditionalist groups

śruti: 'that which is heard'; the Vedas and Upanisads

suchēt: active memory

subhāv: drives, feelings, instincts, affect

sukh: pleasure; happiness

sultān: sovereign

śunyā: nothingness, void

sunṇanā: listening; hearing

suṇaṇ: void; nothingness

Sufī: member of a Muslim mystical order

surat(i): awareness

sūtra: concise text expounding a teaching

Udāsī: member of Udasis, an order of ascetics claiming Sri Chand (elder son of Guru Nanak) as their progenitor

Upanisads: fourth division of Hindu literatures; wisdom texts

Vaisnava: follower of the god Viṣhṇu

vāk: 'saying', randomly chosen passage from the Guru Granth Sahib; in Hinduism early Vedic term for the divine Word and the goddess of speech

varṇa: 'colour'; caste hierarchy comprising Brahman, Kshatriya, Vaishya and Sudra; individual letter in the Sanskrit language

Veda: knowledge; earliest texts of the Hindus

Vedanta: the last part of the Veda; Upanisads

vichār (*vichāraṇā*)

virāsat: psychic inheritance

vismād: wonder; awe

yoga: 'yoke'; system of Indian philosophy and practice in which the mind is brought under control

Notes

Introduction

1 The description of the Guru Granth Sahib from pages 3–6 largely follows the book: Christopher Shackle and Arvind-Pal S. Mandair, *Teachings of the Sikh Gurus: Selections from the Sikh Scripture* (London: Routledge, 2005), i–xvi.

2 Ibid., xvii.

3 Ibid., xviii.

4 Ibid.

5 Ibid.

6 Ibid., xxii.

7 Ibid., xxiii.

8 Ibid., xxiv.

9 Concepts such as sovereign violence and *miri-piri* inevitably point to the fact that Sikh philosophy is also intrinsically political. Due to a lack of space in this book, I decided to develop a detailed discussion of Sikh political philosophy in separate volumes. A first step in this direction can be found in my book *Violence and the Sikhs* (Cambridge: Cambridge University Press, 2022). A more detailed treatment of Sikh political philosophy centring on the concept of sovereignty is worked out in my *War Machines* monograph which is currently in progress.

10 Verne Dusenbery, '"Nation" or "World Religion"': Master Narratives of Sikh Identity', in *Sikh Identity: Continuity and Change*, edited by Pashaura Singh (Delhi: Manohar, 1999), 133–4.

11 Arvind-Pal S. Mandair, *Religion and the Specter of the West* (New York: Columbia University Press, 2009).

12 Dusenbery, '"Nation" or "World Religion"'.

13 My understanding of 'Sikh theology' is more complex than might appear at first glance and may need some clarification here, given that there have been misreadings of my earlier work where I adopted a critical stance towards theology (Arvind-Pal S. Mandair, 'The Passage of Ideas From Trumpp to Bhai Vir Singh: Indology, Native Informancy and the Politics of Translation', *Bulletin of the School of Oriental and African Studies*, 68, no. 2 (2005): 253–74; Mandair, *Religion and the Specter of the West*; Arvind-Pal S. Mandair, 'Sikhs, Sovereignty and Modern Government', in *Religion as a Category of Government and Sovereignty*, edited by Trevor Stack, Naomi Goldenberg and Timothy Fitzgerald (Leiden: Brill, 2015)). This is primarily because in these earlier publications my aim was to gain a keener insight into the nature of the colonial epistemic machinery, and to what extent it was modelled on Christian theological and secular humanist frameworks of

thought. Colonial translators such as Trumpp and Macauliffe, in different ways, prepared the ground for Sikh elites to uncritically adopt 'theology' as a lens for translating and interpreting Sikh concepts even in Punjabi language (see Mandair, 'The Passage of Ideas From Trumpp to Bhai Vir Singh'). What I did in these earlier works was to show that it was possible to decolonize the epistemic machinery and experiment with more productive ways of translating Sikh concepts.

However, this does not render my stance anti-theological by any means. Anybody who reads Chapters 2–6 of this book carefully and without preconceived bias, should be able to see that a *certain kind* of theology is still active in the way I present Sikh concepts. The philosopher of religion Richard Kearney calls this *anatheism* which speaks to a way of speaking about 'God' but from a position of not-knowing. This is not dissimilar to what I'm doing in Chapters 2 through 6, but I would caution against a direct comparison. The boundaries between theology and philosophy are blurred at best, and *gurmat* as concept/category does not translate smoothly or transparently into either the discourse of theology or philosophy. The choice between theology and philosophy ultimately boils down to a question of pragmatism: Which of these two discourses, theology or philosophy, is more suited to doing critical work in the humanities, such that we're able to question the very idea of critique itself? Fortunately, as I show in Chapter 2, the compositions of the Sikh Gurus provide us with strong clues about navigating this seeming impasse. According to the logic of *gurmat*, 'God' and 'self' cannot be in the same place or time, conceptually or otherwise. This is very different from classical Christian theology in which 'God' and 'Man' are made present to each other. European Enlightenment philosophy tried to turn this problem on its head by trumping God with human reason (vis-à-vis the ontological proofs for the existence of God) resulting in humanism. *Gurmat* philosophy takes a step further than both Christian theology and humanistic philosophy because its very logic is premised on *self*-critique. This self-critique (egoloss) does not negate Sikh theology but, rather, puts it in its correct place by manoeuvring within the Anglophone language and consciousness in ways that avoid the oppositional mentality that happens to be the trademark of Christian-secular metaphysics. In a different book I have connected this move to an existential positioning that I have called 'becoming-diasporic' (see Arvind-Pal S. Mandair, *Geophilosophical Encounters: Diasporic Logics, Decolonial Praxis and Sikh Thought* (London and New York: Routledge, 2023), which means accepting the Anglophone consciousness as one's own/home but refiguring the rules by which one thinks and lives. In this way, it is possible to use 'Sikh theology' as a vehicle for presenting Sikh concepts, but only if one accepts that it is an assemblage, just like 'Sikh philosophy'. Where Sikh philosophy scores better as a discourse is its potential for enabling *gurmat* concepts to connect far more widely than 'Sikh theology' which is fine for adoration of the divine. But in the wrong hands theology runs the risk of bolstering the power of clericalism, clerical elites and its advocates who pretend they speak for the Gurus or for 'God', with their 'holier than thou' attitude, their tendency to label critical thinking as 'blasphemy' against the Gurus, or to carry out public inquisitions, spreading rumours and mistruths, to carry out little crusades against members of their own community and other communities, and their tendency to marginalize voices of difference (be they women, members of the LGBTQ community, or those of different caste, race, creed and colour). Sikh philosophy, in contradistinction, remains in the hands of individual readers and interpreters. It has the potential to give power and freedom back to the people.

14 Timothy Fitzgerald, *Religion and the Secular: Historical and Cultural Formations*, edited by Timothy Fitzgerald (London: Routledge, 2007) (see Fitzgerald's Introduction to this volume).

15 T. Fitzgerald, *Religion & Politics in International Relations* (London: Continuum Press, 2011).

16 See Timothy Fitzgerald, *Discourse on Civility and Barbarity: A Critical History of Religion and Related Categories* (New York: Oxford University Press, 2008), 16–41.

17 W. H. McLeod, *Sikhism* (London: Penguin Publishers, 1998), for example, devotes an entire chapter to 'Sikh Doctrine' in which he discusses what would normally be regarded as philosophy or philosophy of religion. In a different book (1968) he simply calls it theology. J. S. Grewal also refers to Sikh thought as 'doctrine' or 'ideology'. A particularly good example is his book *A Study of the Guru Granth Sahib* (2009) where he devotes two entire chapters titled 'Conception of God' and 'Conception of Liberation'. Again these are clearly topics central to philosophy and/or philosophy of religion. Their stance is understandable because both scholars are historians who worked with material, empirical evidence rather than indulge in what they would regard as non-material 'ideality'.

18 See Mandair, *Geophilosophical Encounters*, where I have devoted more space to discussing the marginalization of Sikh thought by the modern knowledge system. Nevertheless, it may be useful to at least register in passing a couple of related reasons for the lack of scholarly interest in Sikh thought. Perhaps the most important reason is an implicit cultural nativism that influences even the most critical scholarship in Sikh studies in addition to many Sikhs themselves. By nativism I refer to a general reluctance to separate Sikh thought and concepts from the ethno-linguistic and cultural soil out of which it emerged. In recent years, some scholars have even given this cultural nativism a name: 'Punjabiyat' (lit. Punjabi-ness, the essence of being Punjabi). Various scholars have tried to define 'Punjabiyat' (M. Dhandha and P. Singh, 'Sikh Culture Punjabiyat', in *The Oxford Handbook of Sikh Studies*, edited by Pashaura Singh and Louis Fenech (New York: Oxford University Press, 2013), 482–94; A. Malhotra and M. Mir, eds, *Punjab Reconsidered: History, Culture and Practice* (Delhi: Oxford University Press, 2012)). Their central thesis seems to boil down to a defence of 'Punjabiyat' as a cultural

identity comprising caste, language, pieties, spiritualities and so on. In regard to the relationship between Sikhi and 'Punjabiyat', what seems to also emerge in the Punjabiyat thesis are the following presuppositions: (i) there is no such thing as a 'Sikh' concept outside of the Punjabi cultural context, (ii) there is no Sikh identity as such that is not already part of 'Punjabiyat' or Punjabi cultural identity which espouses shared pieties, practices and boundaries as opposed to anything Sikh-related which tends to be boundary-forming. The problem with the 'Punjabiyat' thesis is that it is itself an intellectual construction influenced by Marxist intellectuals that began to take root in the 1930s. It came about primarily as a response to religious sectarianism/nationalism that seemed to be emerging from the ideological stances of the reformist movements. As I've argued elsewhere, the 'Punjabiyat' thesis is indebted to a European secularist logic that recognizes difference only in terms of identity. The 'Punjabiyat' thesis is unable to conceive of identity-*as*-difference (and vice versa), which means it sees Sikhism as fitting into a quantitative pluralism of Punjabi cultures, but unable to recognize the qualitative sense of plurality intrinsic to Sikhi and *gurmat*.

It seems that the basic difference between *Sikhī* (or *gurmat*) and 'Punjabiyat' is that the former can posit and fosters concepts that can travel outside Punjabi culture and take root in different cultural soils, yet allow the two (or more) cultures to exist together in a body. 'Punjabiyat' cannot foster its own distinctive concepts, which is why it will remain tied to a particular culture. Because 'Punjabiyat' doesn't have any indigenous epistemology that it can call its own, it also has no concepts and therefore can only refer to the material culture of Punjab. And even when scholars try to speak about 'Punjabiyat' as something *generalizable*, it is forced to borrow a universalism from European thought, specifically Hegel and Marx, which it then imposes on particular cultures of Punjab. My stance is simply this: *Sikhī* (and *gurmat*) may certainly have been born within the Punjabi cultural soil, it has used the cultural idioms of Punjab to express itself, but it is able to *travel* outside the material culture of Punjab by dint of its conceptuality and *translate* into the soil of different cultures. This ability to travel, translate and flourish elsewhere is dependent almost entirely on the work of concepts and the way they interact with material cultures. Which, of course, raises the question: What exactly is a concept? For discussions on this, see endnote 15 and the more detailed discussion in *Geophilosophical Encounters*.

19 Most scholars in Sikh studies have followed the trend set by earlier pioneers of Sikh studies in the West such as W. H. McLeod, J. S. Grewal, N. G. Barrier and others, where Sikh philosophy is labelled as doctrine or ideology. As I have argued elsewhere, this trend stems from the pervasive secularity and positivism of the frameworks in which these scholars were working. While the labelling as doctrine or ideology is certainly not incorrect (see Chapter 2 in this book), it also limits the potential of Sikh philosophy to go beyond the religio-secular frame and develop a notion of *gurmat* that is non-doctrinal and non-ideological.

20 Giani Sant Singh Maskin is certainly not the only philosopher-exegete in the
    Sikh world. But what marks him out is that he travelled widely in the 1980s
    and 1990s and reached large audiences in the Sikh diaspora both in-person
    and through his published books and cassettes. Along with everything that
    was happening in the Sikh world during the difficult period of the 1980s,
    the direct and simple form of Maskin's lectures and commentarial writings
    influenced my own thinking. From the outset, it was clear to me that this
    was a form of Sikh philosophy that briefly went out of vogue but is now set
    for a comeback.

21 A good example, among the dozens of books written or composed by
    Maskin, is: *Guru Chintan* (The Guru's Philosophical Thought). The book
    is composed of sixty-eight short chapters which reflect on key terms and
    concepts in the Guru Ganth Sahib. For example, *dharam até dhan; kām
    até mōkh, dukh até sukh* and so on. He uses a form of free thinking but the
    amalgamated influence of several *sampardaya* and *pṛnālīs* (Giani, Nirmalā,
    Udāsī and Singh Sabha) can be discerned in his style of speaking and
    exegesis.

22 An obvious question here is what is a (Sikh) concept? As I have discussed
    this question at length elsewhere (Mandair, *Geophilosophical Encounters*),
    I will summarize the main points as follows. It may be easier to define
    a concept by first referring to what it is not. Concepts should not be
    understood in the sense of Platonic ideals, that is, as terms with immutable
    meanings that define the essence of phenomena or things in the world
    in order to measure, rank and ultimately control them. Concepts should
    not be considered simply as tools in the service of human knowledge for
    the purpose of controlling the world, other beings and so on. Of course
    concepts help us to organize our thinking, represent our thoughts to
    other people and, in doing so, make our communication a lot simpler
    (C. Stagoll, 'Concepts', in *The Deleuze Dictionary*, edited by Adrian Parr
    (New York: Columbia University Press, 2005), 50–1). But to see concepts
    this way is to prevent them from contributing to the rich variety and
    uniqueness that comprises our everyday encounters with the world,
    what we call lived experience, or simply life. Rather, concepts ought to
    be seen as means by which we extract new possibilities inherent in life
    as it constantly unfolds, in order then to make new and more productive
    connections with the world. From this perspective, concepts can help us
    experience the world anew each time, to see and experience newness in
    the world instead of presenting the same thing to mind over and again.
    In Sikh philosophy this experience of eternal newness is called *nām* and
    the psychic-aesthetic state in which one experiences it is called *vismād*
    (wonder).

    For example, terms commonly used in the Sikh lexicon such *akāl
    purakh* (or simply the term *akāl*), *anhad*, *śabda*, *guru* and *nām* should
    not be understood as static words with fixed meanings that reign for
    all time over specific states of affairs, meanings that can be abstracted

from life. Rather concepts are better considered as critical points, potentialities or simply degrees of force that inhere in specific states of affairs without themselves becoming actual (T. Lorraine, *Deleuze and Guattari's Immanent Ethics* (New York: SUNY Press, 2012), 17–19; Mandair, *Geophilosophical Encounters*). They are potentialities that can shift and change with the unfolding of time. They do not form systems or patterns but work by inducing affective intensities which one learns to channel through contemplative practices. That is, concepts are singular configurations of mental components that affect the landscape of our thinking by leading to certain thresholds rather than others, thresholds that affect how we experience our world and the actions that we engage in (Stagoll, 'Concepts', 50-1). Thus, a concept can never be separated from the concrete movements of thought that actualize it, and yet it allows a liveable approach to a chaotic range of thought possibilities (Mandair, 'Sikhs, Sovereignty and Modern Government'). Basically, a concept is an event of creative meaning-making that can precipitate new avenues of thinking and dwelling, which can in turn induce static situations to be tipped over into actions, thus causing things to happen, events that might not otherwise have occurred. Concepts can therefore only be evaluated in terms of life-experiments (Stagoll, 'Concepts', 51; Lorraine, *Deleuze and Guattari's Immanent Ethics*, 18-19). They open up lived experience by attributing meaning in a different way to states of affairs. In short, far from representing a fixed world, concepts are actually part of temporal becoming.

23 The term 'white epistemologies' corresponds to Jacques Derrida's 'White Mythology' and Robert C. Young's 'White Mythologies'. See Derrida's *Margins of Philosophy*, translated by Alan Bass, (Harvester Wheatsheaf: London, 1982); and Robert C. Young's *White Mythologies: Wring, History and the West* (London: Routledge, 1990).

24 Many young Sikhs are involved in some form or other of activism motivated at least in part by their lived understanding of Sikh concepts and how they apply to the world.

25 The practical aspect of what a (Sikh) concept is and how it works in practice can be adduced ethnographically and philosophically. To do so, however, the scholar/questioner needs some intuitive understanding of the mechanisms that block the flows of meaning between the Sikh life-world and its outside, or simply block the Sikh life-world within itself, hence blocking the potential to create new meaning. This is the function of public space in the contemporary world. Given that the analysis of public space constitutes an entire project in itself, I will limit myself to what might seem a banal example of how the above ideas might apply to the contemporary Sikh life-world and to exemplary Sikh practices. Take *kirtan*, for example. Irrespective of whether such a *kirtani* is a professional or a lay person, s/he should be able to display some level of mastery of the art by being able to play an instrument, having some knowledge of *rāg/tāl* and of

gurbāṇī, and will be able to put these things together in the performance of a *śabda*. Now one might ask this *kirtani*: What is it that specifically constitutes *Sikh kirtan* as opposed to similar devotional practices in other cultures which might also share the emphasis on singing, music and taking the Name? In other words, what is it that makes this a Sikh practice? The answer to this question cannot be reduced to the demands of social identity. At some level it must involve the ability of the practitioner to access Sikh concepts and put them into play. We can repeat this exercise with other practitioners, for example, a Sikh architect, someone building a gurdwara, an oral exegete, someone involved in social or political activism – the examples could be multiplied here. In order to count their activity as 'Sikh', at some minimal level one must have some interpretive ability to explain *why* one does *what* one does, and this interpretative ability must involve some minimal access to Sikh concepts, categories and so on and the ability to operationalize them in a wider world. But although the average Sikh manages to retain this core interpretive ability at some minimal level, it is also the case that his or her ability to actually enunciate Sikh concepts is limited to a private sphere of existence. Any attempt to relate them to the dominant social framework of the modern social imaginary results in them being interdicted. What this means in practice is that one is not allowed to share Sikh concepts with the wider social imaginary, that is to say, with Western concepts.

Of course, the average Sikh is not even aware of this interdiction because the vast majority of Sikhs are supposed to have internalized the laws of the modern social imaginary, and the most insidious form of this law is the principle of identity – that to count as a living, thinking person one must be able to re-present oneself as the same, as an identity rather than something capable of self-differentiation, that is, capable of alteration. Only by acceding to this law does one gain the recognition of the dominant social culture which has, by means of this interdiction, effectively set the Sikh in his or her proper place, that is, as the member of 'religious' group. However, as noted earlier, the mechanism of this interdiction is centred around the imposition of a secular ideology of time as linear-homogenous and the assertion of a universal temporal experience which 'we' are all supposed to share. It works by interdicting the temporality of Sikh concepts, effectively reducing them to representations, that is, clichés or stereotypes that allow the Sikh to be identified again and again as the same kind of thing, namely, 'religious'.

26 A good example is Bernard Harcourt's *Critique and Praxis* (New York: Columbia University Press, 2020).

27 This brief nod towards sovereignty and the political clearly cannot do justice to a need that is becoming increasingly urgent within Sikh intellectual circles and one that is not satisfied by political science. I refer to the desire to articulate a Sikh social and political philosophy which will be examined in detail in a sequel to this book tentatively titled *War Machines*.

Chapter 1

1 For elaborations on assemblage as a concept, see Gilles Deleuze and Felix Guattari, *A Thousand Plateaus: Capitalism and Schizophrenia* (London: Bloomsbury Academic, 2013), 257–60; Rob Shields and Frank Vallee, *Demystifying Deleuze* (Ottawa: Quill Books, 2012), 29–30.

2 Pashuara Singh and Louis Fenech, ed., *The Oxford Handbook for Sikh Studies* (Oxford: Oxford University Press, 2014), 225.

3 Ibid., 226.

4 Roberto Esposito, *Two: The Machine of Political Theology and the Place of Thought* (New York: Fordham University Press, 2015), 9–10.

5 The term 'conceptual personae' was coined by Deleuze and is developed in Chapter 3 of his last major work *What Is Philosophy?* It refers to a perspective beyond the control of a personal self, one that is activated by philosophical thought (see also Lorraine, *Deleuze and Guattari's Immanent Ethics*, 23). JI have adapted the original term by calling it *conceptual* im*personae* as a way of thinking about the function of the *gurmukh*, who cultivates a selfhood that is not a possessive personal container but, rather, a process of connecting to others and the world.

6 Kahn Singh Nabha, *Mahānkōsh* (Patiala: Languages Department, 1990), 945.

7 Ibid., 415.

8 Taran Singh, *Gurbānī dīan Viākhiā Prnālīan* (Patiala: Punjabi University, 1980).

9 R. Singh, 'Works of Bhai Gurdas', in *The Oxford Handbook for Sikh Studies*, edited by P. Singh and L. Fenech (Oxford: Oxford University Press, 2014), 242.

10 Pashuara Singh, *The Guru Granth Sahib: Canon, Meaning, Authority* (Oxford: Oxford University Press, 2000), 240.

11 A detailed elaboration of these modes can be found in Gurnam Kaur, *Reason and Revelation in Sikhism* (New Delhi: Cosmo Publications, 1990).

12 See Singh, 'Works of Bhai Gurdas'.

13 Rattan Singh Jaggi, *Encyclopedia of Sikhism*, vol. 1, 119–20; see also Madanjit Kaur, *Encyclopedia of Sikhism*, vol. 4, 377–8.

14 Jaggi, *Encyclopedia of Sikhism*, 120.

15 Singh, *Gurbānī Dīan Viākhiā Prnālīan*, 93–8.

16 Rattan Singh Jaggi, *Gurbānī Tikke: Anandghān* (Patiala: Punjabi University, 1970), 65.

17 Sher Singh, *Philosophy of Sikhism* (Amritsar: Shiromani Gurdwara Parbhandhak Committee, 1944), 82.

18 Gurdev Singh, 'Gulab Singh, Pandit', in *Encyclopedia of Sikhism*, edited by Harbans Singh, vol. 2 (Patiala: Punjabi University, 1992), 124.

19 Sher Singh, *Philosophy of Sikhism* (Amritsar: Shiromani Gurdwara Parbandhak Committee, 2003), 6.

20 Taran Singh, *Gurbani dian Viakhian Prnalian*, vol. 2 (Patiala: Punjabi University, 1988), 77.

21 Ibid.

22 *Sikhan dī Bhāgat Mālā* and *Giān Ratnāvalī* (Bhāī Mani Singh), *Prayai Guru Granth Sahib* (Bhāī Chandā Singh), *Sri Guru Granth Kōsh* (Bhai Hazarā Singh), *Gurbāṇī Vyākaran* (Bhai Bhāgvan Singh), *Tawārikh Guru Khālsā* and *Giān Prabōdh* (Giānī Giān Singh).

23 Ernest Trumpp, *The Adi Granth* (Delhi: Munshiram Manoharlal, 1877 [1987]).

24 Arvind-Pal S. Mandair, 'Valences of the Dialectic', *Religions of South Asia*, 4, no. 2 (2010): 233–64.

25 Badan Singh, *Farīdkōt Tika* (Patiala: Bhasha Vibhag (1989 edition), 1898), 1 (and Ft Note on p. 1).

26 Ibid.

27 Ibid.

28 See Madhav M. Deshpande, *Sanskrit and Prakrit: Sociolinguistic Issues* (New Delhi: Motilal Banarsidas, 1993).

29 Ibid., 55–74.

30 Harjot Oberoi, *The Construction of Religious Boundaries: Culture, Identity and Diversity in the Sikh Tradition* (New Delhi: Oxford University Press, 1994).

31 Bob Van der Linden, *Moral Languages from Punjab: The Singh Sabha, Arya Samaj and Ahmadiyahs* (Delhi: Manohar Publishers, 2008); Oberoi, *The Construction of Religious Boundaries*.

32 For details see Tejaswini Niranjana, *Siting Translation: History, Postructuralism and the Colonial Context* (Berkely: University of California Press, 1992); Gauri Viswanathan, *Outside the Fold: Conversion, Modernity and Belief* (Princeton: Princeton University Press, 1998).

33 Oberoi, *The Construction of Religious Boundaries*; Arvind-Pal S. Mandair, *Sikhism: A Guide For the Perplexed* (London: Bloomsbury, 2013).

34 Mandair, *Sikhism*.

35 Mandair, 'The Passage of Ideas From Trumpp to Bhai Vir Singh'.

36 Ibid.

37 See Trumpp's 'Sketch of the Religion of the Sikhs', in his *The Adi Granth*, xcv11–cxv111.

38 See Bhai Jodh Singh, *Gurmati Nirnai* (Ludhiana: Academy Press, 1932).

39 A detailed exposition of this is provided in my earlier work *Religion and the Specter of the West*, Chapters 3 and 4.

40 Mandair, *Religion and the Specter of the West*.

41 Talal Asad, *Secular Translations* (Baltimore: Columbia University Press, 2018).

42 Singh, *Philosophy of Sikhism*, 1944.

43 It could be argued that earlier works such as *Gurmati Nirinai* also treated concepts of *gurmat* in a comparative manner (note, for example, Jodh

Singh's effort to place Sikh concepts in relation to important intellectual currents at the time) but the comparativity remains implicit rather than explicit.

44 Sher Singh, *Philosophy of Sikhism*, 2003, i.

45 Ibid.

46 Ibid.

47 Ibid., emphasis mine.

48 See my *Geophilosophical Encounters: Sikh Philosophy, Decolonial Praxis and Diasporic Logics* (London and Delhi: Routledge, 2023).

49 This list is highly selective. The number of works that broadly count as belonging to or related to Sikh philosophy are too numerous to mention. Two other authors whose works contribute to Sikh philosophy are Gurbhāgat Singh (*Sikhism and Postmodern Thought* and *Western Poetics and Eastern Thought*) and Nikky Singh (*Physics and Metaphysics of the Guru Granth Sahib*, 1986).

50 Nirbhai Singh, *Philosophy of Sikhism: Reality and Its Manifestations* (New Delhi: Atlantic Publications, 1990), 14.

51 Ibid., 60.

52 See the Punjabi-English and English – Punjabi Dictionaries, Patiala, Punjab.

Chapter 2

1 Arguably, the most important recent work on the *janamsākhī* genre has been done by Dr Harjeet S. Grewal. For details see Grewal's PhD dissertation (*Janamsākhī: Retracing Networks of Interpretation*) and his forthcoming books on the same subject.

2 J. S. Grewal, *Sikh Ideology, Polity and Social Order* (Delhi: Manohar, 1996); Mandair, *Sikhism*, 19.

3 W. H. McLeod, *Textual Sources for the Study of Sikhism* (Manchester: Manchester University Press, 1984); Mandair, *Sikhism*, 29–30.

4 The following works look closely at the concept of *śabda-guru* from various perspectives: Himmat Singh, *The Philosophical Conception of Śabda* (Patiala, 1985); Verne Dusenbery, 'The Word as Guru: Sikh Scripture and the Translation Controversy', *History of Religions*, 34, no. 4 (1992): 385–402; W. H. McLeod, *Guru Nanak and the Sikh Religion* (Oxford: Oxford University Press, 1968), Chapter 7; Mandair, *Religion and the Specter of the West*.

5 Here I'm thinking of the attribution of prophethood, that he is chosen by God, miracles and so on. These kind of things are more important except to the narrowly pious, or to those who keep the figure of Nanak and his teaching safely protected (or imprisoned, depending on how you look at it) within the sanctum of clerical elites, or to those who stand to gain social benefit from claiming theological proximity and control over the

meaning of his teaching. This is one of the downsides of theology as has long been known. As I argue in this chapter and elsewhere, the focus on exceptionalism drastically reduces the potential of Nanak's teaching for reaching a wider humanity.

6 *Rāg Malār.*

7 W. H. McLeod and K. Schomer, *The Saints: Studies in A North Indian Devotional Tradition* (Delhi: Manohar, 1987).

8 See chapter 3 of *Religion and the Specter of the West.*

9 K. Sharma, *Bhakti and the Bhakti Movement: A Study in the History of Ideas* (New Delhi: Munshiram Manoharlal, 1987); V. Dalmia, *The Nationalization of Hindu Traditions: Bharatendu Harischandra and Nineteenth Century Banaras* (Delhi: Oxford University Press, 1996); S. N. Balagangadhara, *The Heathen in His Blindness: Asia, the West and the Dynamic of Religion* (Leiden: Brill, 1994); R. E. King, *Orientalism and Religion* (London: Routledge, 1999); T. Fitzgerald, *The Ideology of Religious Studies* (New York: Oxford University Press, 1999); Fitzgerald, *Religion & Politics in International Relations*; T. Asad, *Formations of the Secular: Christianity, Islam, Modernity* (Baltimore: Johns Hopkins University Press, 2003); W. Cavanaugh, *The Myth of Religious Violence* (New York: Oxford University Press, 2008); Mandair, *Religion and the Specter of the West.*

10 McLeod and Schomer, *The Saints*, 7–13.

11 McLeod and Schomer's *The Saints*, is a good example of this.

12 Christianity was the premise for the European Enlightenment. The two cannot be separated as they done in normative secular frameworks. See Balagangadhara, *The Heathen in His Blindness*; Asad, *Formations of the Secular*; Fitzgerald, *Religion & Politics in International Relations.*

13 M. Hagglund, *Radical Atheism: Derrida and the Time of Life* (Stanford: Stanford University Press, 2008), 14.

14 Caputo, *On Religion* (Routledge, 2018), 40–56.

15 Ibid., 45.

16 Mandair, *Religion and the Specter of the West.*

17 McLeod, *Guru Nanak and the Sikh Religion.*

18 See Jodh Singh's, *Gurmati Nirnai*, which has an entire chapter titled 'akāl purakh' and consists of a systematic commentary on the attributes and nature of God in the fashion of Christian orientalist theology.

19 McLeod, *Sikhism*, 87–108.

20 I'm thinking here specifically of figures such as Bhaī Gurdās whose life contemporaneous with several of the early Sikh Gurus. His exegetical writings were a major influence on the early Sikh community's self-understanding (see Grewal's *Sikh Ideology, Polity and Social Order*). For a more up to date, thorough and probing analysis of the epistemologies that frame early Sikh sources, see Dr Harjeet S. Grewal's forthcoming book: *The Janamsākhī Tradition: Non-Oppositionality, Allegory, and Transformation in the Sikh Narrative Tradition.*

21 See also Mandair (2022) *Violence and the Sikhs.*

22 Bhaī Gurdās, *Vāran* – Satta and Balwand, *Tikkī di Vār* (Coronation Ode), *Paurī* 2–3.

23 Gandhi, *History of the Sikh Gurus* (Delhi: Gurdas Kapur & Sons, 1978), 168–72.

24 Singh, *The Guru Granth Sahib*; McLeod, *Sikhism*; Harbans Singh, *Heritage of the Sikhs* (Manohar: New Delhi, 1985).

25 I refer to the commonly held theological model inspired by the *Purantan Janamsakhi* (PJS) according to which Guru Nanak receives the cup of communion from God during his apparent disappearance into the river Bein. This encounter is narrated by the PJS as a once-and-for-all revelation from God. Sikh theologians and historians treated this revelation as the fundamental 'timeless' event which sets the tone for the unfolding of Sikh history in linear time. As I have argued in *Religion and the Specter of the West*, pages 366–7, one of the problems with this model is that all Sikh action and all events become ever-weakening mimetic echoes of the sacred origin, which subsequently try to retrieve this origin. The resort to mimesis is an indication of the assumption that the only time available to is linear, historical time (or what I have referred to as *kāl*-centrism).

26 Jacob Sherman, *Partakers of the Divine: Contemplation & the Practice of Philosophy* (Minneapolis: Fortress Press, 2014), 2–7.

27 Nikky Singh gives wonderful expression to this in her books and translations. See, for example, *The Name of My Beloved: Verses of the Sikh Gurus*, 1999.

Chapter 3

1 Esposito, *Two.*

2 Martin Heidegger, 'The Age of the World Picture', in *The Question Concerning Technology and Other Essays*, translated by William Lovitt (New York: Harper Torchbooks, 1977), 128.

3 Wael Hallaq, *Restating Orientalism* (New York: Columbia University Press, 2018).

4 See, for example, Esposito, *Two*; Hallaq, *Restating Orientalism.*

5 Mandair, *Religion and the Specter of the West.*

6 S. N. Radhakrishnan, *Indian Philosophy*, 1924; Julian Bagini, *How the World Thinks: A Global History of Philosophy*, 2019.

7 The term 'siddha' is used widely in Indic spirituality and philosophy. Generically, it refers to ones who have perfected body and mind, often through the attainment of *siddhis* or paranormal capabilities. Thus *siddhas* can belong to various traditions, for example, Tantric Buddhist, Nath Yogic, Kashmir Saivism, South Indian *lingayat* and so on. The siddhas mentioned

in Guru Nanak's Siddh Gosth were part of the influential Nath orders associated with the great yogic master Gorakh Nath.

8   Mandair, *Religion and the Specter of the West*, 2009; *Sikhism*, 2013.

9   E. Grosz, *The Incorporeal: Ontology, Ethics and the Limits of Materialism* (New York: Columbia University Press, 2017).

10 What I present here in the four-step explanation may not be immediately recognizable to most Sikhs who simply recite these stanzas from Japji and, if they do reflect on it as they are supposed, mostly allow the reflection to remain within the 'Punjabi' sphere of meaning. My explanation not only exercises a certain degree of artistic experimentation (which is part of how I understand hermeneutical practice) but is also an acknowledgement of the fact that 'we' are all thinking and reflecting in translation; indeed, we are thinking-between cultures as 'we' reflect on the meaning of theses stanzas, and that this mode of thinking-between is as 'authentic' as any 'original' Punjabi domain. In fact I want to go one step further and assert that this manner and style of explanation is for me part of my devotion to *gurbāṇī*. The explanation therefore narrates and participates in a devotional logic. In other words, as I recite these verses each morning (or whenever else I feel like it) the result of the recitation-reflection-meditation is not simply to praise or ponder the nature of a theistic entity (it certainly begins with this), but to force my mind to look into itself critically. What begins as theistic adoration turns into annihilation of the self or mind (the two are absolutely connected). It is one thing to simply recite the stanzas, but another thing altogether to contemplate it, which entails enacting the instruction upon one's own mind. To contemplate it is to think upon it in such a way that the teaching is put to work in this time and world that I'm living in, that we all share, but most importantly Guru Nanak's instruction (his *gurmat*) is to apply this to our own mind or self. This is what I'm trying to do with this kind of four-step explanation. It is part of my devotion, what some might call an application of my 'faith', initially to my mind, before it is then applied to the world.

11 As an act /thought/desire, the 'I am not' can also be considered a *desistance* (to use Lacoue-Labarthe's phrase – see *Typography: Mimesis, Philosophy, Politics* (Harvard University Press, 1989), which is an act-thought-desire of self-naughting, a becoming-nothing of the self. To see this in an ethical sense, the 'I am not(thing)' is an act-thought-desire of absolute humility. In *gurbāṇī* the Sikh Gurus regularly invoke the sense of 'I am not(hing)' through phrases that equate their self with the 'dust on feet of the Saints'. Now, in actual practice the '[I + not-I . . .]' formula can be seen in the religio-spiritual performativity of adoration, *bhakti*, *matha-tekkana* or any other act of self-surrender either to the divine or to one's fellow beings-in-the-world. From this perspective, the experimental figuration [I + not-I] is very similar to a central thesis of Ubuntu (African philosophy) which states that: 'I am because you are'.

12 Hagglund, *Radical Atheism*.

13 B. Allan Wallace, *Contemplative Science Where Buddhism and Neuroscience Converge* (New York: Columbia University Press, 2007), 1.
14 Sher Singh, *Philosophy of Sikhism* (Amritsar: Shiromani Gurwara Prabandhak Committee, 1944), 152.
15 Nirbhai Singh, *Philosophy of Sikhism* (New Delhi: Atlantic Publishers, 1990), 171.
16 Singh, *Philosophy of Sikhism*, 152–5.
17 The exegete Bhai Kahn Singh Nabha renders *dhur ki bani* as 'akal pason bani or *mukh asthan ton aye*', which literally mean coming from the place of the absolute or words from the timeless origin. See *Mahānkōsh*, 670.
18 The purpose of this heuristic method is simply to enable readers to experiment with ways of applying the terminology of *gurmat* in ways that allow you to discover something for yourself. The juxtaposition of *manmukh* theory with modern psychology is merely meant to help contextualize the discussion of consciousness in the contemporary world. I have found this heuristic particularly helpful in class discussions.
19 Sudhir Kakar, *The Indian Psyche* (Delhi: Oxford University Press, 1996), 16–23.
20 Indicate verses in *Japji*.
21 Brian Massumi, *Parables of the Virtual* (Duke University Press, 2002).
22 See Kaur, *Reason and Revelation in Sikhism*.
23 Nirbhai Singh, *Philosophy of Sikhism*.

Chapter 4

1 See Singh, *Philosophy of Sikhism: Reality and its Manifestations*.
2 W. Mignolo and C. Walsh, *On Decoloniality: Concepts, Analytics, Praxis* (Durham: Duke University Press, 2018), 135.
3 A translation of the Rāg Mārū composition on pages 1035 to 1037 in the Guru Granth Sahib is provided in the Appendix section.
4 This view of creation as an actual event is discussed in works such as Sher Singh, *Philosophy of Sikhism*, 1944; Singh, *Philosophy of Sikhism*; Bhai Jodh Singh, *Guru Nanak's Gospel* (Patiala: Languages Department, 1968); McLeod, *Guru Nanak and the Sikh Religion*. A longer and slightly different version of my argument in this chapter can be found in my *Geophilosophical Encounters*, Chapter 5 (forthcoming).
5 The notion of the One immersed in self-enjoyment (*vigsaii* means to rejoice, or to enjoy as one self-contemplates) can be interpreted philosophically as a reference to the absolute self-proximity, or absolute auto-affection of the One. Though expressed in theistic terms, *aapai aap vigsaii* and similar expressions such as *aape karta aape bhugta* (stanza 14, 1035) are references to the nature of pure consciousness as being without distance or spacing.

6 See Appendix.

7 By ontogenesis I refer to the idea that the processes by which the self is formed are the same as those by which the cosmos is formed. The implication is that if we're to continue to use the term 'ontology' (the science of determining what is, what exists, etc.), we have to do it and think about it differently. Different varieties of ontogenesis can be found in traditions of thought or in thinkers as culturally different as the Stoics, Spinoza, Nietsche, Simondon, Ruyer, Deleuze and Guattari, Derrida (on the one hand), and Jain, Buddhist, Kashmir Saivism, mystical Islamic though (especially Ibn Arabi) and the Sikh philosophies (on the other hand).

8 I have treated the problem of theological versus historical explanation in greater detail in *Geophilosophical Encounters*.

9 Avtar Singh, *Ethics of the Sikh* (Patiala: Punjabi University, 1983), 226.

10 Ibid., 227.

11 See Ibid who argues that action and grace are both translations of *karam*.

12 Singh, *Ethics of the Sikh*, 253.

13 Ibid., 254.

14 Jorge Ferrer, *Participation & Mystery* (New York: SUNY Press, 2012), 74.

15 Grosz, *The Incorporeal*, 251.

16 GGS, 287.

17 GGS, 280.

18 Raymond Ruyer, *Neo-Finalism*, trans. Alyosha Edlebi (Minneapolis: University of Minnesota Press, 2015).

19 See Raymond Ruyer, *NeoFinalism*, trans. Alyosha Edlebi (Minneapolis: University of Minnesota Press, 2012), ix–xii.

Chapter 5

1 Sant Singh Maskin, *Guru Chintan* (Ludhiana: Amritsar: Pustak Bhandar, 1987), 49.

2 Todd May, *Death* (Oxford: Blackwells, 2006), 4.

3 See Paul Ricouer, *Time and Narrative*, 3 vols. (Chicago: Chicago University Press).

4 Jodh Singh, *Gurmat Nirnai*, 248–61.

5 This section in parentheses has been translated less literally to help tease out the more important point in Bhai Jodh Singh's text.

6 Jodh Singh, *Gurmat Nirnai*, 253–4.

7 The implication here is that *hukam* might be confused for the inexorable iron law of *karma* held by classical Indian philosophies. But *hukam* is not an inexorable and transcendental law – it operates immanently and is interactive in relation to individuation (*haumai*). *Hukam* and *haumai* are therefore intrinsically related as explained in Chapters 2 and 3.

Chapter 6

1 K. Surin, 'Liberation', in *Critical Terms in Religious Studies*, edited by Mark
   C. Taylor (University of Chicago Press, 1999), 173.
2 Ibid., 177.
3 Ibid.
4 Ibid., 179.
5 Ibid., 180.
6 Ibid.
7 At a glance, these terms can be transliterated as follows: *muktī* (freedom/
   liberation), *mōkh* (freedom/liberation), *mōkh-duār* (door of liberation),
   mōkh-padvī (liberated state) and *jīvan-mukt* (liberated in the stream of
   life).
8 Literally, producing ego.
9 Nirbhai Singh, *Philosophy of Sikhism*, 157.
10 Rāg Āsā, GGS, 466.
11 Antonio Damasio, *The Strange Order of Things* (New York: Vintage, 2018).
12 Ibid., 25 (emphasis mine).
13 Ibid. (emphasis added).
14 Ibid., 25.
15 Ibid., 108.
16 Ibid., 114.
17 Ibid., 120.
18 See Jon Kabat-Zinn, 'Some Reflections on the Origins of MBSR, Skillful
   Means, and the Trouble With Maps'. *Contemporary Buddhism*, 12, no. 1
   (2011): 281–306. doi:10.1080/14639947.2011.564844. ISSN 1463-9947
19 Singh, *Ethics of the Sikhs*, 57.
20 Nabha, *Mahānkōsh*, 77.
21 GGS, 1142.

Chapter 7

1 W. H. McLeod, *Exploring Sikhism: Aspects of Sikh Identity, Culture and
   Thought* (Delhi: Oxford University Press, 2000), 103–34. See also McLeod's
   Sikhism.
2 In fact it is generally accepted that if the codes of conduct conflict with
   the precepts of the Guru Granth, or if they are simply silent, they should
   be disregarded in relation to the former. However, as we noted in earlier
   chapters, the aesthetic grounding of Sikh scripture renders it somewhat
   resistant to the dominant metaphysical schemas characteristic of modern
   imaginary, irrespective of whether these are theological or secular
   rationalization. As such it does not allow the reader to form normative

responses to issues that many of us are concerned with in daily life. In such schemas, which are routinely associated with 'religions' and their belief systems, life itself is valued only in relation to its transcendental or sacred ground.

3 Grace Jantzen, *Becoming Divine: Towards A Feminist Philosophy of Religion* (Manchester: Manchester University Press, 1998). See also Nikky Singh, *The Birth of the Khalsa* (New York: SUNY Press, 2005).

4 Singh, *The Birth of the Khalsa*.

5 https://en.wikipedia.org/wiki/Sikhism_and_sexual_orientation; https://feminisminindia.com/2017/01/05/sikhism-homosexuality/.

6 http://www.bbc.co.uk/Sikhism/euthanasia.

7 Singh, *Ethics of Sikhism*, 31.

8 Harold Coward and Tejinder Sandhu, 'Bioethics for Clinicians: Hinduism and Sikhism', *Canadian Medical Association Journal*, 163, no. 9 (31 October 2000): 1167.

9 http://www.bbc.co.uk/religion/contraception/contraception_abortion.shtml.

10 Kāla Singh, 'The Sikh Spiritual Model of Counseling', *Spirituality and Health International*, 9 (2008): 32–43.

11 Ibid., 35.

12 See, for example, http://www.bbc.co.uk/Sikhism/organ donation.

13 Kamaldeep Bhui, ed., *Racism and Mental Health: Prejudice and Suffering* (London: Jessical Kingsley Press, 2002).

14 A. Ivey, 'Counseling Psychology: The Most Broadly Based Applied Psychology Speciality', *The Counselling Psychologist*, 8, no. 3 (1978): 3–6. See also, Bhui, *Racism and Mental Health*.

15 Bhui, *Racism and Mental Health*.

16 See Susan Prill, 'Sikh Ecotheology', *Sikh Formations: Religion, Culture, Theory* (2015). Prill cites Bauman et al. who developed the threefold schema of 'Recovery, Reform and Replacement' to categorize the responses of various world religions and the communities associated with them (Bauman, W. A., R. R. Bohannon, and K. J. O'Brien, 'Ecology: What is it, Who Gets to Decide, and Why Does it Matter?', in *Grounding Religion: A Field Guide to the Study of Religion and Ecology*, edited by W. A. Bauman, R. R. Bohannon, and K. J. O'Brien (London: Routledge, 2011), 49–63. I have adapted this schema slightly to better address the nature of Sikh responses to the climate crisis.

17 S. Weintrobe, *The Psychological Roots of the Climate Crisis* (London: Bloomsbury Press, 2020).

Epilogue

1 Monika Kirloskar-Steinbach and Leah Kalmanson, *A Practical Guide to World Philosophies* (London: Bloomsbury Academic Press, 2021), 35.

2   My sense of the term un/inherit is borrowed from Derrida for whom the concept of inheritance plays a crucial role in many of his texts. The term's importance for my work revolves around the fact that it allows us to perform undecideability that is intrinsic to passing on and receiving any legacy, allowing individuals or societies to enact inherit acceptance and refusal in the same gesture. A novel adaptation of this can be found in Ananda Abeyesekara's *The Politics of Postsecular Religion* (New York: Columbia University Press, 2008) in which he talks of un-inheriting the name democracy as an identity. See also Samir Haddad's extended discussion of this term in his *Derrida & the Inheritance of Democracy* (Indiana: Indiana University Press, 2013).

3   In contemporary popular parlance the term 'influencer' refers the deployment of social media as a marketing tool involving 'endorsements and product placement from people and organizations who have a purported expert level of knowledge or social influence in their field'. However, I think the term can also be usefully adapted to look at the role of individuals and groups who have been successful in influencing their own communities in one way or another through social media, radio and related media. A few examples of such influencers who work with *gurmat* as a form of Sikh thought include individuals and organizations. One of the more interesting examples is the Sikh Human Rights Group (SHRG). Led by Dr Jasdev Singh Rai since the late 1980s this group has official NGO status at the United Nations. Broadly inspired by ideas of Sikh philosophy, SHRG has done much work over the past three decades on issues pertaining to sustainability, environment, diversity and racism, and women's rights. Other examples include Eco-Sikh, *Nanak Nam*, *Gurmat* Psychology (Dav Panesar), Naad Pargaas, SikhNet, SikhRI and any number of visual artists and musicians.

4   See Mignolo and Walsh, *On Decoloniality*, 229.

5   I started looking at political sovereignty in an earlier publication Mandair, 'Sikhs and Modern Government'. A more sustained effort to think through this question is undertaken in a sequel to this book, tentatively titled *War Machines* – which is basically an investigation of Sikh social and political philosophy as based on its institutions, ideas and practices. See Mandair, 'Sikhs, Sovereignty and Modern Government'.

Bibliography

Ahluwalia, J. S., *Sikh Chintan: Darśanak ate Sansthāmik Vikās*, Chandigarh: Lokgeet Parkashan, 1985.

Ahluwalia, J. S., *Sikh Falsaphé di Bhumikā*, Chandigarh: Lokgeet Parkashan, 1978.

Ahluwalia, J. S., *Sovereignty of the Sikh Doctrine*, 2nd edn, Amritsar: Singh Brothers, 2006.

Asad, T., *Formations of the Secular: Christianity, Islam, Modernity*, Baltiitmore: Johns Hopkins University Press, 2003.

Asad, T., *Secular Translations*, New York: Columbia University Press, 2018.

Balagangadhara, S. N., *The Heathen in His Blindness: Asia, the West and the DymanicDynamic of Religion*, Leiden: Brill, 1994.

Barrier, N. G., *The Sikhs and their Literature*, Delhi: Manohar, 1970.

Bauman, W. A., R. R. Bohannon, and K. J. O'Brien, 'Ecology: What Is It, Who Gets to Decide, and Why Does it Matter?', in *Grounding Religion: A Field Guide to the Study of Religion and Ecology*, edited by W. A. Bauman, R. R. Bohannon, and K. J. O'Brien, 49–63, London: Routledge, 2011.

Bhogal, B., 'The Animal Sublime', *Journal of the American Academy of Religion* , 80, no. 4 (2012): 2–53.

Bhui, K., *Racism and Mental Health: Prejudice and Suffering*, edited by Kamaldeep Bhui, London: Jessica Kingsley Press, 1996.

Caputo, J., *On Religion*, Routledge, 2018.

Cavanaugh, W., *The Myth of Religious Violence*, New York: Oxford University Press, 2008.

Coward, H. and T. Sandhu, 'Bioethics For Clinicians: Hinduism and Sikhism', *Canadian Medical Association Journal*, 163, no. 9 (2000): 1167–70.

Dalmia, V., *The Nationalization of Hindu Traditions: Bharatendu Harischandra and Nineteenth Century Banaras*, Delhi: Oxford University Press, 1996.

Damasio, A., *The Strange Order of Things*, Vintage, 2018.

Deleuze, G., and F. Guattari, *A Thousand Plateaus: Capitalism and Schizophrenia*, London: Bloomsbury Academic, 2013.

Deleuze, G. and F. Guattari, *What is Philosophy?*, London: Verso, 1994.

Derrida, J., *Margins of Philosophy*, translated by Alan Bass, London: Harvester Wheatsheaf, 1982.

Deshpande, M., *Sanskrit and Prakrit: Sociolinguistic Issues*, New Delhi: Motilal Banarsidas, 1993.

Dhanda, M. and P. Singh, 'Punjabiyat', in *The Oxford Handbook of Sikh Studies*, edited by Pashaura Singh and Louis Fenech, 482–93, New York: Oxford University Press, 2013.

Dusenbery, V., '"Nation" or "World Religion": Master Narratives of Sikh Identity', in *Sikh Identity: Continuity and Change*, edited by Pashaura Singh, 133–4, . Delhi: Manohar, 1999.

Dusenbery, V., 'The Word as Guru: Sikh Scripture and the Translation Controversy', *History of Religions*, 34, no. 4 (1992): 385–402.

Esposito, R., *Two: The Machine of Political Theology and the Place of Thought*, New York: Fordham University Press, 2015.

Ferrer, J., *Participation & Mystery*, New York: SUNY Press, 2012.

Fitzgerald, T., *Discourse on Civility and Barbarity: A Critical History of Religion and Related Categories*, New York: Oxford University Press, 2008.

Fitzgerald, T., *Religion and the Secular: Historical and Cultural Formations*, edited by T. Fitzgerald, London: Routledge, 2007.

Grewal, H., 'Janamsakhi: Retracing Networks of Interpretation', Doctoral Dissertation, University of Michigan, 2017

Grewal, J. S., *A Study of Guru Granth Sahib: Doctrine, Social Content, History, Structure and Status*, Amritsar: Singh Brothers, 2009.

Grewal, J. S., *Sikh Ideology, Polity and Social Order*, Delhi: Manohar, 1996.

Grewal, J. S., *The Sikhs: Ideology, Institutions and Identity*, Delhi: Oxford University Press, 2009.

Grosz, E., *The Incorporeal: Ontology, Ethics and the Limits of Materialism*, New York: Columbia University Press, 2017.

Hagglund, M., *Radical Atheism: Derrida and the Time of Life*, Stanford University Press, 2008.

Harcourt, B., *Critique and Praxis*, New York: Columbia University Press, 2020.

Ivey, A., 'Counseling Psychology: The Most Broadly Based Applied Psychology Speciality', *The Counselling Psychologist*, 8, no. 3 (1978): 3–6.

Jaggi, R., *Encyclopedia of Sikhism*, vol. 1, Patiala: Punjabi University, 1992.

Jaggi, R., *Gurbani Tikké: Anandghana*, Patiala: Punjabi University, 1970.

Kabat-Zinn, J., 'Some Reflections on the Origins of MBSR, Skillful Means, and the Trouble With Maps', *Contemporary Buddhism*, 12, no. 1 (2011): 281–306.

Kakar, S., *The Indian Psyche*, Delhi: Oxford University Press, 1998.

Kaur, G., *Reason and Revelation in Sikhism*, New Delhi: Cosmo Publications, 1990.

Kaur, M., *Encyclopedia of Sikhism*, vol. 4, Patiala: Punjabi University, 1986.

Kearney, R., *Anatheism: Returning to God After God*, New York: Columbia University Press, 2010.

King, R. E., *Orientalism and Religion*, London: Routledge, 1999.

Lacoue-Labarthe, P., *Typography: Mimesis, Philosophy, Politics*, Cambridge, MA: Harvard University PressHarvard Stanford University Press, 1989.

Lorraine, T., *Deleuze and Guattari's Immanent Ethics*, New York: SUNY Press, 2012.

Mahboob, H. S., *Sahje Rachio Khalsa*, Amritsar: Singh Brothers, 1988

Malhotra, A and M. Mir, eds, *Punjab Reconsidered: History, Culture and Practice*, Delhi: Oxford University Press, 2012.

Mandair, A.-P. S., *Religion and the Specter of the West*, New York: Columbia University Press, 2009.

Mandair, A.-P. S., *Sikhism: A Guide for the Perplexed*, London: Bloomsbury, 2013.

Mandair, A.-P. S., 'The Passage of Ideas From Trumpp to Bhai Vir Singh: Indology, Native Informancy and the Politics of Translation', *Bulletin of the School of Oriental and African Studies*, 68, no. 2 (2005): 253–2745.

Mandair, A.-P. S., 'Valences of the Dialectic', *Religions of South Asia*, 4, no. 2 (2010): 233–66.

Mandair, A.-P. S., *Violence and the Sikhs*, Cambridge University Press, 2023.

Massumi, B., *Parables of the Virtual*, Duke University Press, 2002.

McLeod, W. H., *Exploring Sikhism: Aspects of Sikh Identity, Culture and Thought*, Delhi: Oxford University Press, 2000.

McLeod, W. H., *Guru Nanak and the Sikh Religion*, Oxford University Press, 1968.

McLeod, W. H., *Sikhism*, Penguin Publishers, 1998.

McLeod, W. H., *Textual Sources For the Study of Sikhism*, Manchester University Press, 1984.

McLeod, W. H. and K. Schomer, *The Sants: Studies in A North Indian Devotional Tradition*, Delhi: Manohar, 1987.

Mignolo, W. and C. Walsh, *On Decoloniality: Concepts, Analytics, Praxis*, Durham: Duke University Press, 2018.

Nabha, K. S., *Mahankosh*, Patiala: Languages Department, 1990.

Narotam, T. S., *Sri Gurmat Nirnay Sagar*, 2nd edn [1955], Lahore: Sanskrit Press, 1887.

Niranjana, T., *Siting Translation: History, Post-structuralism and the Colonial Context*, Berkely: University of California Press, 1992.

Oberoi, H., *The Construction of Religious Boundaries: Culture, Identity and Diversity in the Sikh Tradition*, New Delhi: Oxford University Press, 1994.

Panesar, D., *Gurmat: Practical Self Realization*, Birmingham: DTF Publishers, 2018.

Prill, S., 'Sikh Ecotheology', in *Encountering Sikh Texts and Practices: Essays in Honor of Christopher Shackle, Sikh Formations: Religion, Culture, Theory*, edited by Pashaura Singh and Arvind-Pal S. Mandair, 223–42, London: Routledge, 2015.

Randhawa, D., *Unsettling Boundaries: Rethinking Culture, Religion, Literature After Postmodernism and Globalization*, Amritsar: Naad Pargaas, 2015.

Ricoeur, P., *Time and Narrative*, vol. 3, Chicago University Press, 1990.

Ruyer, R., *Neo-Finalism*, translated by Alyosha Edlebi, Minnesota University Press, 2015.

Shackle, C. and A. S. Mandair, *Teachings of the Sikh Gurus: Selections From the Sikh Scripture*, London: Routledge, 2005.

Sharma, K., *Bhakti and the Bhakti Movement: A Study in the History of Ideas*, New Delhi: Munshiram Manoharlal, 1987.

Sherman, J., *Partakers of the Divine: Contemplation & the Practice of Philosophy*, Minneapolis: Fortress Press, 2014.

Shields, R. and F. Vallee, *Demystifying Deleuze*, Quill Books, 2012.

Singh, A., *Ethics of the Sikh*, Patiala: Punjabi University, 1983.

Singh, B., *Faridkot Tika*, Patiala: Bhasha Vibhag (1989 edition), 1898.

Singh, B. J., *Gurmati Nirnai*, Amritsar, 1932.

Singh, B. M., *Gian Ratnavali*, Patiala: Bhasha Vibhag.

Singh, B. M., *Sikhan di Bhagat Mala*, Patiala: Bhasha Vibhag, 1972.

Singh, B. V., *Santhya Sri Guru Granth Sahib*, New Delhi: Bhai Vir Singh Press.

Singh, D., *Sikhism: A Comparative Study of its Theology and Mysticism*, New Delhi: Sterling Publishers, 1979.

Singh, G., *Sikhism and Postmodern Thought*, Amritsar: Naad Pargaas, 1999.

Singh, G., *Western Poetics and Eastern Thought*, Delhi: Humanities Press, 1984

Singh, H., ed., *Encyclopedia of Sikhism*, 4 vols., Patiala: Punjabi University, 1986.

Singh, H., *Heritage of the Sikhs*, Delhi: Manoher, 1985.

Singh, H., *The Philosophical Conception of Śabda*, Patiala: Punjabi University, 1985

Singh, I., *The Philosophy of Guru Nanak*, New Delhi: Atlantic Publishers, 1983.

Singh, K., 'The Sikh Spiritual Model of Counseling', *Spirituality and Health International*, 9 (2008): 32–43.

Singh, K. S., *Gurpartap Suraj Granth*, Patiala: Bhasha Vibhag, 1841.

Singh, K. S., *Guru Nanak Parkash*, Patiala: Bhasha Vibhag, 1823.

Singh, N., *Philosophy of Sikhism: Reality and Its Manifestations*, Patiala: Punjabi University Patiala, 1990.

Singh, N., *Philosophy of Sikhism: Reality and Its Manifestations*, New Delhi: Atlantic Publications, 1990.

Singh, N., *The Name of My Beloved: Verses of the Sikh Gurus*, New Delhi: Penguin Books, 2001.

Singh, N.-G. K., *The Guru Granth Sahib: Its Physics and Metaphysics*, New Delhi: Sterling Publishers, 1981.

Singh, P., *The Guru Granth Sahib: Canon, Meaning, Authority*, Oxford: Oxford University Press, 2000.

Singh, P. and L. Fenech, eds, *The Oxford Handbook for Sikh Studies*, Oxford: Oxford University Press, 2014.

Singh, R., 'Works of Bhai Gurdas', in *The Oxford Handbook for Sikh Studies*, edited by P. Singh and L. Fenech, Oxford: Oxford University Press, 2014.

Singh, S., *Philosophy of Sikhism*, Amritsar: Shiromani Gurdwara Parbandhak Committee, 1944.

Singh, S., *The Seeker's Path*, Bombay: Orient Longmans, 1959.

Singh, T., *Gurbānī dīan Viākhiā Prnālīan*, Patiala: Punjabi University, 1980.

Singh, T., *Shabadartha Sri Guru Granth Sahib*, 4 vols, 4th edn, Amritsar: Shiromani Gurdwara Parbhandhak Committee, 1988.

Stagoll, C., 'Concepts', in *The Deleuze Dictionary*, edited by Adrian Par, New York: Columbia University Press, 2005.

Surin, K., 'Liberation', in *Critical Terms in Religious Studies*, edited by Mark C. Taylor, 173–85, Chicago: University of Chicago Press, 1999.

Trumpp, E., *The Adi Granth*, Delhi: Munshiram Manoharlal, 1877[1987].

Van der Linden, B., *Moral Languages From Punjab: The Singh Sabha, Arya Samaj and Ahmadiyahs*, Delhi: Manohar Publishers, 2008.

Verran, H., 'Engagement Between Disparate Knowledge Traditions: Towards Doing Difference Generatively and in Good Faith', in *Contested Ecologies: Dialogues in the South on Nature and Knowledge*, edited by L. Green, 141–61, Cape Town: HSRC Press, 2013.

Viswanathan, G., *Outside the Fold: Conversion, Modernity and Belief*, Princeton: Princeton University Press, 1998.

Wallace, B. A., *Contemplative Science Where Buddhism and Neuroscience Converge*, New York: Columbia University Press, 2007.

Weber, M., *The Sociology of Religion*, translated by Ephraim Fishoff, New York: Beacon Press, 1922[1963].

Weintrobe, S., *The Psychological Roots of the Climate Crisis*, London: Bloomsbury Press, 2020.

Young, R., *White Mythologies: Writing, History and the West*, London: Routledge, 1990.

Index